THE KURANKO

MICHAEL JACKSON

The Kuranko

Dimensions of Social Reality
in a West African Society

ST. MARTIN'S PRESS · NEW YORK

To the Kuranko People

Contents

Photographs

Tables

Figures

Diagrams

Maps

Acknowledgements

The field research on which this book is based was carried out in Sierra Leone, November 1969-October 1970 and January-March 1972. The first period of field work was generously funded by the Nuffield Foundation. Further field work was made possible by a travel grant from the British Universities Travel Association and by a Henry Ling Roth Fellowship awarded by the Faculty of Archaeology and Anthropology at the University of Cambridge. I would like to record my gratitude for the financial support which I received from these organisations.

I owe special thanks to Professor Jack Goody who supervised my doctoral research and gave me valuable advice and help throughout my years at Cambridge, and to Professor Meyer Fortes without whose timely assistance my second period of field work would not have been possible.

In Freetown, Sierra Leone, my wife and I enjoyed the hospitality and friendship of several members of the University of Sierra Leone—Fourah Bay College. Mr. J. Edowu-Hyde of the Institute of African Studies gave me advice and help in planning my field work among the Kuranko. Jim and Lenore Monsonis, Moses Dumbuya, Albert and Cathy Tuboku-Metzer, Ken Wylie, Sewa Bokari Marah (member of parliament 1957-67), Corporal Ali Bokari Marah (Sierra Leone Police Force), all made our sojourns in Freetown memorable and rewarding.

In the field, countless Kuranko helped me as informants and as friends. The kindness, generosity and hospitality with which my wife and I were received in Kuranko country made our stay in northern Sierra Leone far more than anthropologically worthwhile. I would like to note a special debt of gratitude to Chief Sewa Marah of Barawa section, to Chief Pore Kargbo of Kamadugu Sukurela, to Chief Keli Kargbo of lower Kamadugu section, and to the chiefs and people of Barawa and Kamadugu sections, Dankawali, Kondembaia, Benekoro and Kabala. To my friends, Keti Ferenke Koroma, Abdul Marah, Bundo Mansaray, Duwa Marah, Morowa Marah, Fode Kargbo, and the late Alpha Kargbo II, I owe a special debt. My deepest gratitude is to Noah Bokari Marah who was my field assistant, teacher and companion throughout the period of my field work. I hope that this book will both fulfil the expectations which he had for it and vindicate the confidence which he placed in me—that I would prove equal to the task of recording for posterity the culture of his people.

To my wife Pauline, who endured the long and arduous months of field work with me and who, at every stage, has helped in the preparation of this book, I address this final note of thanks and love.

M. J.

Preface

. . . Obviously there is no classification of the universe that is not arbitrary and conjectural. The reason is very simple; we do not know what the universe is . . . But the impossibility of penetrating the divine scheme of the universe cannot dissuade us from outlining human schemes, even though we are aware that they are provisional.

—Jorge Luis Borges, *Other Inquisitions*

It was largely fortuitous that I came to study the Kuranko. When I first outlined my programme of doctoral research at the University of Cambridge, I intended to carry out field work among the Mende of southeast Sierra Leone; my interest lay in the sociological implications of the transition to literacy.[1] Within two weeks of arriving in Sierra Leone I revised these plans. The prospect of studying the Kuranko appealed to me for several reasons, most of them arbitrary and even banal: the Kuranko area was anthropologically almost unexplored, the drier climate and remoteness of the northern province attracted me, and, in view of my intention to study the effects of literacy, the short history of schooling in the Kuranko area offered me the opportunity of studying these effects among a first generation of school pupils.

My wife and I arrived in Kabala (the administrative headquarters of the northern province) in early December 1969. I was immediately fortunate in gaining practical advice and encouragement for my research from a Kabala primary school teacher, Noah Marah. Noah took leave of absence from the school and became my full-time field assistant. All my research was carried out with his help. He mediated relationships between villagers and myself with tact and diplomacy, he tutored me patiently in the Kuranko language, assisted me as an interpreter and guide, and supported me as a friend.

Between December 1969 and April 1970 my field work was carried out in Firawa (Noah's home town and the largest town in Barawa section, situated at the heart of Kuranko country). During this period I made regular trips back to Kabala to visit Pauline, my wife. In May 1970 Pauline and I returned to Freetown where our daughter was born. This respite from field work enabled me to make a preliminary assessment and analysis of the data that I had already collected. I read the available literature on the Kuranko and on other tribes of Sierra Leone, and formulated plans for further research.

During the rainy season I divided my time between field work in more accessible Kuranko villages and a research programme which, until then, I had neglected: a study of the impact and consequences of literacy among the Kuranko. With the support of the Principal of the Kabala Secondary School and with the cooperation of teachers at this school and at the District Council Primary School, I began this research. My continuing field work was centred mainly on the village of Kamadugu Sukurela, some ten miles from Kabala, and I made regular excursions to Kondembaia. A recently-made 'bush' road (the work of the men of Kamadugu Sukurela) and the willing cooperation of the villagers enabled me to do invaluable work in Kamadugu Sukurela until

xi

September when illness forced my wife and I to return to Freetown. It was to Kamadugu Sukurela that I returned for my second period of field work in early 1972. At this time my doctoral thesis had been completed and I discussed at length with village elders the content of the thesis and my plans to rewrite it as a book. The positive reception of my preliminary work confirmed for me the importance of trying to write a book which would be acceptable both to the Kuranko and to anthropologists.

Most of the observations concerning Kuranko society and most of the first-hand illustrative and descriptive material in this book are based upon my work and experience in Firawa (Barawa section) and Kamadugu Sukurela (lower Kamadugu section). I spent brief periods in several other Kuranko villages, and these will be mentioned from time to time in the text. I made several visits to Dankawali in upper Kamadugu to record oral traditions, and I also spent a total of about fifteen days and nights in Kondembaia (Diang chiefdom) where I recorded Kuranko folk-tales and traditions. These texts gave me insights into many of the problematic and officially 'unrecognised' aspects of Kuranko social life. They proved valuable as means of furthering my knowledge of the language and its idioms as well as providing rewarding subjects for discussion when my research passed beyond the surfaces of ideology and informants and friends became more willing to speak freely and anecdotally about real events. I will have occasion to mention Kuranko folk-tales in this book but a complete account of the place of these narratives in Kuranko culture will form the subject of another monograph, projected as a sequel to this one.

Apart from one trip to Bandakarafaia in the foothills of the Loma mountains (Woli section), I made occasional visits to many other villages and hamlets in the course of helping people or when a passing acquaintance afforded me a formal introduction.[2] In Kabala, my wife and I spent much of our time with Kuranko friends, neighbours and guests, but the research on which this book is based does not (and is not intended to) reflect Kuranko social life in Kabala.[3]

In the field, much of my time was not involved in the business of collecting data or making scientific observations. This is undoubtedly consonant with the experience of most ethnographers. Yet the everyday concerns of village life such as preparing and sharing meals, helping a neighbour, attending the sick, advising in a dispute, participating in farm work, visiting and socialising are all peripheral to the anthropological report. These events and experiences usually constitute merely an anecdotal undercurrent in the academic mainstream. They are, none the less, the invisible and imponderable elements that determine the authenticity, the humanity, and the quality of that report. I have, somewhat reluctantly, excluded from this book much of this kind of episodic and 'private' material. But I have endeavoured to make it clear where my own personality (and the idiosyncratic personalities of informants) intervene. Even allowing for 'subjective bias', this account of Kuranko society should still be regarded as provisional; here I allude to such factors as the limitations of my linguistic competence (limitations which were perpetuated, ironically, as a result of the reliance I placed upon the bilingual competence of my field assistant), the paucity or inadequacy of my data on certain subjects, the comparatively short period of my field work (about twelve months in all), and the inevitable personal problems such as illness, loneliness, dietetic maladaption, and the mild paranoia of the cultural stranger which persuaded me at times that the anthropological project is founded upon arcane considerations and a kind of self-deception.

Methodological Perspectives

One of the recurring problems in anthropological field research arises from a division which tends to isolate and polarise two kinds of data.

First, the ethnographer relies heavily upon the exegetical accounts of his informants and upon ideas intuited in the process (and stress) of day to day life in another culture. Because his key informants are often also friends and allies, the anthropologist's understanding of their culture is largely mediated by them. But the choice of informants often depends upon fortuitous encounters and personal compatibilities. Reliance upon informants may hinder neutrality because of the randomness and uniqueness of the personal relationships out of which exegesis develops. The anthropologist's account of another culture may thus be an 'invention' by means of which he inadvertently projects prejudices and intellectual persuasions of his own.[4] This 'invention' of the other culture may be produced in collusion with certain informants in whom he discovers compatible predilections. With reference to this monograph, which I have already declared to be provisional, I accept that it is an 'invention', the product of a dialogue between myself and the Kuranko. It is a synthesis of this interaction, presented systematically in the dispassionate language of social anthropology, and, in some instances this synthesis is not exactly superimposable on that which the Kuranko have worked out.[5] Yet, it is neither I nor the other whom we encounter in this work. Like most anthropological monographs, it is in part a thinly-disguised allegory of culture contact mediated by personal relationships. Just as the Kuranko enabled me to understand myself in another way, so this book may offer them a novel perspective for contemplating themselves. Rather than deny the element of creativity and invention in the writing of this book, I am more interested in drawing attention to these same elements in the context of Kuranko social life, for it is my view that *their* social world is just as provisional and negotiable as the social world which I have represented in this book.

Second, the ethnographer employs techniques which are more characteristic of other social sciences. He collects and amasses data on such topics as residence and marriage patterns, economic activity, legal disputes and settlement using surveys and questionnaires that tend to relegate the informant to a peripheral role. Here the methodology depends upon impersonal techniques rather than personal mediations. The narrow exactitude of a world of facts based solely upon measurable data is often arrived at only by diminishing the significance with which individuals invest that data. Those methods which lead most directly to quantification also support, with least chance of refutation, those theories in which persons are equated with roles, in which people-as-objects (cast in a passive role) are given greater sociological significance than people-as-subjects (accorded an active and purposeful role in shaping and reshaping their social world). We have only to remember that every observation is also a choice[6] and that the objectivist mode of theoretical knowledge is no less partial and culture-bound than a personal prejudice to become aware that the relationship between the observer and the observed is always characterised by uncertainty.[7]

In this book I have endeavoured to avoid both the extreme phenomenological and objectivist positions; neither the notion of the autonomy of the individual nor the notion of the 'social' as a category of external causation constitutes the basis of my approach. My aim is to develop a praxeological perspective which emphasises the dialectical relationship between subject and object.[8] I share the view of Merleau-Ponty, that the process of 'joining objective analysis to lived experience is perhaps the most proper task of anthropology, the one which distinguishes it from other social science'.[9] Anthropologists have long been faced with the task of appreciating the experiential realities of human beings in society while at the same time seeking to elucidate the order and infrastructure which unite them, of understanding the interplay between socially-constituted knowledge and individual experience. By urging us to study relationships between social facts rather than the social facts themselves, and by placing emphasis on the dialectic between the mind and its productions, the structuralist method has opened up new possibilities for exploring the transformations at the heart of social life. A reawakened interest in the sociology of knowledge has encouraged us to treat the socially-constituted knowledge of a given society, the shared meanings that are taken for granted as sets of unquestioned assumptions, as problematical.[10] This approach has also curbed the tendency to understand the mind or the 'social' as 'a collection of permanent schemata' rather than as 'the as yet unfinished product of continual self-construction'; structures 'are not eternally predestined either from within or from without'.[11]

My aim in this book is to present an anthropological account of Kuranko social reality, working systematically from Kuranko conceptions of the world, seeking to relate to these ideas the rules of their society and the patterns of activity observeable within it. Areas of ambiguity and inconsistency, both within ideology and between the ideal and the actual, are examined in order to show *both* how Kuranko thought and activity are determined by anterior and given conditions (accomplished acts) *and* that these conditions are mediated, manipulated, transformed and created through *praxis* (the practice of accomplishing).

Finally, I would like to draw attention to certain related problems of a literary rather than theoretical kind. In writing this book I often found myself using such phrases as 'The Kuranko say . . .' or 'The Kuranko believe . . .' as if there was in reality some profound consensus or simularity of opinion to justify such generalisations. Again, I have had recourse to such phrases as 'One informant commented . . .' or 'Tamba told me . . .', thereby omitting those biographical amplifications which might make a comment or opinion explicable in a very particular sense. These various conventions of ethnographical reportage belie, to some extent, the idiosyncrasies and variabilities which one encounters through living in another culture. Yet, because the variability occurs within certain limits, some anthropological generalisation is warranted. What must be made clear is that the relation between knowledge and event is indeterminate, and it is for this reason that the difference between exegesis and direct observation should be always obvious. When Kuranko villagers replied to those of my persistent questions which may have betrayed an overeagerness for pattern and form, it was often to remind me of the existence of choice and the variability of attitude. I would be told, for example, that in the case of relations with one's mother's brothers or father's brothers or joking partners 'everything depends upon personal liking' or 'it all rests upon the amity between you.' In other words, affect is not *necessarily* determined by formal categorisations or schematisations. It is therefore the indeterminate character of the interplay between patterns and preferences which I hope will be conveyed in this book, despite a grudging reliance which I have placed upon the idioms of a general science.

xiv

A Note on Orthography

In other publications of mine on the Kuranko I have, in transcribing Kuranko words and phrases, used the script recommended by the International African Institute.[12] This same orthography has been used in two mimeographed grammars of the Kuranko language.[13] Unfortunately the present high costs of book publication have made it impracticable to use phonetic characters or diacritical (tonal) marks in this book. I have endeavoured nevertheless to be as systematic as possible in my transcriptions of Kuranko words and phrases. Dialect differences posed another problem but wherever possible I have used the western dialect (Sengbe-Barawa) or indicated alternative spellings. Many informants wished their names to be spelt in accordance with Sierra Leonean usage and I have sometimes employed local spellings, particularly of clan names: e.g. Marah (Mara), Sisay (Sise), Mansaray (Mansare).

The following is a general guide to the orthography used in this book.

Vowels have continental values except in the following cases: 'o' is open (ɔ) before consonants 'g', 'r', 'l', 'n', 'm'; 'e' is open (ɛ) before consonants 'g', 'r', 'l', 'n', 'm'; 'i' is open (ɔ) before consonant 'm'.

'g' has the value ɣ after 'or', as in *morgo*, and, in some instances, after 'o': e.g. *doge, dogoma, logoma, sogoma, toge, togoma*.

In Kuranko the plural is formed with the suffix *nu*. Rather than give both singular and plural forms I have, in most instances, transcribed Kuranko nouns in the singular.

Elisions of vowels and the addition of consonants to facilitate fluency are characteristic of the Kuranko language. Such elisions are usually marked in the text by an apostrophe; added consonants are usually separated from the associated words.

Doubling of vowels signifies a falling voice tone and lengthening of the vowel, e.g. *saan* (year), *san* (sky).

Notes

1. I had previously carried out research on this subject in the Maori field (Jackson 1967).
2. During my first period of field work I had a Landrover which enabled me to help villagers truck their goods to market in Kabala.
3. Another proviso should be stated here. The international boundary between Guinea and Sierra Leone divides the Kuranko area into two regions; it is difficult to assess the extent to which my account of the Kuranko in Sierra Leone is also valid for the Kuranko and Sankaran peoples of upper Guinea. This monograph should therefore be read as an interpretive ethnography of the Kuranko of Sierra Leone.
4. See Wagner 1975 for an excellent discussion of this problem. La Barre's comments are also relevant to this issue: Successful fieldwork . . . constitutes a kind of cumulative triumph of personality—such that, very commonly, the anthropologist comes out of the field experience with a mildly fanatic love for 'his' particular primitive people, and even with deeply gratifying personal friendships that over-ride great cultural and age differences. It is possible, however, that the anthropologist's need and effort contributed more to these friendships than did spontaneous native admiration for his uniquely valuable personality. They have merely rescued his humanity, for which, in context, he is perhaps overly grateful (1972:52). For a further discussion of 'counter-transference' in the field work situation see Devereux 1967.
5. See Lévi-Strauss 1967:14.
6. Pouillon 1971:74.
7. I refer here to the principle of uncertainty as described by Heisenberg. Science no longer confronts nature as an objective observer, but sees itself as an actor in this interplay between man and nature. The scientific method of analysing, explaining and classifying has become conscious of its limitations, which arise out of the fact that by its intervention science alters and refashions the object of investigation. In other words, method and object can no longer be separated (Heisenberg 1958:16).
8. In developing this view I have been influenced by the writings of Simmel (1968), Mannheim (1968), Merleau-Ponty (1964:1965), Sartre (1963; 1967) and Bourdieu (1972).
9. Merleau-Ponty 1964:9.
10. See Berger 1963; 1969 and Berger and Luckmann 1971.
11. Piaget 1971:4, 9.
12. International African Institute, Memo 1 (1962).
13. *Kuranko Grammar* (n.d.), mimeographed in two volumes and produced by the American Mission in Kabala.
   Kuranko Grammar, mimeographed as a set of lessons and produced by the Freetown Teachers Training College.

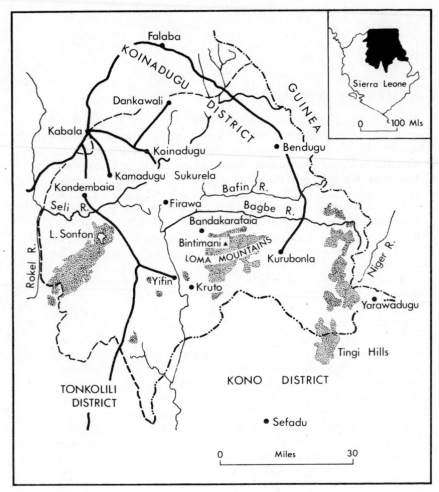

Map 1: The Kuranko Area in Northern Sierra Leone.

PART I

1. Introductory: The Kuranko People

In the late 15th century a series of Mossi invasions precipitated the collapse and fragmentation of the Mande empire. Maninka fled the anarchy in Mande and moved west and south, overwhelming the Yalunka in Upper Guinea and occupying the Circles of Kankan and Sankaran. Kuranko oral traditions suggest that the Sankaran region was the area of dispersal for the Maninka peoples who, in the late 16th century, entered Koinadugu and northern Sierra Leone. When asked from whence they came, the Kuranko invariably reply, 'From Mande, from up'; 'up' (*teliboi*, literally 'sun comes from') signifies the east, by contrast with 'down' (*teliyige*, literally 'sun go down') which signifies the west and south.

According to Yves Person, who has chronicled these migrations and dispersals, the first Maninka incursions were led by the Mara.[1] The Mara were probably a warrior group belonging originally to the Konde clan. Kuranko traditions refer frequently to a great warchief—Yilkanani[2]—who established the Mara hegemony in Koinadugu and later allowed other clans of Maninka extraction (notably the Kargbo and the Koroma) to establish other areas of control. A Kuranko proverb states that 'A clan might be older than the Mara, but it is under a cotton tree planted by the Mara that they were raised' (*morgo sikina yan mara kode, koni i ma ku l ta maran ku l finyan bandan koro*).

Following the Mara incursions, the autochthonous Kono and Limba were pushed back and the Kuranko consolidated their position in Koinadugu. Throughout the 17th century the Kuranko attacked and invaded the peoples of the Guinea Highlands, notably the Kissi. Person notes that the Kuranko have always been the traditional persecutors of the Kissi, and Kuranko traditions bear this out.[3] Many Kuranko have Kissi ancestry and many Kuranko villages, founded during the 19th century, have names which can be traced back to Kissi—Firawa, Woli, Bendugu, Serafilia, Mongo, Yamadu, Kamaron.

In the early 17th century another Malinke (or Maninka) clan, led by Tenen-Tamba Koroma, attacked the Kissi from the north. Joining up with the Mara on the Niandan, they became an important part of the Kuranko bloc. One of the Koroma clan totems—a large eagle or hawk—is called Tamba Koroma after this warrior chief. The Koroma came first to Diang as traders (according to Diang traditions), finding the Tegere clan already living in the vicinity of Lake Sonfon. Later the Koroma established the chiefdom of Nieni to the south; today the Nieni Koroma speak of the Diang Koroma as their 'elder brothers'.[4]

1

Towards the end of the 17th century the Sano attacked the Toma, coming from the 'country of Kong'. The Toma resisted, but the Sano in alliance with the Mara finally conquered them. The Kuranko pushed as far as Upper Makona. Later still the Kargbo, accompanied by a group of Sise (another Maninka clan), entered Koinadugu under Mansa Kama. Kargbo clan traditions indicate that they first came as hunters but stayed on to found a new chiefdom—Kamadugu—between the Mara areas to the south and the Yalunka to the north.

Throughout the 18th and 19th centuries other clans of Maninka, Susu and Bambara extraction migrated into Koinadugu and settled under the protectorate of ruling Kuranko clans. It is likely that the Tokolor *jihads* forced many 'pagan' refugees into the mountain fastness of the Kuranko bloc.[5] During this period the Kuranko waged intermittent wars against neighbouring peoples; Limba, Kissi and Kono slaves became in time assimilated.[6] It is also probable that Kuranko chiefs founded new areas of power and influence among the Temne.[7]

During the 19th century the Kuranko were themselves invaded or influenced by new forces from the east. Islam, introduced by Fula cattle-herders and Maninka traders, had some impact.[8] In fact, a Fula line of chiefs has ruled in the southwestern Kuranko chiefdom of Sambaia since the mid-19th century.[9]

Invasions from Temne, Kono and Yalunka (Sulima) occurred throughout the 18th and 19th centuries. Even the Mara hegemony in Barawa succumbed to the Konike Temne in the late 19th century and the Barawa rulers sought refuge in the Kabala area, repulsing the Limba who were settled there.[10] In the late 1880s Samory's Sofas invaded Kuranko country. These invasions were already presaged by the Sankaran refugees who had sought protection under both Kuranko and Limba chiefs.[11] When Samory was finally defeated and the British set up their administration in Koinadugu there were approximately twenty petty chiefdoms in the Kuranko area of Sierra Leone, all but five of them ruled by Mara chiefs.

This brief survey of Kuranko history makes it clear that we should not regard the Kuranko as an isolated cultural unit 'protected from and unacquainted with the vicissitudes of history'.[12] The fragmented political order which the British found in Koinadugu after the Sofa wars had not always existed. When Laing journeyed through Kuranko country in 1825 he met a powerful Mara war chief—Balansama— whose name is still renowned in Barawa genealogies. Laing described the 'kingdom' of Kuranko as follows.

The capital of south-western Kooranko is Seemera, and that of the north-western, Kola Konka, where Ballansama, the present King resides; he is a man of considerable influence and property, and is the most powerful chief between his country and Sierra Leone; his authority extends as far as the banks of the Niger, and his capital is visited by the natives of Sangara for the purposes of trade. The kingdom of Kooranko must extend a long distance to the eastward, as the natives of the district through which I passed could give no definite idea of its extent in that direction. . .[13]

The Kuranko were evidently a part of a vast trading network which extended over the Upper Niger as far as Kankan. Camwood was a principal trade product, being exchanged for salt from the south. Native-dyed cloth was also important as a trade commodity.

The historical oscillation which is in evidence here, from consolidation to fragmentation, from centralised to decentralised political organisation, has been noted for other Mande peoples.[14] Thus, when referring to Kuranko descent structure I prefer to speak of lineage 'fragmentation' rather than 'segmentation'; fragmentation emphasises discontinuities in space rather than a model of levels of segmentation through time.

The complex and confused history of the Kuranko is also reflected in the cultural and social heterogeneity of the tribe. The Kuranko refer to their tribe as a whole as *ferensola,* or as 'the four corners of the *ferensola*' (*'ferensola tunko nani'*).[15] However, there are distinct dialect differences within the Kuranko area as well as distinct social groupings or estates; different chiefdoms each have their own traditions and heritage. The many Kuranko patriclans (*sie*) have diverse origins: some as war refugees, some as slaves, some as conquering warrior groups, some as traders (*dyula*), and some as bands of hunters. While some clans remain avowedly 'pagan'[16] (Mara for example), others are associated closely with Islam (Koroma, Kargbo, Sise, Dabu and Sano). Yet the assimilation of 'strangers' (*sundan*) has characterised Kuranko history. Maninka clans which have settled in Koinadugu as recently as fifty years ago, are regarded without equivocation as true members of the *ferensola.* Although domestic slavery was abolished only fifty years ago, it is rare to find Kuranko who recollect slave origins; the adoption of the 'master's' clan name facilitated the assimilation of slaves into the established order.

Population and Language

The Kuranko occupy a vast, broken and frequently mountainous region of the western and northwestern Guinea Highlands. Of a total population of over 125,000 some 80,732 live in Sierra Leone (1963 Sierra Leone population census). In Guinea the Kuranko area extends east as far as Beyla where the Toma and Konianke peoples form the eastern margins of the Kuranko territories. To the south, also in Guinea, the Kuranko are neighbours of the Kissi, and to the north the Malinke and Sankaran occupy the plains of the Upper Niger and its tributaries.

In Sierra Leone the Kuranko area is roughly coincident with the Koinadugu South and Tonkolili North political constituencies. To the south the Kuranko meet the Kono, the north the Yalunka (or

Dialonke), to the west the Limba, to the southwest the Temne. With the exception of the Temne and Limba all the peoples who are neighbours of the Kuranko, both in Sierra Leone and Guinea, belong to the Mande (or Manding) grouping. Murdock identifies the Kuranko as 'nuclear Mande'.[17]

The Kuranko language is classed with the Mande language group[18] and within this general class Kuranko belongs to the Malinke-Bambara-Dyula dialect cluster which is itself classed among the Mande Tan group.[19] Kuranko is generally described as a Maninka dialect and it is inter-intelligible with Malinke and Susu, and to a more limited extent with Bambara and Yalunka. Within the Kuranko area of northeast Sierra Leone five minor dialect clusters can be distinguished. These dialect differences are easily recognised by the Kuranko, although to an outsider, unfamiliar with the language, they are often difficult to differentiate. They are: (1) the western area (Sengbe, Barawa, Diang); (2) the Loma mountains area (Woli); (3) the northeastern and eastern area (Mongo); (4) the southeastern area (Neya); (5) the southwestern area (Nieni). Although these dialect differences are small they enable a Kuranko to identify a stranger's provenance. These minor dialects undoubtedly reflect the tribal mixing and cultural heterogeneity that characterises Kuranko history; they also indicate the extent to which various chiefdoms were, in the past, relatively isolated and autonomous.

In Sierra Leone the Kuranko are the fifth most numerous tribal group (3.70% of the total population). But inhabiting the most inaccessible regions of the north, lacking an adequate road system (no road actually traverses the Kuranko area), on the periphery of the main areas of modern economic development, and having only in the last twenty years begun to send their children to school, the Kuranko have remained socially isolated, although indirectly their culture has succumbed to the forces of change spreading first from the Colonial administration and more recently from the independent national governments. Nonetheless, Kuranko people still feel isolated, bypassed, poorly represented in the affairs of the nation, and to most Kuranko villagers, Freetown (which they call *Saralon,* i.e. Sierra Leone) is another country of which they do not yet feel a part.

Landscapes

Geologically the Koinadugu plateau is a region of granite and acid gneisses. On this granite base a reddish-brown laterite soil has built up, mixed with recent quartz sand.

To the east, in the mountainous terrain of the Loma mountains, huge granite inselbergs dominate the broken foothills. The highest peak in Sierra Leone (Bintimane, 6,390 feet) is located in the Loma range; the Kuranko call it Loma Mansa (the Loma chief). Further west the country extends in a series of laterite tablelands, divided by small

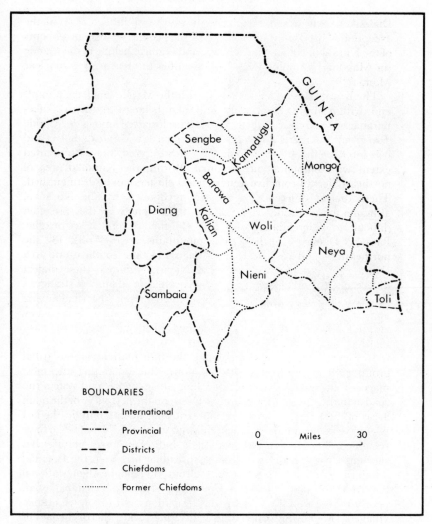

Map 2: The Kuranko Area and Major Chiefdom Boundaries.

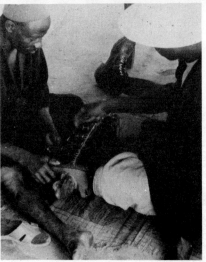

1. Duwa Marah, *keminetigi* of Kamadugu
Sukurela, broadcast sowing rice on a
recently-cleared farm site about three
miles from the town. 2. Noah Marah with
his son Kaima at Firawa. 3. Morowa
Marah at Kamadugu Sukurela. 4. Bundo
Mansaray (in whose house the author
lodged at Kamadugu Sukurela) plays *wari*
with the visiting townchief of Fasewoia.

5. *Luiye* in Firawa. Note the ground loom (*dugumayei*) and the mat-making. The house porch in the foreground has just been repaired. 6. *Luiye* in Firawa. 7. A weaver winds cotton thread (which his wife has carded and spun) onto a shuttle. 8. The Chief's courthouse (*barri*) at Firawa (walls were built later). Barawa Chief Sewa Marah is sitting in the hammock; the Firawa townchief occupies the chair at the right of the picture.

10

12

9

11

9. **Street scene, Kamadugu Sukurela. 10. House-building.** A circular trench is hoed for the wall foundations. **11.** The walls are made from poles and elephant-grass canes. **12.** The walls are daubed with mud.

streams which drain into the Seli river, which then flows south into Temne country where it is known as the Rokel. The other major river in the region—the Bagbe—rises in the Loma mountains and flows south to join the Bafin.

Kuranko social and economic life is closely related to the marked seasonal contrast between the rainy season (May to November) and the dry season (December to April). The mean annual rainfall for the Kuranko area is 80-100 inches in the north and 100-110 inches in the south where the country is more mountainous and more densely forested. About 90% of the total rainfall falls in the rainy season. For most of the dry season, warm dust-laden winds (the Harmattan) blow off the southern Sahara.

Practically all of the northern area of Sierra Leone is covered by savannah woodlands with extensive tracts of elephant grass in the northwest where more frequent burning has taken place for farming and cattle-grazing. Such areas often indicate the domains of the pastoral Fula. On higher ground abandoned village sites are frequently found (known locally as *tumbon*), associated with stands of heavy bush with huge silk cotton trees reminding the visitor that such sites date back to an epoch of almost continual warfare when defensive positions formed by pallisades of hardwood trees, fences and earthworks, were necessary to survival. The town of Koinadugu is a good example of this kind of 'war town'.

In the vicinity of the Seli river there are still areas of dense forest. Along the Bagbe and beyond, into the foothills of the Loma, is a forest reserve and it is in this area that hunting remains an important ritual activity for the Kuranko.

Most of the Kuranko area is outside the zone of the oil palm and the difficulty in obtaining palm oil is a common complaint among villagers. For wine-tapping the Kuranko rely mainly on the Raphia Palm, locally known as the 'bamboo'. Apart from the many trees and shrubs whose roots, bark and leaves have medicinal use, the most important trees for the Kuranko are the *nere* or Locust tree, Kola, Mango, Coconut, Papaya, Orange, Lime, Indigo, Cotton, Banana and Plantain. All these trees are 'protected' and occasionally cultivated.

The Kuranko live in a zone where the Sudanese savannah encroaches upon the forest belt of the West Atlantic coast. Migrating from the former regions into the latter, the Kuranko have steadily deforested large areas through slash and burn farming. Although there are few areas which are completely treeless, successive and sometimes uncontrolled burning has reduced vast tracts of country to sparse orchard bush (dominated by Lophira scrub) and grassland (dominated by elephant grass).

Economy

The Kuranko area is sparsely inhabited. The population density does not exceed twenty-five persons per square mile, except in the southeast where it rises to between twenty-five and fifty persons per square mile. The reasons are numerous: the topography, the large areas still under barely penetrable bush, the poor communications, the absence of 'new' towns and of any major industries or economic development, the still evident effects of the campaigns of the Maninka warrior Samory (who laid waste large areas of Kuranko country in the 1880s, decimating and scattering the population[20]), and last but not least the continual migration of young Kuranko men towards the urban and industrial centres in the south (notably the diamond districts of Kono). It is unusual, even in remote villages, to find more than a few young men who have not spent some time in Kono or elsewhere outside Kuranko country.

The low population density and ready availability of land for farming may explain certain aspects of Kuranko economy. Land is not individually owned, nor is it inherited. The only exception to this rule is that if a man dies during the farming season his heirs 'inherit' the farm until it has been fully exploited (this may involve harvest and then another year growing secondary crops on the land). The land is then allowed to revert to bush. The fact that land is not included in the category of inheritable property (*che*) at once indicates that kinship groupings lack one of the most important elements of corporateness. As we shall see, labour recruitment for rice farming is also only partly based upon kinship groupings. The land is 'owned' by the Paramount Chief (*manse*) in a particular chiefdom or 'country' (*nyemane* or *dugue*). One of the titles of a Paramount Chief is *nyeman' tigi* (owner/ master/protector/lord of the land). Disputes over land boundaries, claims and allocations, are all settled by the chief and he has a customary right to a portion of all produce from the land, including meat from animals killed by hunters.

Abundant farming land also means that shifting cultivation can continue without restriction. But farmers often have to make their farms five or six miles away from their village; traditions indicate that many new villages and hamlets have been founded by men seeking new areas in which to farm.

The Kuranko are primarily subsistence agriculturalists. Their livelihood is based upon shifting cultivation of upland rice with some secondary crops being inter-cultivated with the rice or grown in gardens in and around the villages. The steep hill slopes and the long dry season make burning an efficient way of clearing the bush on farm sites. And burning makes the soil more friable in addition to restoring nutrient elements to it. After one growing season the land is used again for secondary crops: groundnuts, millet, cassava. It is then allowed to revert to bush and five or six years must elapse before it is farmed again.

Because farming families must often travel several miles from their village to their farms, they usually spend much of the rainy season living on the farm. A single square building is constructed from branches and thatched with palm leaves; the ground floor is the living area while the upper floor (under the thatched roof) is used for a granary. During the rainy season, when individual families live in these temporary farmsteads, relationships among villagers are in abeyance. But during the dry season, following the rice harvest, families return to their village and resume their lives within the wider community of neighbours, affines and kin. This annually-alternating pattern of dispersed settlement followed by a return to the village community where initiations, marriages, court cases and festivities take place, directly reflects the contrast between rainy season and dry season. To the Kuranko the rainy season is, moreover, a period of hard work, isolation, hunger and uncertainty; the dry season heralds a time to relax, to readjust to community life, and to enjoy the blessings of full granaries.

Rice

The Kuranko distinguish and name some sixteen to twenty indigenous varieties of rice, classifying each variety according to taste, colour, shape, size, smell and growing time. About ten other varieties of rice are called 'stranger' (*sundan*) varieties since they have been introduced from outside, usually purchased in market towns (like Kabala) on the edge of Kuranko country. Most are Chinese varieties. One of these imported grains (*bako*) is very popular, partly because it is 'sweet', partly because it is easily marketed. The Kuranko also make a distinction between upland rice (*kore*) and swamp rice (*yaka*). Swamp rice is considered to be inferior. Farmers point out that it takes too long to mature (five months), has an inferior taste, and that swamp rice cultivation is impracticable on a large scale because swamps are too few, too remote from most villages and too small to make adequate farms. Customarily, women cultivate swamp rice, men upland rice. This signifies the secondary value of swamp rice, and its association with women is one reason why Kuranko farmers reject the idea of turning more attention to its cultivation.[21]

After harvest each year (late October to early January) most farmers sell some of their rice on the markets. The sale of rice is the sole source of money for many Kuranko and money is needed to pay taxes, buy blankets and clothing, lamps, zinc sheets for roofing, cement, and other imported commodities. In many cases the farmer must also purchase seed rice for the next growing season. The demands for cash have meant an increase in indebtedness in Kuranko villages and a transition from a barter economy; many men have become partly dependent upon sons who migrate south and earn wages in the diamond districts. The scarcity of rice for consumption has, in turn, also meant an increase in hardship during the growing season which the Kuranko refer to as the 'hungry time' (*same konke*—literally 'rainy season hunger'). Normally, however, this term reflects the monotony of available foods rather than the absence of any food at all. The only year in living memory when food was completely unavailable and when villagers had to resort to grubbing bush yams and living off wild fruits was about twenty years ago. It is the shortage of rice, the staple food, which is referred to when the Kuranko speak of hunger. A shortage of rice, it is alleged, can lead to a breakdown of goodwill and reciprocity within the wider kin group and within the local community.

Other Crops

Kuranko farmers intercrop sesame, millet, maize, peppers and cotton with the upland rice. Farmers often say that it is because one cannot intercrop in swamp farms that they do not consider seriously the idea of devoting more energy to swamp rice cultivation.[22]

Other crops are gardened rather than farmed, and most gardening is done by women. The traditional term for garden was *nakoe* (mother gift/act), but nowadays the Kuranko speak of *gardennu* (gardens). The association of the staple food—rice—with men's labour and of subsidiary crops with women's labour is consistent with the status distinction between men and women. On the outskirts of the villages the women of individual household groups make cassava, groundnut, millet and sweet potato gardens. These crops may also be grown during the second year of cultivation on the upland rice farm.

Gardens and farms are fenced, with animal traps concealed in the fencelines to keep marauding animals out. In many areas monkeys, baboons, cutting grass and even elephants are still a menace to farmers. Within the village each household has a perpetual right to cultivate land adjacent to the house site, and in these small garden patches the women of the household grow a variety of other supplementary crops: groundnuts, maize, cotton, sweet potato, cocoyams, onions, tomatoes, pumpkin, cowpeas, okra, peppers, sorrel, indigo, and occasionally some rice. Old men often make tobacco gardens along the banks of a stream near the village. Apart from these crops, every household owns certain fruit trees in and around the village, notably bananas, mangoes, papaya, orange, lime, and coconut trees. Pineapples are also grown. Each household head is the custodian of a kola grove planted by an ancestor of the family or sub-clan. These trees are usually protected by fetishes.

The Upland Rice Farm and the Seasonal Cycle

Each household group, under the direction of the household head, makes its main rice farm (*senbe*—'big farm') anew each year. The enormous labour required for slashing and burning the secondary bush quickly and efficiently (about 100 man-hours are involved), together with the size of the farm (6-10 acres) and the steepness of the hill slopes which must be cleared mean that the labour supply of a single household is insufficient to meet the demands. Nor is the labour potential of a compound (*luiye*)—comprising close agnates—sufficient.

Of the sub-clan group (*kebile*), the Kuranko claim that it is too small to be a viable farming unit. They also point out that if the farming work were based on the sub-clan alone then this would lead to divisions within the village community. The system of farm labour therefore involves occasional groups which comprise large numbers of village men, generally organised on an age-set and friendship basis. These groups, operating in terms of a cooperative-reciprocal principle, cross-cut clan and sub-clan lines, and are called *kere*. The *kere* system both meets the demands for labour during the crucial periods of the farming year—clearing, burning, harvesting, hoeing—and serves to maintain some kind of community solidarity during the farming season when most individual households transfer their residence from the village to remote bush sites. The *kere* system also involves men in the bride-service commitments of other members. When a man's father-in-law approaches him for help on his farm, the man will notify his *kere* and they will work together to discharge his affinal obligations. In this instance the *kere* is known as *biranye* (in-lawship). *Mansan* refers to occasions when a *kere* works to help a chief make his farm. As one young man put it, 'We help the chief to make his his farm so that the chief will look after us in the future; a head not in the hands of someone else is a rotten head.' This obligation is the only levy or tribute still exacted by Kuranko chiefs; it is no longer mandatory for farmers to give part of their crop to the chief after annual harvest. Nor do chiefs not make farms as may have been the case in pre-colonial times.

The economic factors which I have outlined above affect the corporate identity of the sub-clan (*kebile*) and the household (*dembaiye*) since from the point of view of labour demands for farming, the demands of bride-service, and the obligations of hospitality within the local community, *kebile* and *dembaiye* are too small to be effective corporate groupings. Affinal, cognatic and neighbourhood or friendship ties within the village compensate for this deficiency and at the same time serve to create locality-based economic groupings that transcend 'divisive' kinship and clanship ties. This creates village solidarity and articulates ties of mutual obligation and indebtedness *throughout* the entire community. This is why Kuranko will often prefer to employ the *kere* system, even when it is not economically necessary to do so. Thus, in preparing rice for consumption during initiation rituals, women work collectively in *kere* groups, and the building of bridges and other public works (road building is particularly important) are carried out through the *kere* system. The spirit of community is noticeably strong on occasions when people work together in *kere* groups. The Kuranko emphasise that 'it makes the work lighter'. During hoeing, drummers and flautists play while others work (the hoeing cooperative is known as *kondon*) and light-hearted competitions are organised to see who can hoe the most ground in a given time. Sometimes these cooperatives number over fifty men.

The seasonal cycle of farming activities is divided, by the Kuranko, into five main periods:

(1) Late January to early March: *firalamfan* (bush clearing, underbrushing). The household head searches for a suitable farm site, often located near the previous year's farm. He then checks with his village chief and with any former farmer of the site to make sure that he is permitted to farm there. He then clears a small plot with a machete to signify his intention to farm that site. Much preparatory work will be done by men of the household but the main work of clearing will involve the *kere* to which the farmer belongs, or to which his sons belong.

(2) Early March: *kontege* ('tree felling'). Large trees are felled with axes, smaller trees with machetes, about 18 inches or two feet above the ground. From these stumps some of the hardier trees, such as Lophira, will later regenerate.

(3) March: *senemintan* ('farm burning'). After the land has been cleared and brushed it is left to dry for about two weeks. After burning, the farm is cleared of unburnt sticks and charred logs. This period is known as *wonkorekoi* ('gathering the unburnt sticks').

(4) April to May: *senewore* ('farm hoeing'). The soil is loosened up by hoeing and the rice seed (together with some maize, sesame, cotton and sometimes sacrificial earth) is broadcast sown by the household head. Women then work the seed into the soil with smaller hoes. With the coming of the rains in May the major work is completed, but the farming family resides on the farm for the remainder of the growing season. The women are occupied with weeding (*bindan*) and the children are employed in scaring birds from the maturing crop (*kon'ma denye*—'children's bird scaring'). They keep vigil on high platforms (about ten feet above the ground) with slingshots, or make scarecrows among the rice. The farmers build fences to keep marauding animals away.

(5) Late September to early December: *koretege* ('rice harvest'). The rice is cut, tied in bundles, then dried in the sun. After threshing the grain is stored in large clay-lined cane baskets which are placed in the farm granary. About half the grain is usually taken to the village for dry season requirements, the rest is left in the farmhouse granary for security reasons and for use during the next rainy season.

The Farming Group: Labour and Consumption

Every household has its main farm (*senbe*). If a compound (*luiye*) happens to be a single extended household occupying several houses, the main farm may be 'owned' by the senior man in the compound (the *lutigi*). Married sons of the household head who are either resident in the household or recently married and living in their father's compound will have smaller farms called *logoma sene* ('occasional day farm'). From such farms a young man will supplement the rice produced from the main farm; his own farm also gives him a measure of independence from his father's household. When a man's father dies he is theoretically obliged to devote most of his labour to working on the farm of his father's brother, but in practice this will depend on several factors— whether or not he is living independently of his father's brother (i.e. in another *luiye*), whether or not he is married, and whether or not relations between his late father and father's brother were amicable.

Generally speaking an unmarried man works full time on his father's farm; he is regarded as a dependent. A married man achieves partial independence by making his occasional day farm, for which he relies on his wife, his children and his *kere* for labour. Usually he works 3–4 days on his father's farm, then 2 on his own. But he may also work full time for his father before taking full time off to make his own farm. In some cases an unmarried son will have a small farm too, the rice from which he will use to entertain his friends.

In addition to his commitments to his father, a married son residing in his father's house or compound will have to work on his father-in-law's farm and on his chief's farm. He will also give help to his maternal uncle if called upon to do so. If he is in fact living with his maternal uncle or married to his mother's brother's daughter, his major commitments will be of course to him. Often too, sisters will ask their brothers to help them clear their farms (usually this involves the heavy work of preparing a swamp for cultivation), and a man helps his wives and sisters with the hoeing of potato, yam and cassava plots. This network of labour commitments means that men often have to travel long distances during the farming season. From a sociological point of view this pattern of labour cooperation and assistance offsets the pattern of dispersal in the rainy season when individual families scatter far and wide through the countryside to make their farms.

Unmarried sons and women of the household have their own garden plots, the produce from which is in theory 'owned' by the household head. In practice this garden produce or supplementary rice is stored in separate granaries; both dependent sons and women sometimes sell part of this production to buy clothes and other imported paraphernalia. This economic independence of women and their ability to determine how they will use their production from gardening is certainly not customary, but it is increasing in importance as Kuranko villagers get access to roads and markets and as trading shops are established in the villages. In pre-colonial times market centres did not exist within the Kuranko area of Sierra Leone; most large scale trade centred on market towns on the Upper Niger such as Kankan and Faranah.

Other Sources of Food

There is usually at least one hunter (*donse*) in every Kuranko village and larger villages have several who form a hunters' cult. Although hunting is nowhere a full time specialisation, in the forested regions of the Bagbe river and the Loma foothills, hunting is an important ritual activity.

Hunters use traps and deadfalls for catching small animals (porcupine, cutting grass, squirrel, rabbit) but the native gun—locally made by blacksmiths—is used for hunting large game animals (bushcow, deer, monkey, elephant, wild pig, wild goat). When a hunting trip is successful the hunters sacrifice the blood of an animal at a shrine (*Mande Fabori bon*), named after the great ancestral hunter, *Mande Fabori*. The meat is distributed within the hunter's village: the forequarters (formerly the head) to the chief, the heart and liver to 'an honest man as a special favour' or retained by the hunters for making hunting medicines, and other cuts to household and sub-clan heads. In the past, the stomach (*yonki bore*—'slave bag') was given to household slaves. Hunters consider it important to share the meat among as many villagers as possible so that animosity or envies will be avoided.[23] Today, however, it is common for a hunter to sell meat for cash, a change which is often justified by the high cost of gunpowder.

Fishing is also an important part time activity and Kuranko women are skilled in many fishing techniques: using nets, dams and weirs, herbal anaesthetics, scooping by hand. Apart from groundnuts and chicken, fish are the major source of protein.

Hens and chickens are kept by every household, but mainly used for gift giving. Wealthier families (usually Muslims) keep some cattle, but in most cases, when cows are required for bridewealth or sacrifice they are purchased outside the chiefdom from Fula cattle herders.

Craft Specialisations

Certain craft specialisations (none of which are associated with particular clans) are important: hunting, blacksmithing, leatherwork- ing, mat and basket making, weaving. Except for basket-making(done by both men and women), these crafts are all male occupations. Although non-hereditary, blacksmithing (*numuye*), hunting and leatherworking require apprenticeships during which the practical and mystical aspects of the occupations are taught.

Cloth making is an important occupation in the dry season. Women pick the cotton, card it and spin it. Men then weave it into cloth. The weaver (*yesidane*) either uses an upright loom supported on a frame (*samayesi*) or sits on a small stool, using a smaller weaving frame made of a tripod of sticks (*dugumayesi*). The long strips of woven cloth are then sewn into garments and dyed (by either batik or tie-dying processes), using extracts of the indigo plant, kola, or acacia root.

Blacksmiths are mainly occupied with the manufacture of guns and agriculture implements. They also make drums for chiefs. But the techniques of iron ore smelting are now forgotten. Smiths use scrap metal to forge implements over a charcoal fire, using hand-worked hide bellows. Other metal-working crafts (such as goldsmithing) are only practiced by Maninka specialists; yet every Kuranko woman possesses some gold ornaments among her heirlooms. The manufacture of xylophones is carried out by the *jeliba* group that uses them. The making of medicines and fetishes is also done by ritual experts—Mori men, medicine owners (*besetigi*), or old women renowned for their knowledge of herbs.

Summary

The ecological, historical and economic factors described in this chapter must be taken into account if we are to understand Kuranko social organisation.

First, settlement patterns today reflect the exigencies of the economy. In the past they also reflected the needs for adaption to warfare and defence. Moria, a village three miles from Firawa in Barawa section, was founded about fifteen years ago as a cattle camp; a Sano man was given responsibility for organising the settlement and he was later joined by other emigrants from Firawa. The village of Moria is now a sizeable community of about 100 people. Other Barawa villages were founded as farming settlements. A man who opened up new farming lands remote from his own village might build a permanent house in that locality; subsequently a small hamlet of farm huts (*senbekinu*) would be established, in time to become a separate village. Economic independence could always be achieved through emigration, for there were always new areas to move into. Sons might leave their natal *luiye* and set up a new *luiye* in the same village. Dispossessed brothers might leave their village and found new settlements. Political and economic independence (difficult to achieve within the village) could thus be attained gradually through emigration and dispersal. It is also noteworthy that when schisms developed within a ruling lineage, often as a result of competition for high office, the disadvantaged or dissatisfied could (and did) move away from the main village of the chiefdom, establishing sub-lineages (or 'houses') elsewhere. In time such divisions would become established genealogical facts. The population of Kuranko villages seldom exceeds 1,000; one reason for this is that accessible farmlands become scarce as the village reaches this optimum size. Many hamlets have been founded by individuals, simply because they wanted to be close to their farmlands. Second, residential mobility is also facilitated by the fact that land holding is not vested in the kinship group; usufructuary rights in land are not inherited and descent ties are only partially involved in labour recruitment and farming. Food production is, therefore, partly based upon the household group (not always a kinship group, strictly defined) and partly upon village cooperatives in which affinal, cognatic and friendship ties predominate. Food consumption and distribution follow the same pattern. Each household produces a certain amount for use in exchange outside the domestic sector. Much of this exchange is carried out within the context of marriage transactions, and bride-service commitments are fulfilled through the *kere* system. A great deal of exchange, borrowing and lending also take place within the context of neighbourhood and friendship networks.

The significance of community networks is even more marked when we realise that Kuranko descent groups are seldom 'locally anchored' beyond the level of household organisation; it is this interplay between local and lineage identifications which I will explore in the following chapters.

Notes

1. Person 1961. See also Sayers 1927:42.
2. Although the Kuranko do not admit the derivation Yilkanani (in Maninka Djoulou kara Naini) is probably a corruption of the Arabic 'Dhul Quarnein', i.e. Alexander the Great. Muslim informants often link the name of Yilkanani with the names of Sulaiman (Solomon) and Mohammed. See Niane 1965:90; cf. Sayers 1927:80.
3. Person 1961:9; Kup 1961:145.
4. The Koroma refer to Sara n' Tamba, Sara being the ancestor of the Diang Koroma, Tamba the ancestor of the Nieni Koroma. They are thought of as 'brothers'; in fact, as a general rule Kuranko regard the founding ancestors of sub-clans or 'houses' of a ruling lineage as brothers. The tendency for ruling clan genealogies to emphasise lateral (and putative) links as a way of conceptualising the points of schism over time is noteworthy (cf. Person 1962:469; Hopkins 1971:100).
5. Kup 1961:153.
6. See Laing 1825:195; Trotter 1898
7. Thomas 1916:26.
8. According to Barawa traditions, in the reign of Marin Tamba (mid-19th century) Muslim Fula came to Barawa and converted the pagan Mara to Islam. In time the Fula (Thoronka) were given cheiftaincy in the neighbouring chiefdom of Kalian. Kup cites evidence of the Islamisation of Kuranko in the early 18th century (1961:154).
9. Sayers (1927:49-56) gives a mid-17th century date.
10. Barawa traditions omit to mention that they were in fact forced from Barawa by Temne invasions. See Koinadugu District Intelligence Diary (September 14th, 1907) for details.
11. These Sankaran clans are located on the Kuranko-Limba borders, especially in the towns of Senekadugu, Mamudia, Sulimania, Yataia, Koromansilaia, Musaia and Kabala. They are closely asssociated with Islam and tend to regard the Kuranko as 'pagan'; very little Kuranko-Sankaran intermarriage occurs.
12. Balandier 1966:53.
13. Laing 1825:195.
14. See Hopkins 1971:99.
15. The etymology of the word is unknown (see Drummond and Kamara 1930), but the Kuranko stress that it refers to those who speak the pure language (kan gbe—literally 'white/pure language') or 'all those that say n'ko (I say or speak) in Kuranko'.
16. The word sunike may be used to describe chiefs or it may, in a more general sense, be used to describe a non-muslim or 'free thinker'.
17. Murdock 1959:71-2.

18. Dalby 1962.
19. Westermann and Bryan 1970:31.
20. During his journey through Kuranko country in 1895-6, Trotter reported that 'Hardly a town in the whole country escaped destruction; except Kurubundo, every town we saw had been built within the last year or two by Kuranko who had escaped from the Sofas, hidden in the bush, and returned when the country was clear' (1898:84). The village of Kondembaia (Diang chiefdom) was, according to Trotter, one of these 'new towns' (1898:34).
21. This resistance to innovation is far less strong in some other areas (e.g. Alkalia). See Haas 1974.
22. Cf. Haas 1974:31.
23. Similar distribution patterns follow the butchering of domestic livestock at household and sub-clan sacrifices. See Jackson 1977a.

2. The Conformation of Time

Ernest Gellner has noted that 'the way in which time and its horizons are conceived is generally connected with the way . . . society understands and justifies itself' (1964:1). In this chapter I present a brief account of Kuranko conceptualisations of time; this then serves as an introduction to some of the main principles of Kuranko social organisation.

The Kuranko regard customary modes of behaviour to be the legacy of the ancestors, the 'first people'. This is why the terms *namui* (custom) and *fol' koenu* (literally 'first/past things or events') are synonymous.[1] In the Kuranko view, social conformity and harmony are secured by living up to and honouring the words and deeds of the past. When the Kuranko offer an explanation or rationalisation of social mores they invariably say 'that is how it happened' (*maiya ta ra nya na*) or 'that is what we met' (*maiya min ta ra*) or 'that is how our ancestors let it happen' (*ma bimban' ya to nya na*). Both the maintenance of social order and the sustenance of individual life depend upon respect for (*gbiliye*) and continuance of the customs prescribed by the 'first people' (*fol morgonu ko dane,* literally 'the things which the first people did'). This belief is summed up in the catchphrase 'long life comes from attending to the elders' (*sie tole l to,* literally 'long life is in the listening'). Conversely it is sometimes said that a shortlived person is one who does not listen to or heed the advice of his or her elders (*si' bant to l sa,* literally 'short life ear has not'). Misfortune, premature death, disgrace and impoverishment (*yarabiye*) are frequently attributed to a person's failure to abide by the advice of elders; this also implies disrespect (*feeye* or *nyeebuye*) and a failure to honour the dead, one's ancestors.[2] A Kuranko proverb expresses the idea as follows: *Kon gbale timbi soni kon kuran ai ke la woi tegala a kore l ma* (if a dead tree is standing and a living tree has fallen then there must be a reason for it).

In other words, if a young healthy man dies while a frail old man is still alive, then the cause of the death will be found in some infraction of customary values, notably rudeness towards elders, indifference to local rules, and failure to offer sacrifices to the ancestors. Ignorance of or disrespect for the ancestral code (*kume kore,* literally 'word old/senior') will lead to death, impoverishment or misfortune because the ancestors will withhold their blessings (*duwe*) from the offender. Kuranko fathers impress upon their children such sayings as these:

I toli kina i bimba ko (your ear is as wise as your ancestor's words, i.e.

17

what one learns from listening to the words of the elders is wiser/senior than oneself).[3]

Ni morge ya tele mi taran i bimba gbelan ma i sa fo wo ma a sume i toro la? (if a person finds an ulcer on his grandfather's shin, should he then say that he finds the smell offensive? i.e. one should respect the *status* of elders even when an individual elder is infirm or incapacitated).

Kuranko ethics are thus founded upon the assumption that once a rule is established (given legitimacy and authority by the elders or ancestors) one should respect and maintain it. The highest purpose in social life is the emulation and recapitulation of the order of the past. By contrast, the future is full of uncertainty. the expression *tumado ke ma l manse la i malo* (perhaps this person will become a chief, you do not know) implies that the future is never entirely predictable, especially when government influence in Kuranko politics is an inescapable fact. One informant elaborated upon this saying by pointing out that a man will not mistreat his children lest they grow up bearing a grudge against their father.

In a sense, the future is virtually absent 'because events which lie in it have not taken place, they have not been realized and cannot, therefore, constitute time'.[4] The younger generation who, in the eyes of their elders, seem to pay little heed and little respect to the mores and norms of the past, are often regarded as foolhardy, endangering their lives by stepping outside the pale of the past.

When two young Kuranko men were killed in a lorry crash in Kono and word of the accident reached the village where I was staying, one old man remarked that by cutting themselves off from the traditional way of life (by becoming wage labourers in the diamond fields) the young men had in effect wished their own destruction. What was implied in the remark was that the young men, by neglecting to offer sacrifices to their ancestors and by repudiating their filial responsibilities, had alienated themselves from the protective blessings of the ancestors. The vulnerability of people who elect to pursue non-traditional courses of action is often commented upon. Nemesis is observed to be a function of implacable fate (*latege*), and once a person has isolated himself from the traditional order (conceived in terms of the protective powers of ancestors) there is no action possible to prevent fate. *Latege saraka saa* (there is no sacrifice to prevent fate).

In a way the Kuranko dilemma in the contemporary world lies in trying to compromise between a heritage which urges conformity to past values and norms (and which customarily refuses to accommodate the new possibilities of a changing world) and a vision which entails innovations and choices for which there are no known precedents. In Eliade's words one could say that insofar as Kuranko ideal values acquire 'a certain reality through the repetition of certain paradigmatic gestures, and acquires it through that alone, there is an implicit abolition of profane time, of duration, of "history" . . .'[5]

I have alluded briefly to the transformations which time concepts undergo as the Kuranko move from a closed, preliterate, tribal environment to an open, literate, national environment. In very general terms this movement is from domination by an idealised past to an orientation towards an uncertain future. Kuranko ideology implies a recapitulation of the past and the annulment of 'history'. By contrast, modern western society tends to live and think in terms of irreversible change and the imminent future. In tribal societies such as the Kuranko, bondage to the past affords a collective security and generates the illusion of cultural continuity. In western society, living in the future often means insecurity and cultural discontinuity. For the Kuranko, plummeted into such a world by force of historical circumstance (and at the same time deprived of real participation in it and control over it) adjustment is extremely problematic.

Two concrete examples will illustrate the problems of social change to which I am referring.

Under the Amalgamation Acts of the 1920s Barawa chiefdom became part of the expanded Nieni chiefdom with its headquarters in Yifin. The former Nieni chiefdom (ruled by Koroma chiefs) retained the staff of chieftaincy and so Barawa (ruled by Mara chiefs) became relegated to 'section' status and the Barawa chiefs divested of paramount authority. Within the new Nieni chiefdom, Barawa became an isolated and inaccessible district. Today the Barawa rulers look forward to two changes: (1.) the bridging of the Seli river and an access road made into Barawa, (2.) the return of full chieftaincy to Barawa. Despite the visits of delegations to the President in Freetown and considerable effort on their part (such as brushing a road from Firawa to the Seli crossing—a distance of 10 miles) these hopes remain unrealised. Without access to markets the people of Barawa feel that they have little hope of participating in the benefits of the modern-day economy. They are obliged to wait for change to come to them; they are powerless to play an active role in generating these changes.

Throughout the dry season of 1969-70 the men of Kamadugu Sukurela, under the direction of the town chief (Manse Pore Kargbo), brushed and made a rough road to their village, a distance of 4 miles over swamp, hill and through heavy scrub. The people of Kamadugu Sukurela, like the people of Barawa section, see the problem of communications as their main problem. They want to be able to market their rice, to have a road link with Kabala, to encourage trading and marketing in their own locality. Their efforts in this direction reflect a unanimous choice on the part of the elders to involve their village more deeply, more successfully, in the market economy, and to control and determine the future of their own village. In March 1970 I took my Land Rover over the new road to Kamadugu Sukurela, the first vehicle to go there. Two years later I was able to note the changes which the road had brought to the village. A Fula trader and a Fula baker had started business in the town, but that was all. Vehicles seldom came to the village, the cost of hiring transport to take rice to the Kabala market (10 miles away) was prohibitive, and there were no signs that educational or medical facilities would reach there for some years. To the town chief, the effort put into making the road was incommensurate with the benefits which had come to the village as a result of it. Young men see one way out of this impasse; it is the leave the village, taking the road out as an avenue of adventure or escape, to seek a personal fortune in the diamond districts of Kono. One might call this the Dick Whittington syndrome. For the older men and chiefs (certainly for the women) political and social commitments in their villages immobilise them.[6] Consumer goods, materials for house-building, better agricultural implements and clothing are purchased with money that the young men send back to the village. It is in this way that the elders, exemplifying the values of the past and a conservative attitude, have come to depend upon the young men, who symbolise the future. And it is this inversion of roles (relative to command over resources and communications[7]) which explains why the powers of the chiefs and elders over the young are today so tenuous.

Despite these problems, many traditional patterns of social life endure in a major part of the Kuranko country. One of the criteria of traditionalism is, as I have stressed, the degree to which a society maintains itself and orients itself in terms of the past. I have indicated how the future prepossesses and also alienates the Kuranko; here I have been speaking of what Eliade calls 'the terror of history'.[8] But the domination of the past is, by contrast, far from being an alienating force in this sense. This is because the Kuranko can will the past back into being although they are powerless to determine the shape of the future. Society-as-past can be recapitulated time and time again. And since society-as-past is unrecorded and not recollected in every detail, it can be, and is, continually adjusted to the exigencies of the present.[9] Although the idealised past appears to have a coercive and all-constraining hold over Kuranko thought, it is important to recognise that the *idea* of the past, at any given time, is a product of contemporary concerns. Moreover, in every generation this apparent subjection to the rule of the past (i.e. the dogmatic or ideological expressions of the ideal social order) is something actively enjoined and deliberately approved. The Kuranko are not the passive or blind vehicles of an already established social order; at every turn they must actively work to recreate that order. It has no reality outside of the individuals who comprise it. As Lévi-Strauss observes:

One can speak of explanations only when the past of the species constantly recurs in the indefinitely multiplied drama of each individual thought, because it is itself the retrospective projection of a transition which has occured, because it recurs continually.[10]

It is in Kuranko ritual that one sees best the operation of the recapitulative, reversionary and revitalisation principle. Ritual is essentially conservative. The actions of ritual align people in terms of common values, values which are invariably sanctioned and explained by reference to the past.[11] The consensus required and attained in ritual is a result of a shared view that the words and deeds of the past are exemplary, even sacred. Once that view is shattered or brought into doubt ritual often becomes sham or defunct. It is probably because of the loss of power and status of elders (as a consequence of changes discussed earlier) that Kuranko male initiation rituals (but not female initiation rituals) have almost become moribund.[12] Only random circumcisions of small groups of boys (many pre-pubescent) are carried out today. But these are hardly 'rites', for they do not involve the community at large and they are not integrated with the system of cult associations. The solitariness of these 'initiations' now is an ironic reflection on the fact that a boy's future will probably lie outside his natal village and be influenced by contingent factors and individual choices.

Another important function of ritual is the transcending of certain social divisions and the resolution of recurrent conflicts. Elaborated accounts of divination, sacrifice, and mortuary ritual have been presented in other publications and the ritual process has been related to Kuranko time concepts as well as to the functional significance of transcendent categories in the Kuranko worldview.[13] A comparable analysis of initiation ritual is presented in chapter 11 of this book.

Social and Biographical Time

Although the Kuranko term for time (*wati*)[14] may refer to many contexts (generations, periods of the day, phases of the moon, seasons, years, or the stages in the individual life cycle), it is always seen as 'a repetition of repeated reversals, a sequence of oscillations . . . In such a scheme the past has no "depth" to it, all past is equally past; it is simply the opposite of now'.[15]

The beginning of the world is associated with Eden and Mande, both of which are regarded as coextensive in time and space. A narrator of a myth or folktale will stress the difference between mythological time and contemporary time by using the expression *wulai yan la* ('far away, long ago') in prefacing his account of past events. The time of the first people (Adam and Eve, heroes of Mande such as Sundiata, Mande Fabori, Yilkanani, and Islamic figures like Mohammed and his slave Bilali) up to the time of one's grandfathers is thought of as a single epoch, chronologically undifferentiated and referred to as *bimbanu tile* (grandfathers' or ancestors' time/day). The shallowness of genealogical knowledge which, with the exception of chiefly genealogies, seldom goes back beyond three generations, helps sustain this view of the past. Present time (the time of one's consociates and contemporaries— *bimorgonu*—by contrast with the time of one's predecessors—

folomorgonu—), defined genealogically, usually comprises only five generations:

> *ma bimbanu tile* (my grandfathers' time)
> *ma fannu tile* (my fathers' time)
> *ma tile* (my own time)
> *ma l dannu tile* (my children's time)
> *ma mamanenu tile* (my grandchildren's time)

Other descending generations are thought of, not so much as generations but in terms of kinship categories: *tolobire* (literally 'earhole')—3rd descending; *kegiye* (literally 'the branch')—4th descending; *kinkinkegiye* (literally 'the extra branch')—5th descending; *fu fa fuye* (literally 'for nothing')—6th descending.

Within contemporary time, time is specified by reference to certain memorable events such as a person's initiation, the year a chief was installed or died, the number of farms a man has made. Use of a calendar based upon natural phenomena is more characteristic of Muslims than of Kuranko generally. A seven day week (*lokun*) is recognised, comprising seven 'suns' (*teli* means both 'day' and 'sun') and seven nights (*suiye*—night). Friday is a day of rest, and Saturday (*simbire*) is the first day of the week; many rituals, notably stages in initiation ritual, are commenced on a Saturday. Although most Kuranko customarily divide the day into three main parts—*sorgoma* (morning), *teli la fe* (noon, literally 'sun full') or *teli ro* (literally 'in the daytime'), and *teli ko kere* (evening, literally 'sun back breaks') or *wure* (evening or dusk)—, Muslims refer to four separate times of the day when prayers are said: *walha, sanfana, lansaran* ('when the evening meal is prepared'), and *fitire* (about seven in the evening). A lunar calendar is also used and different times of the month are related to phases of the the moon: *kerei la tege* ('the moon is cut')—first quarter; *a la ra fa* ('it is full'); *kerei al ta la* ('the moon has divided')—halfmoon; *kerei l la ban* ('the moon has finished')—the last quarter. Each month is called a 'moon' (*kerei*) and twelve months make a year (*saan*). Stars (*lolei*) and stellar constellations are not individually named except for venus which is referred to as the 'beloved or senior wife (*baremusu*) of the moon'; observations of the movements of the stars are not made.

The Kuranko generally, however, use the distinction between the rainy season (*same*) and the dry season (*telme*) to refer to events during the year. And the year is divided into two main periods: 'the rainy season is six months and the dry season is six months' (*same keri woro, telme keri woro*). For most practical purposes reference is made to the recurring sequence of particular farming activities (see chapter 1) rather than to the lunar months, the names of which are generally known only by Muslims. Much more important than the lunar months are such events as the beginning of the harmattan (*foein kun na boi*, literally 'the wind's head has appeared') and the coming of the rains (*banda yi fole*, literally 'the first rain water').

Some Kuranko celebrate the Islamic New Year (called *yonbende*). It is said that the old year (*saankore*) and the new year (*saankure*) meet in the sky and that the old year gradually retires as the new year takes its place. Many people stay awake all night, singing and gorging themselves on food because it is believed that the angels (*malaika*) weigh people and then record the names of the underweight in a great book, so selecting them for death in the coming year. However, it is generally only Muslims who celebrate the New Year in this manner and the festival does not seem to be as important among the Kuranko as among other West Sudanic peoples.[16]

The stages in the individual life cycle can be quickly summarised:

(1.) *dinyene* ('child young/little')—up to the time of weaning (about 3 years after birth). This period of early infancy is also referred to by the expression *a susunia* ('to be suckling').

(2.) Weaning (*a da ra ka*, literally 'its mouth off the breast'). The weaning stage is sometimes referred to by the phrase *ala ra beli* ('God has saved him') meaning that the child has survived the most critical period of its life.[17]

(3.) Childhood for a girl (*dimusu*) or for a boy (*bila kore*) lasts until puberty. Early pubescence is sometimes referred to as *bara ma soe* ('on a raised platform'). At this time a boy is called *bila kore mensa* ('smaller boy') and a girl *dimusu mensa*. During the year prior to initiation a boy is referred to as *bila kore kumba* or *bila kore l belne* ('grown/bigger boy'), while a girl is called *dimusu kumba* or *dimusu l belne*.

(4.) After initiation a young man is called *kemine* (*keminye*—manhood) and an initiated young woman is called *musuba* ('woman big'). Womanhood is *musubaye*. A young initiated woman may also be called *sunkuron*, a term which, like *kemine*, can also connote 'lover'.

(5.) Middle-aged and elderhood (*koroya*).

The Kuranko conceptualise the series of events in the individual life cycle in terms of the all-important ritual divide of initiation. But initiation changes the 'time track' of the individual life from a progressive to a retrogressive frame of reference.[18] After initiation an adult moves towards old age, but the irreversibility of biological ageing and the experience of decline are countermanded by the conviction that this movement is, more significantly, towards the world of ancesterhood (*lakira*). As elder, and later as ancestor, a person comes to exemplify and embody the values associated with the past; his role is to define, maintain and recreate those values. A child (who in Kuranko thought is any uninitiated individual) is free from or not mindful of this commitment. As a consequence children live in subjective time rather than in social time. Initiation assimilates the individual to the objectively-defined social order; it is the capstone of the socialisation process. From this point on, the individual's lifetime moves backwards, ideally identified with the values and order of the past. Initiation therefore imposes upon the individual lifetime a cyclical definition of

time, a social conceptualisation of time movement. It is in this way that
the discrepancy between subjective or biographical time (progressive
and irreversible) and objective or social time (recreative and cyclical) is
made good.

Time and Social Structure

The lineal (or vertical) dimension of Kuranko social structure is a
reflection of growth and change through time. But this process has been
characteristically one of fragmentation rather than segmentation, or, as
Barnes puts it 'catastrophic segmentation' rather than 'chronic
segmentation'.[19] In chapter 1 I noted some of the historical background
to this process and observed that the turbulence of the Kuranko past
must explain, to some extent, the lacunae and disruption in what may
once have been a coherent segmentary system. It is certainly not
possible to elucidate Kuranko social organisation in terms of the
segmentary lineage model. Discontinuities in space as well as
continuities over time must be taken into account. The complementary
principles of social organisation which are variously called—
lineage/locality, kinship/residence, ancestors/Earth, descent/
territoriality—can be abstractly and heuristically polarised as a
distinction between temporal and spatial modalities of structuring.
Descent essentially defines modes of relationship between predecessors
and successors; by contrast, the socio-spatial dimension can be viewed
in terms of modes of relationship between consociates and
contemporaries.[20] There are not, of course, absolute categories; our task
is to elucidate the dialectical interplay between them.[21] The following
account of Kuranko social organisation emphasises the temporal
modality of structuring and makes reference to the cognitive aspects of
structure rather than the behavioural aspects of it. As we shall see, it is
more useful in the Kuranko case to regard descent as a cognative
category rather than as an all-pervasive and constraining jural notion.
The model presented in the following pages will be compared later with
the model of social organisation which emerges from an understanding
of Kuranko concepts of space. Taken together, the temporal and spatial
models will serve as a framework for the study of Kuranko social
organisation in action.

Clanship[22]

About thirty patronymic groups or clans are widely distributed
throughout the Kuranko area. Kuranko oral traditions emphasise that
at the beginning of the world, in Mande, God (*Ala* or *Altala*) created
each clan and gave a particular profession to each.[23] According to one
account the Mansaray were made chiefs, the Mara were given wealth,
the Sise were made the 'moris', the Konde were warriors. 'All the names
of clans are names of professions; they go back to the beginning of the
world.' Today, however, such clear associations between certain clans

and certain professions exist only in some cases. What is still important is that the clan which first conquered or settled a particular area rules in that area. Being the first to lay claim to a territory means seniority and priority in the context of the social organisation of that territory. Thus, the land is 'owned' by the Paramount Chief (*manse*) in a particular chiefdom or 'country' (*nyemane* or *dugue*). One of the titles of a Paramount Chief is *nyeman' tigi* (owner/master/protector/lord of the land).

Within a chiefdom or large town several patriclans will be represented. But it is important to note that, apart from ruling clans, Kuranko clans are not associated with or identified with particular areas. Clans are widely dispersed and this dispersal carries clanship identifications far beyond the Kuranko area itself.[24]

Each patriclan (*sie*) is identified by a common name or patronymic (agnatically inherited), by one or more totems which clan members may not injure, kill, or eat, and by a prohibition against marrying-in. Each clan is also linked to one or more clans in a joking partnership (*sanakuiye* or *sanakuiye tolon*). But these *sanaku* links, like the individual clan totems, vary from locality to locality. Clan traditions and myths concerning the origins of *sanaku* links and totemic usages also vary from place to place, and even from person to person. What is consistent is that the same totem (*tane*) and the same *sanaku* links will be recognised by members of a single clan section (*kebile*). Unlike the clan, the *kebile* is usually localised and clan symbols will be identical and consistent within this localised clan section. In fact, the Kuranko rarely speak of clan (*sie*); in practice the clan is the *kebile*. In this way the clan heritage undergoes continual modification over time, being adjusted to such factors as co-residence and territorial contiguity.

But like the clan, the *kebile* is a non-corporate grouping. Members cannot trace actual descent to the founding ancestor of the sub-clan, and members of a *kebile* seldom act conjointly for any purpose. Nominally the *kebile* is a property-holding group, the largest kinship group in which property is inherited. Although the term probably comes from Arabic, the Kuranko derive it from *ke* or *che* (inheritable property). Thus, *ke-bi-le* is literally 'inheritance sharers/takers'. But when inheritable property is distributed *kebile* kin are given only token shares to symbolise the unity of the group. The *kebile* has no headman and never acts together for defence, ceremony or mutual aid. This may have been different in the past when the *kebile* sometimes formed a vengeance group; such feuds (usually between *kebile* of the same clan but from different chiefdoms) were known as *kebile kele* (*kebile* fights/quarrels). Moreover, when a family group or household offers a sacrifice, *kebile* kin often attend (if they are living nearby) or are invited to attend because remote family ancestors whose names will be invoked are in fact *kebile* ancestors.[25]

At the level of clan or sub-clan organisation there is an ideology of identity. Although the *kebile* is not a corporate group it is thought of as a family. While *kebile* brothers acknowledge, in principle, an obligation to assist one another in times of need, clanship ties are far more diffuse. As a rule, clan and *kebile* figure most prominently in the conceptualisation of rights and reciprocal obligations, even if they have only marginal or attenuated operational significance.

The system of clan totems exemplifies this conceptual dimension. The clan totems represent for each clan 'the ideal and permanent values of agnation'.[26] Respect for the clan totem (not injuring, killing or eating it) is metaphorically linked with the idea that one should respect the laws and usages which were laid down by the clan ancestor long ago. For the clan totem once saved the life of a clan ancestor who then decreed that it should never be harmed by any of his descendants. To injure, kill or eat the clan totem would be tantamount to denying kinship amity and contravening a custom established in ancestral time; death or misfortune would result. Clan solidarity is also expressed symbolically by the way in which men take oaths on their totem. If a man is offended he might declare: 'If you offend me again, then if we do not fight, may I eat my totem'. Or, should a man be insulted or offended he might say: 'You have touched my totem', meaning 'You have offended against my clan'.

Ruling Clans

Within the chiefdom or larger villages a vertical or hierarchical dimension of social organisation exists, based upon three major estates:

(1.) The rulers (*sunike* or *tontiginu*—'law owners'). The ruling clan is politically and demographically dominant. Historically, it is said that its members are descended from the first founders of the chiefdom.

(2.) The commoners (*furunyorgonu*, literally 'the ones we mingle with'). Included in this category are traditionally Muslim clans—the *morenu* or 'moris'.

(3.) The *nyemakale* or 'low born/last born' clans who are the praise-singers, xylophonists and genealogists to the rulers. Some informants suggest that the *nyemakale* estate once included the cobblers and leatherworkers (*karanke*) and the blacksmiths (*nume*), but it now comprises only *finas* and *jelis*. It is said that the term *nyemakale* is derived from *nyema* (a crowd/gathering/assembly) and the verb *a l kala* (to cease speaking/pray silence).[27] *Finaba* and *jeliba* convey the words and decisions of the chief to an assembly and serve as court ushers.

Intermarriage is prohibited between rulers and *finas*, though a ruler may marry a *jeli*. The *nyemakale* estate is not endogamous, but the *finas* are sub-divided into two groups—the *Musa kule finas* and the *Finaningbe* ('little white/pure *finas*')—which may intermarry; *Finaningbe* may also intermarry. Clans of the Muslim grouping are not endogamous; patrilateral cross-cousin marriage rarely occurs and one finds only a loose preference for marriage with other Muslims.

Members of a non-ruling clan in any particular chiefdom usually comprise a single *kebile*. The ruling *kebile* in one chiefdom is, however, usually related to other ruling *kebile* of the same clan in other chiefdoms. Thus, the present chiefdom of Mongo was once five separate chiefdoms, each one ruled by a separate *kebile* of the Mara clan. These five *kebile* are said to have been founded by sons of a famous warrior chief, Mansa Morfin. Mara rulers in Mongo understand their relationship with Mara rulers in Barawa, Sengbe and Woli in terms of common descent from the semi-mythical clan founder, Yilkanani. In Kamadugu chiefdom there are seven *kebile* of the ruling Kargbo clan; these *kebile* all stem from sons of the chief who first conquered the country, Mansa Kama. But these *kebile* are often called houses (*bonnu*). In order to elucidate the relationship between 'houses' and *kebile* let us look briefly at the organisation of the ruling Mara clan in Barawa.

The Mara in Barawa are subdivided into five lineages or 'houses' (*bon loli*—'five houses'). The lineage ancestors are reckoned to have been sons of Mamburu who in turn was a direct descendant of the Mara clan ancestor, Yilkanani. At this level of organisation all genealogical links are putative.

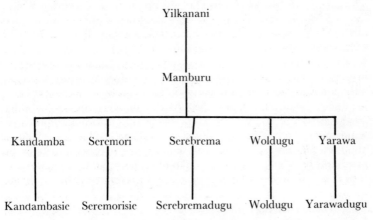

Figure 1. Ruling Clan Lines in Barawa

These five lineages all once had the right to contest for chieftaincy in Barawa, but for about 100 years the Woldugu (renowned as a warrior group) have alone had this right.[28] Thus, chieftaincy in Barawa is invested in this single lineage who 'own Barawa'. Mara informants do not agree on the question of whether or not these five lineages are five *kebile* or simply branches of one *kebile*. In theory the *kebile* can never split, but it is clear that territorial dispersal and schisms following from political contests can, over time, lead to the recognition of separate *kebile*. Such is the case in Kamadugu, and with the Serebremadugu and the Yarawadugu in Barawa.

The Serebremadugu are localised today in Barawa Komoia, a breakaway village about one third the size of Firawa (the main town of the chiefdom) and situated about 3 miles away. The Yarawadugu are likewise localised in other Barawa villages, notably Korokoro and Bambakalia. The three remaining lineages are either localised in Firawa itself, each with different and distinct compound areas or wards (*luiye*). The original dissociation of these three lineages from a common stock is said to have occured when each founding lineage brother set up an independent *luiye* following a schism over competition for high office.

By the early 19th century even the Woldugu lineage had become large enough to accommodate a further division. After the death of Marin Tamba (alias Sewa) his two sons, Balansama and Morowa, each founded separate houses. The elder son, Morowa, became the eleventh chief of Barawa and the second son, Balansama, became the twelfth chief (about 1820). Since Balansama's time the Barawa chieftaincy has remained in this, the junior line.[29]

Although the Woldugu alone have the right to contest for chieftaincy, the delegation of other political offices to other lineages has served to keep the Barawa Mara unified as 'owners' of the country. Thus, the town-chiefs in Firawa are always members of the Seremorisie 'house'. And in other Barawa villages the town-chiefs are members of other Mara 'houses'. e.g. the Serebremadugu in Barawa Komoia. Other non-ruling clans may hold minor political offices in a chiefdom. In Barawa there are villages and hamlets in which the town-chiefs belong to clans other than the Mara. The office of speaker (*kande*), although a 20th-century innovation in the court of a Paramount Chief, is always held by a non-ruler. Moreover, the council of elders (*morgobasebene*, literally 'council of big men') always comprises the senior men of all *kebile* represented in a village or chiefdom. Political and legal matters are settled by the chief acting in concert with his 'big men' and his speaker. The Kuranko often note the saying: *Manse ma yugu fo a fe sigilenu*—'a chief is no better or worse than his advisors'.

The Minimal Lineage

In Kuranko the same term—*dembaiye* (from *demba*, a suckling mother)—refers to the minimal lineage and to the household. *Dembaiye* refers to 'everyone in your care, especially your wife and children'. The household group, under the authority of the senior man of the house (*dembaiyetigi* or *bontigi*), is the basic production and consumption unit, the basic property-holding unit, and the primary group for finding bridewealth for marriages.

The politico-jural domain is defined, by Kuranko, in terms of a distinction between the householder sector and the village sector. *Bonna kume* ('house talk/palavar') is a category of domestic disputes which are all settled within the household, by the household head. Where a group of households in a single compound are closely related by agnatic ties, the senior man of the compound (*lutigi*) may settle any disputes that arise. In this case the category of disputes is known as *luama kele*, rather than *bonna kele* (*kele* means 'fight', 'quarrel' or 'dispute'). However, if disputes involve two separate lineages or *kebile*, then the town chief and his council of elders must intervene and mediate its settlement. In such cases disputes are known as *Mansa Bolola kume* ('chief's courtyard talk/palavar'). Since colonial times a further category and province of politico-jural action has been defined: *Goementi kume* ('Government talk/palaver').

Kuranko note that if a case or dispute arises which involves the *luiye*, then one should drop petty household palavers and tackle the more important *luiye* matters (*Luama kele wa na, wo ni bonna kele sa ka luiyema kele ke*). This same principle obtains when matters concerning the local community or the entire chiefdom arise. We can therefore define two sectors of politico-jural organisation, the first based upon the authority of the heads of minimal lineages, the second based upon the authority of chiefs.[30] Chiefs belong to the senior clan of the country or chiefdom; their right to rule and their authority derive, as we have seen, from the fact that they settled or conquered the country first. All other clans are subordinate, related to the rulers on the basis of a patron-client relationship. They are regarded as later settlers. This concept of historical priority is frequently compared, by Kuranko, with the seniority and authority that comes from being first-born. Within the minimal lineage the *dembaiyetigi* or *lutigi* is the eldest man. He is at the same time closest to the ancestors of the lineage and the 'first-born' of all living members of the group.

Notes

1.   Kuranko make a distinction between *namui* (those customs which are the same throughout the *ferensola*) and *seria* or *seriye* (laws and usages which differ form locality to locality).
2.   The word *bimba* means both 'ancestor' and 'grandfather'.
3.   It is believed that a person should never touch his grandfather's ear lest the grandfather die.
4.   Mbiti 1969:17.
5.   Eliade 1959:35.
6.   Data on sex ratios and age structures are given in Clarke (1966: 44 and 46). In 1963 sex ratios for Koinadugu district were 1,073 females per 1,000 males.
7.   Cf. Nadel 1957:116.
8.   Eliade 1959
9.   See Horton 1971:256.
10.   Lévi-Strauss 1969a:491.
11.   Cf. Stanner 1956:51-65; Lévi-Strauss 1966; Horton 1971:252-6.
12.   The Kuranko cite other reasons too: the expense of the rituals, the waning of the associated cult systems, the indifference of the young men to initiation.

13. See Jackson 1975; 1977a. An essay on Kuranko mortuary ritual and ancestorhood will also amplify this general subject (in preparation).

14. Examples of the use of *wati* are such phrases as: *ke soronta wati nyuma* (literally 'this one born time when?', i.e. 'when was this person born?'), *ke soron' wati ar saan tan bo* (literally 'this one born time ten years ago). When asking at what time of the day a certain event took place, one says *ke mara wati nyuma* (literally 'this happen time when'). It is also noteworthy that *folo* means 'past' as well as 'first'; *ma bimban bimban tile* ('my ancestor's ancestor's day') is thus synonymous with *folo morgonu tile* ('first/original people's day'); here *wati* and *tile* are interchangeable terms for time. As a general rule adverbs of time and time and place 'modifiers' come at the end of a sentence: *bi* (today); *kaka* (now) as in the phrase *kaka wati ro* ('now time in', i.e. at the present time); *nyina* or *nyina saan* ('this year'); *kunu* ('yesterday'); *serun saan* ('last year'); *folo* ('in the past') and *folofolo* ('in the beginning'); *sina* ('tomorrow'); *yari* ('next year'). These modifiers and derived forms enable fairly precise time references to be made.

15. Leach 1971:126.

16. Trimingham 1962:76-7.

17. Infant mortality rates (birth to 3 years) are in the neighbourhood of 54% (Kamadugu Sukurela 1972).

18. Cf. Pocock (1967) on the Hindu theory of cycles of time. He notes that the Indian '*experience* of change and duration (is) set against a *system* of values that appears to deny it' (1967:313, italics in text).

19. Barnes 1962:9.

20. See Schutz 1962:17-18.

21. See Jackson (1977a) for an extended analysis of related problems in the context of West African social organisation.

22. I have published elsewhere a complete analysis of the structure and significance of Kuranko clanship (Jackson 1974). Comparable data on the Malinke *sanaku ya* is summarised by Denise Paulme (1973).

23. See Dieterlen 1957:125.

24. Refer Jackson 1974:401.

25. Further data is presented in Jackson 1977a.

26. Lienhardt 1970:135.

27. Paulme records that in Malinke the word *nyamakala* means 'stalk' of 'manure'; *nyama*, in its original sense, means a 'pile of grass or leaves which have been swept up—fallen leaves, dead leaves, cut grass, sweepings, piles of rubbish, detritus, dung heaps, scurf. *Nyamakala* are the "little people, men of no account, commoners, persons of servile origin, people belonging to a caste".' (1973:90-1).

28. There is no evidence that the Kuranko ever had a system of circulating succession. See also Person 1962:467.

29. Balansama was installed as chief in Barawa around 1820 (see Laing 1825:195). Nine chiefs (including the present Barawa chief, Tala Sewa Mara, who was installed in the late 1950's) have ruled since that time. Thus, over a period of 135 years each chief has, on the average, ruled 15 years. This makes it possible to calculate roughly the date of Mamburu's rule (first chief in Barawa); it would be circa 1640.

30. Cf. Trimingham 1962:34.

3. The Configuration of Space

In the previous chapter I showed how the Kuranko construct and arrange social categories on the basis of a conceptual distinction between past and present. In some contexts this distinction is construed as a contrast between necessity and contingency, prior and successive. But from the point of view of social relationships, Kuranko time concepts always imply a model based upon elder-younger or senior-junior category distinctions. In this chapter I am concerned with Kuranko concepts of space and their social correlatives.

Kuranko space concepts are founded upon an essential and pervasive distinction between inner and outer. the following table lists some of the most important category distinctions which spring from this initial contrast; all may be understood as transformations of an even more fundamental opposition: self and other.

INNER	OUTER
self	other
town	bush
kinsmen	neighbours
village	other villages
chiefdom	other chiefdoms
tribe	other tribes

Clearly these categories are relative ones and in the course of social life different frames of reference are called into play in different circumstances. All these social categories and identifications are confirmed in various Kuranko protective rites. The essence of the protective rite is an action which makes inner space inviolable. As we shall see, Kuranko ideology is, in part, developed from the assumption that social order requires a subtle balance and a clear distinction between these spatial categories.

The verb *ka kandan* means to protect, enclose or safeguard, as in *ka i nyere kandan* ('to self protect'), *ka bon kandan* ('to house protect'), *ka sene kandan* ('to farm protect'), *ka luiye kandan* ('to *luiye* protect'). The main categories of Kuranko social space are: self, house/household, *luiye*, village, farm, and chiefdom. The boundaries of these areas are made inviolable by charms, fetishes and medicines which are collectively called *kandan li fannu* ('protective or enclosing things').[1] Their purpose is to isolate a socio-spatial category by making it impossible for uncontrolled external forces to trespass across the boundry line. For

31

example, in the past, when going forth to wage war, a pale-skinned virgin girl was often sacrificed to protect the country and safeguard the warriors. The victim was buried alive, her mouth stuffed with gold, her head covered with a copper container (*baramawulan*). In Kuranko terms this was not a human sacrifice but a means of protecting the chiefdom during the absence of its warriors. Sacrifice (*sarake*) differs from protection in so far as it involves an offering which mediates between the areas or categories which are distinguished. The sacrificer is thus brought obliquely into a social relationship with external powers; the dangerous and quixotic aspects of this communication explain why an intermediary (the victim) is used.[2] Protection (*kandan*) denies its object while sacrifice demands a dialogue with it, implying a recognition that the external powers can be manipulated, addressed and appeased. Most Kuranko sacrifices are made in order to establish a form of enduring reciprocity between man and spirit (sacralization), while protective rites serve to separate opposed categories (desacralization). While sacrifice constitutes an attempt to extend social communication across the boundaries of time and space, protective rites serve as defences against forces with which there can be no reciprocity, no pact: predatory animals, enemies (called *morgo finye*, literally 'black people'), witches (*suwage*, literally 'night owners'), sorcerers, and the more intractable of the bush spirits (*nyenne*).

Every Kuranko man possesses a small 'armoury' of protective fetishes and medicines which he guards jealously; should their identity or whereabouts be divulged to outsiders, enemies or women, then a man would be vulnerable to mystical attack.[3] Many are made and distributed by the male cult associations and, in the past, to divulge the secrets of their production was to invite punishment by death, the judgement being carried out by the cult itself. Others can be aquired from mori-men. A friend in Firawa once showed me his own collection of *kanda li fannu*. He had chosen a time when his wives were away from the house, but even then he made sure that the door of his room was bolted before he took out the box containing his medicines. He then showed me *gbogure* ('padlock'), acquired from a mori-man some years before. A page of Koranic verses had been folded lengthwise and wrapped around the padlock; this had then been bound with thread. As the bar of the padlock is closed one wraps first white, then red, then black thread around the padlock, reciting words from the Koran and the name of the person whom one is 'tying' or 'locking' up. White symbolises oneself, red symbolises the zone of interminacy or danger between self and other. The 'padlock' allegedly has the effect of making the victim dumb or immobile; it is often used surreptiously in court cases. Another device was said to have a similar use. Called *yuluba* ('rope'), it consisted of a knotted cord with a noose at one end. The cord is smeared with cow's milk butter. To use it one holds the knotted end away from the hand, words from the Koran and the victim's name are spoken, and the noose is pulled tight within the clenched hand. In this way the victim is mystically bound and immobilised. The third device which I was shown was called *fele*, made of twisted black and white cotton thread. it is usually placed across the threshold of one's room so that any person harbouring evil intentions will be unable to cross it. The white thread again symbolises self, the black thread stands for the other—the potential enemy. The fourth medicine was known as *nisi* which is a general term for liquid concoctions made from water and the erased verses of the Koran (first written on a slate—*walan*—and then dissolved in water). The concoction is rubbed on the body. *Lesemorge* or *sebe* are small paper charms (on which Koranic verses are written) which are sewn into leather satchets and worn around the neck.

The Kuranko often make reference to angels (*malaika*) which are believed to be spirits in human form. It is said that everyone has two guardian angels, one which stands at one's feet, the other which stands at one's head while one is asleep. People also have special or personal angels which helped create them; these are known as *danmalaika* ('making angels'). The guardian angel is called *kanda malaika*. Guardian angels are sometimes held responsible for a person's conduct and if a person behaves badly, then the expression *i danmalaika yugu* ('your making angel is bad') may be used.

Even today, most men seek to protect themselves against poisoning, witchcraft and sorcery by amassing a collection of protective medicines, some of which are acquired from Islamic medicine 'owners, some from 'pagan' cults. May non-Muslim Kuranko fear the powers of the Muslim alphas or mori-men. And informants stress that envy and evil can never be predicted. One can only anticipate possible mystical attack by taking precautions. It is as if the randomness and unpredictability of the human temperament (subjective states) can only be confronted by order and control when medicines and other 'objective' devices are employed to stand between self and other, to create a boundary line between discrepant subjective worlds, so minimising the possibility of destructive trespass or invasion. Even when individuals decide not to use destructive medicines themselves (a common occurence) this is no guarantee that others will not use such medicines against them. This is the usual Kuranko rationale for maintaining a collection of personal protective medicines.

The protection or symbolic enclosing of household, farm, garden and chiefdom areas also requires the use of *kanda li fannu*. In these cases Muslim specialists (alphas or mori-men) are called upon to supply the medicines and to direct their ritual use. The appropriate medicine is usually placed in a prominent position on the margins of the area to be protected, or buried within the precinct. If the medicines are placed on the margins of the area they will be found in such places as the fenceline or gateway of a garden or farm, on the lintel of a house, on the trunk of a fruit tree. The alternative manner of siting the medicine is parallel to the manner in which personal protective medicines are used: either swallowed/eaten, or placed against the skin (pendants and ointments).

The wilderness

In Kuranko thought the wild is the direct opposite of village life, and their distinction between bush or wild (*fera*) and village or domestic space (*sue*) expresses this principle of opposition in many ways.

It is the belief of many Kuranko Muslims that monkeys once lived in towns with people and behaved like them. As a result of their proclivity to steal, the monkeys were driven from the towns by God and permanently banished to the bush. Cursed in this way, the monkeys continue in their anti-social habits by stealing food from farms and raiding gardens. The use of animal metaphor to express anti-social behaviour is very common: enemies are likened to predatory beasts, unbelievers (*kafiri*) are likened to dogs, a thief is a 'monkey', a traitor is a 'snake'. But the metaphor becomes even more forceful in the Kuranko belief that certain people have the power of transforming themselves into animals in order to harm others. These shape shifters (*yelamafentiginu*, literally 'change-thing-masters') are greatly feared. Almost everyone can tell some anecdote concerning an incident wherein a person changed himself or herself into a leopard (commonest) or elephant, and then, in that form, killed another person's livestock. Moreover, witches are associated with various animals which symbolise the various attributes of witchcraft (*suwa'ye*): predators (leopard), scavengers (hyena, vulture, palmbird), black animals (black cats), dangerous and treacherous animals (snakes), night animals (bat, owl).[4]

A libellous form of insult is to refer to someone as a 'bush person' (*fera morgo*), implying that he or she is anti-social or marginal to one's own social frame of reference. Similarly an ignorant person might be referred to as a 'bush person' or as a 'farm person' (*sen' to morgo*), meaning that he or she shows no ability to grasp the principles of correct social conduct (associated with town life). Thus: *fera ro morgo ke a sa ko kal ma* (literally 'bush-in-person, he not events grasp'). It is significant that these forms of insult are often used among clan joking partners: anomalous status distinctions are thereby implicitly compared with anomalous category distinctions, i.e. the overlapping of the category 'town' and the category 'bush'.[5]

The nyenne

The wild is not only the realm of animals, a metaphor for anti-social behaviour. In Kuranko belief the bush, rivers and streams and mountains are the domain of the *nyenne* (cf. Arabic *djinn*), quasi-human beings who are rarely seen but which influence Kuranko in various ways. Bundo Mansaray told me that '. . . the *nyenne* have towns as we do, even in the bush. They are like people, some are good, some are bad. There are male and female *nyenne*, and they have children, just as we do.

And they have their chiefs. But they live in the bush. They think that we are living in the bush. At times they fear us because we eat our food hot. They cook their rice but eat it cold the next day. They make farms and they offer sacrifices so that they will be saved from evil, especially the evil of the white men. For some white men travel to the Loma mountains to find them and capture them. But the *nyenne* always escape.'

Some people have special gifts of vision which enable them to see and make contact with the *nyenne* and even to enlist their help in various undertakings. However, an alliance with a *nyenne* is considered dangerous, since in return for help given the *nyenne* will often demand some impossible or outrageous favour in return, such as the life of one's child. The quixotic temperament of the *nyenne* makes Kuranko people wary of them. When walking in the bush you should not call a companion's name lest a malevolent *nyenne* use the name to harm that person. And when brushing a farm in the bush, a Kuranko farmer invariably offers a sacrifice to the *nyenne* who may inhabit the surrounding forests.

Some *nyenne* are sympathetic to man, others are harmful and vengeful. Although it is alleged that there are 'as many *nyenne* in the world as there are human beings', two main kinds are distinguished: *nyenne* and *kome*. The *kome* may be 'mastered' or 'owned' by the leader of a male cult— the *kome* cult—and the powers of *kome* can be tapped to give ultimate sanction to the rules of the cult. But *kome* is refractory, unpredictable and unsympathetic by comparison with most *nyenne*. Mastery of *kome* requires exceptional gifts and when the *kometigi* (master of the *kome* cult) in the village of Kamadugu Sukurela died in March 1970 he left no sucessor. When I returned to the village in January 1972 the cult was still in abeyance, awaiting a new leader.

The difference between the dread of *kome* and the more amenable *nyenne* is expressed in a Kuranko saying: *Morgo benta nyenne bolo komo ko* (a person is better off in the hands of a *nyenne* than in the hands of *kome*). The saying implies that it is preferable to be ruled over by someone you know than by a complete stranger. We shall later examine the contrast between the secular powers of chiefs and the mystical powers of cult leaders in terms of this distinction between village authority and the powers of certain bush spirits.[6] The saying also implies that the greater the socio-spatial distance between self and other, the less predictable and trustworthy the other becomes. The idea is contained in many *jeliba* praise-songs, such as 'A man's worth will be known best in his home; in a strange country they will not know him', and 'You only really know a person in his own home.'

Different *nyenne* and *kome* have different names, such as *kome kunde* (a formidably strong 'dwarf demon' who may give boys strength in wrestling), *nyennawulan* ('red *nyenne*'), *kelsokole* ('bone of the *kole* fish'), and *faralungbon* ('stone pole').[7] These all have powers to counteract sorcery and witchcraft. But the influence of most *nyenne* is, despite their occasional usefulness as allies, capricious. Sometimes they appear in dreams in the form of a beautiful woman or handsome man; the dream seduction by succubus or incubus which may occur will cause a pregnant woman to miscarry, will cause a woman to become barren, or will cause a man to become impotent as a result of the *nyenne* 'eating his seed'. Sudden fits of delirium or insanity may also be attributed to the influence of *nyenne*. And accidents on the farm—injuring oneself with a machete or hoe—may be blamed on a malevolent *nyenne*. On trek through the bush, Kuranko will often relate anecdotes about the *nyenne*, and many times, crossing a treacherous bridge or grinding up a steep hill in low gear in my Land Rover, Kuranko companions told me that my powers were being pitted against those of the *nyenne* who dwelt in the vicinity. But despite their volatile disposition, *nyenne* have sometimes allied themselves with people and brought them fortune. This kind of benevolent association is common in Kuranko stories where mystical aid compensates for some social misfortune (being an orphan, being mistreated by a tyrannical older person, etc.). If a person has exceptionally good fortune in political life people may comment, 'a *nyenne* has come out for him' (*nyenne a boa ye*), and in at least two Kuranko chiefdoms (Woli and Upper Kamadugu) the ruling lineages still offer sacrifices to certain *nyenne* who have, for several generations, allied themselves with the rulers and helped make the chiefdom prosper. Near Bandakarafaia, the main village of Woli, there is a large granite boulder called *Mantenefara* (Mantene's stone). The *nyenne* associated with the stone is 'owned' by the chief of Woli. This stone can bestow prosperity on the land and its inhabitants, and people offer sacrifices beside it (bananas, rice, white cloth, kola etc.) as they pass by it on their way from the farms to village or when they are afflicted by misfortune. Oaths are also taken here by men seeking political position. I asked the Woli chief, Damba Lai Mara, to tell me the story of the origin of the stone.

A *nyenne* came here in my grandfather's time. The *nyenne* was with my father, then with my elder brother, and now it is with me (i.e. the last three Woli chiefs). The *nyenne* used to be at Kombili where there was a woman who used to praise it. She was called Fora Kamara. My grandfather went to Kombili to attend a sacrifice there; then that woman was given in marriage to my father, and she came here to Bandakarafaia. But there was no one at Kombili to praise the *nyenne* and so it decided to come here. It is called Mantene. That is her stone.

The mystical association of chieftaincy and the land which is, in this instance, symbolised by an alliance between a ruling lineage and a bush spirit, is also found in Upper Kamadugu. At Dankawali, the main town in the chiefdom, the chief (Fakuli Kargbo) explained that . . .

The chief who founded Dankawali was Fina Bala. He owned a *nyenne* which helped him achieve power and fame (during wars against the Sofas near Falaba). After his death nobody achieved such fame and everyone here hopes that some day the *nyenne* will ally itself with a man of the ruling lineage and make him chief again.'

The last comment refers to the amalgamation of Kamadugu chiefdom and Sengbe chiefdom (a Mara chiefdom) in the reign of Morlai Kargbo; this led to the loss of paramount status among the Kargbo rulers in Kamadugu. Today the Kargbo hope that they will regain Paramount chieftaincy within the amalgamated Sengbe chiefdom. This is why annual sacrifices are made to this *nyenne*. Large quantities of rice and fish are cooked and eaten sacrificially by the river side. The *nyenne* is said to take the form of twin crocodiles[8] which live in a granite box on the river bed, or of twin water snakes called *nyen'kinanke*. Handfuls of rice are thrown on the riverbank as offerings to the *nyenne*. The site is outlawed to women, non-initiates, and persons not of the ruling clan or its joking-linked clan, the Sise.

Many chiefly lineages derive some of their authority and power from the spirits of the land, but in most cases the only time when sacrifices were offered to the *nyenne* was when the country was first settled. Muslim officiants wrote Koranic verses on a piece of paper which was then buried. If it remained unearthed for several days, this was taken as a sign that the autocthonous *nyenne* approved of human settlement. Thus, Kuranko chiefs govern and inhabit their countries through the approval of the *nyenne*, the original 'owners' of the land. Once human settlement took place the *nyenne* 'went far into the bush' But since Kuranko must continue to encroach upon the bush, to make their farms, to hunt, or to journey to other places, it is considered imperative that continued respect be shown to the *nyenne*. This is why, at the commencement of the farm season, farmers sacrifice rice, kola and food to the *nyenne* of the surrounding forests. In return for untroubled occupation of the bush, gifts must be given.

The foregoing account of the *nyenne* makes it possible to define an area or category which lies part way between the wilderness (inhabited by animals) and human society (the village). Like the animal world, the domain of the *nyenne* constitutes an inverted image of the human world. But unlike the animal world, the domain of the *nyenne* is, through mystical means, accessible and coextensive with the world of man. By possessing exceptional gifts, certain human beings can see *nyenne* and enter into social relationships with them. Through dreams, the *nyenne* may even have sexual relations with people. But the *nyenne* remain, nonetheless, marginal and mysterious. Most Kuranko think that the domains of the *nyenne* and man should be kept segregated. Even the *nyenne* are, for the most part, supposed to share this attitude. 'We seldom if ever see them', one informant told me; 'we are blind to their presence and could easily tread on them or injure them without knowing it; so when they see us approaching they usually run away and hide.' What makes this segregation difficult is the fact that Kuranko must go periodically into the forests, to farm or to hunt. Sacrifice to the *nyenne* not only serves the purpose of appeasing them; it is a means of maintaining a respectful distance and boundary between two different worlds.

Within the Village

The contrast between *fera* (the bush or wild) and *sue* (village)[9] is often phrased as a contrast between 'out of town' (*sue ko ma,* literally 'town back on') and 'in town' (*sue bu lon,* literally 'town belly in'). The Kuranko conceptualise social space as the domain that one faces (where one is fed and born); extra-social space is the domain which one turns one's back on. 'In town' may be expressed also as *duge ro* and 'out of town' as *a ra ta dugu ro* ('he has gone to the country'). The latter phrase is used to refer to people who have left their home village and migrated to other parts of Seirra Leone. Similar divisions between inner and outer space describe the precinct of the house or compound area (*luiye*). Thus, the inside of the house is described as the area one faces ('the belly-side'), the outside of the house as the area one turns one's back on. If a man leaves his natal *luiye* and goes away to found his own *luiye* elsewhere, then Kuranko say *a ra ta a ta luiye da tege* ('he has gone and cut his mouth off from his own *luiye*'). These figures of speech imply that outer space is an inhospitable domain, by contrast with inner space where one is fed and nourished as if a child or dependent. This belief is consistent with the idea that the child is more vulnerable after birth than in its mother's womb, or that the farming season (bush space) is characterised by hunger and hardship while the dry season (village space) is a period of abundance, of sharing and hospitality.

Domestic Space

A child is always born inside the house and the birth is attended by women only. A woman usually gives birth to her first child in her parents's house. She returns home for the birth of her first child 'so that she can be cared for by her own kin'. During the period of a woman's confinement men may not go anywhere near the house. When the child is born, the women in attendance pound camphor (*kene*) in a mortar and chant three times, *kembo ken,* to announce the birth. The mother and child remain indoors for seven days; on the seventh day the child is brought outdoors for the first time—a baby girl through the back door, a baby boy through the front door. This signifies the locations of male and female activities or domains. Until initiation, the child remains within the domestic domain, marginal to the politico-jural world of the wider community.

If a child dies it is buried in a rather perfunctory way. Only kin attend the burial, the grave is shallow, obsequies are brief. It is significant that children should be buried at the back of the house, in that area which is the centre of domestic activities, where food is prepared, rubbish is discarded, and which marks the boundary between one household and another, i.e. where the household space meets the space of the wider local community. Since only initiation can create a 'whole person'. children are thought to be only half-alive (partly socialised) up to that time. Burying a dead child among domestic refuse gives symbolic

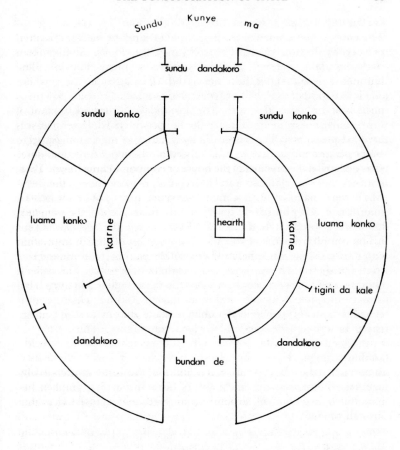

Diagram 1. The Kuranko House

expression to its marginality: the rubbish comprises material which is also part way between life and death—groundnut husks (no kernels), husks of winnowed grain, ash from cooking hearths, sweepings from the house, discarded scraps of food.[10]

The rubbish heap (*sundu* or *sundu kunye ma*, literally 'behind head on') at the back of the house is contrasted with the front or belly of the house, and this metaphor is sustained in the names given to various parts of the house itself (see Diagram 1). The door at the front of the house is the 'mouth' (*bundon de*, literally 'granary mouth'), the rooms are hollowed-out spaces' (*konko*). The back rooms are the rubbish heap-side spaces' (*sunda konko*), and the front rooms are the '*luiye*-side spaces' (*luama konko*). Other analogies with the human body are indicated by the name for the top of the thatched roof (*bonsore, sore* being the word for a braid of hair) and by the name for the threshold of a room (*tigini da kale*, from *de*—mouth). The women of the household occupy the back rooms, the men occupy the front rooms. The backyard is the women's domain, the front verandah (*dandakoro*) and the *luiye* are the men's domains. The Kuranko believe that it is the male seed which brings or creates life; the female is regarded as a shell or receptacle in which the seed grows. So the back of the house, like the shell of a groundnut or the husk of a grain, is the domain of women. Men are the life-providers while women are the food-preparers. The house 'belongs' to the man (the *bontigi*). Women and children live in it as subordinates, dependent upon and governed by the male head. However, a woman retains, even after marriage, her own clan name and also continues to sustain relationships with her own natal group; a woman thus remains marginal to as well as subordinate in her husband's household. In this sense too, the women's domain is appropriately the 'back' of the house—the *sundu kunye ma*.

The complex scheme of role distinctions is quite clearly associated with the socio-spatial distinctions between the back of the house and the front of the house. The *sundu kunye ma* also defines the boundary between domestic and village space. In a sense this area mediates between the primary life-giving category (minimal lineage and household) and a secondary category wherein the obligations of sharing and nurturing tend to be weaker (the *kebile* and the local community). This contrast is transformed into various other oppositions such as domestic-wild, familiar-strange, close-distant. In the next chapter I will give further attention to the manner in which sharing the same space (living together) influences the ideology of kinship (which implies an unmodified extension of structure and sentiment across space and through time).

To summarise some of the crucial socio-spatial contrasts, let us picture their relative positions in this way:

NATURE		CULTURE
animals	*nyenne*	man
bush	rice farms	town
	.kola groves	
wild plants	raw rice flour	cooked food
	kola[11]	
bush animals	domesticated	animals of the
	livestock	household (cats and dogs)
world of the dead	*sundu kunye ma*	world of the living
outer space	'middle ground'	inner space
	luiye	

The anomalous character of the *sundu kunye ma* makes it both literally and symbolically 'dirty' or 'dangerous'. This is borne out by the Kuranko custom of 'swearing' or cursing on the *sundu kon*. For example, if some petty theft is commited by a member of the household then the owner of the property can curse (*danka*) the unknown thief on the hearthstones or rubbish heap. The curse can only be lifted if the thief digs a gutter from the *sundu kon* to the village stream and then fills the gutter with water until a single purifying flow connects the *sundu kon* and the stream. Although I have never heard of this particular curse being invoked, the dread of it acts as a powerful sanction against theft within the household. Moreover, the belief is instructive in itself for understanding Kuranko concepts of space. Apart from the exploitation of the powerful forces associated with the *sundu kon,* it is common for Kuranko to use materials or objects from this area in preparing fetishes destined to protect domestic space or property. Thus, a calabash drilled with holes (and with the holes stuffed with cotton wool), a mat and dead fire-stick, salted water containing a fire coal, hearthstones, and tree bark are often used to protect or enclose household gardens. Bodily exudations, urine and excreta, are also commonly used to make harmful medicines. The logic underlying these usages will be discussed further when I come to consider in greater detail the relationships between danger, dirt, cursing and marginal space.

Space and Social Organisation

The Kuranko conventionally identify themselves in terms of the village where they live and the kinship group into which they are born. These locality and descent identifications are further illustrated by the Kuranko observation that a town or village (*sue*) comprises one's kin (*nakelinyorgonu,* literally 'mother one partners/relatives') and one's neighbours (*siginyorgonu,* literally 'sitting together partners'). *Nakelinyorgonu* includes, in this general usage, both kin and immediate affines. The distinction between 'kin' and 'neighbours' implies a distinction between people with whom one is connected by relationships of clanship, kinship and immediate affinity, and people who are co-resident in the same community with whom no kinship or affinal connections are traced. A further category of persons— 'strangers' (*sundan*)—includes recent immigrants or visitors who have no kinship or affinal ties within the local community.

Large villages may number between 500 and 1,000 people (Kamadugu Sukurela has a population of about 530, Firawa about 800), but some towns which have become chiefdom headquarters and market centres have populations which are even larger (Yifin—1,576, Alikalia—2,118).[12] But within each chiefdom there are always several small villages or hamlets, the smallest of which may comprise only a single *luiye* of 10-15 houses. Many of these hamlets have evolved from a farmstead in a remote area; a man may decide to establish a permanent settlement in the area where he and his agnates have made their farms for several successive seasons. Others have evolved as a result of political factionalism. For example, when the senior Woldugu 'house' lost the paramountcy in Barawa they established a new town—Kurekoro— some ten miles from Firawa. About 1920, the Woldugu decided to return to Firawa to contest for the paramount chieftaincy again. Kurekoro was then abandoned. Again, when warfare destroyed a town and led to a dispersal of the population, new towns might arise when peace came. Thus, before the Sofa wars the main town in lower Kamadugu was Tungbaia (named after its founder—Tawule Tungba Kargbo); Tungbaia was destroyed in the Sofa wars and the chieftaincy of lower Kamadugu moved to a new town—Kamadugu Sukurela (Sukurela means 'new town'). Few large towns seem to be more than 100 years old (Koinadugu and Kurubonla are notable exceptions) Today, new towns tend to grow up on the roads to market centres. This usually means that the traditional *luiye* pattern (clusters of houses facing in on a circular compound area) is giving way to a 'street' layout or linear development.

One such town, only four years old (in 1969), was founded by Momori Sise. Momori was born in Yusumaia but went to Guinea as a young man to study the Koran. He returned home in the late 1960's, an old man. He has three wives and an adult son (Braima). Since he was too old to farm any more, he decided to plant an orange grove, planning ultimately to sell oranges in Kabala, about four miles away. He selected a site on the Kabala-Sukurela road. The Sengbe chief then granted him permission to settle there and to farm in the vicinity. The hamlet comprises five houses (one for each of his wives, one for his son and son's wife, and one for himself).

In this case the *luiye* is the settlement; everyone is related to the head man through agnatic kinship or marriage. But in the case of larger villages there will be many *luiye* and the likelihood that all people in the village can reckon kinship or affinal connections with one another grows remote. This is partly because genealogies do not (except in the case of ruling clans, who do not, anyway, recollect non-agnatic links) extend beyond the third or fourth ascending generation. While clanship ties and a common clan name identify agnates in terms of putative or totemic ancestry, affinal and cognatic connections are not generally known beyond the range of living memory. Although many 'neighbours' are remotely connected through affinal links, genealogical amnesia renders these links conjectural or superfluous.

Larger villages tend to admit further divisions as well because they comprise clans of the various estates. Rulers, commoners, Muslims, *jelibas* and *finabas* each tend to be located in separate *luiye*.

The Kuranko frequently describe the *luiye* as a group that is based upon *kebile* ties. 'It comprises close relatives', one is told, with the implication that these 'relatives' are close agnates. But space always limits the extent to which a *kebile* can also be a co-residential grouping. When one studies the residence patterns in a large Kuranko town, it becomes apparent that the ideal coincidence of *luiye* and *kebile* (even the ideal that close agnates should live together) is seldom realised. Descent groups tend to be fragmented and scattered, forming a number of 'local lines'.[13] Migration accounts in part for this process of dislocation. But other tendencies and stresses, built into the developmental cycle, are also significant.

Firawa

Firawa (see Map 3) is the largest and most important town in the former Barawa chiefdom (now Barawa section). In 1969 the population was about 800. The total number of occupied houses was 110. There were also many abandoned houses and house sites, and most houses had detached huts built around the *luiye* or behind the main house. These huts served as secondary dwelling units, lavatories, cooking sheds, or storage huts. Of the 110 houses occupied, 40 were constructed in the modern style with concrete floors, plaster walls (although the wall structure is usually mud brick), hardboard or matting ceilings, and zinc roofs. But 35 of these houses incorporated traditional methods of construction: wattle and daub walls, roofs made from trimmed and lashed poles, open or matting ceilings.

FIRAWA

□	New-style pan-roofed house	● ■	Abandoned or recently demolished	▲	Muslim mosque
O	Traditional round house	/	Tracks, paths etc.	■ ●	Chief's house
▫	Out-house	ꭨ ꭨ	Banana grove	◉	Sutigi's house
○	Out-house	v v	Cassava garden	▣	Courthouse
⌒	luiye	◉	Grass, gardens, trees, scrub etc.	▲	Chief's luiye
		◢	Blacksmith's forge		

The groundplan of Firawa reveals the traditional pattern of compound or ward organisation. In Firawa there are 17 major *luiye* and each clan or *kebile* in the village is concentrated in one or more of these ·listinct wards.[14]

Mara	Woldugu	5 *luiye* (3 for the non-ruling senior 'house', 2 for the ruling junior 'house')
	Seremorisie	1 *luiye* (the *luiye* of the town chief
	Kandambasie	1 *luiye*
Wulare		2 *luiye* (Wulare are linked to the Mara in a clan joking partnership)
Kuyate		1 *luiye* (Kuyate are the *jelis*—praise singers of the Mara rulers)
Yaran		2 *luiye*
Mansaray		1 *luiye*
Sise		1 *luiye* (Muslim clan)
Dabu		1 *luiye* (Muslim clan)
Sano		2 *luiye* (Muslim clan)

Total   17 *luiye*

Over one third of the population of Firawa is Mara, representing three of the five Mara 'houses' in Barawa. The two unrepresented 'houses' are localised in other Barawa villages. The Muslim clans (Sano, Dabu, Sise) are all localised in the western section of the town.[15]

When referring to a particular *luiye* in Firawa, a person will name its founder as a way of identifying it (e.g. *Na Misa Boloya luiye ma*, Misa Bolo's *luiye*), or if the founder's name is not known, the *luiye* will be identified by the clan that 'owns' it, e.g. Yaran *na luiye*, Sanoia *luiye*. Sise *la luiye*. In the centre of each *luiye* a post for tethering sacrificial animals marks the location of the grave of the *luiye* founder. Alternatively, the grave may be marked by a rectangle of lateritic gravel bounded by logs and upturned bottles. In the past it was not uncommon for a *luiye* founder to plant an orange tree in the middle of the new compound.

Each *luiye* is a discrete spatial unit. The houses are joined to each other by 6-7 feet high fences made of elephant grass or palm fronds. Each house is oriented so that the front verandah faces onto the central compound area. Narrow paths run through the village, interconnecting each *luiye* area. While each house opens onto the *luiye*, the area at the back of each house is usually closed off by fences of thatched grass,

Luiye	Relationship of household head to lutigi							Occupants of houses without a resident household head			
	Son	Class son	Grandson	Brother	Class. brother	Sister's son	Stranger	Son's wife	Wife/wives	Class. mother	Class. sister
1					2	1				1	1
2	1	1									
3a		1							1	2	
3b					1		1		1		
4		2							2		
5a	1	1	2		1	1					
5b	2							1			
5c	2										
Totals	6	5	2		4	2	1	1	4	3	1

Table 1. The Composition of 8 *luye* (Kamadugu Sukurela).

palmleaf, or zinc sheets. There is never any public right-of-way through the backyards of houses.

Luiye *Composition*

The composition of the *luiye* can be studied in Table 1.

This analysis of the composition of 8 *luiye* in Kamadugu Sukurela (2 *luiye* have spread so that they are now regarded as comprising subsidiary *luiye*) indicates that actual sons and brothers of the *lutigi* seldom live in the same *luiye*. The four sons (*luiye* 5b and 5c) listed in the first column do not live in the same *luiye* as their father, the *lutigi* (5a). There is a tendency for the *luiye* to comprise classificatory agnates and their wives and children. And it is not unusual to find men living in the same *luiye* as their maternal uncle. This residential pattern reflects the Kuranko emphasis on good-will and cooperation among *luiye* members. If a son fails to 'pull well' with his father, he may take up residence in his maternal uncle's *luiye*, either temporarily or (especially if he marries his mother's brother's daughter) permanently. Brothers who fail to 'pull well' together may also decide to split up, one brother subsequently establishing an independent *luiye* in the village or choosing to reside in another *luiye* of the same *kebile*, i.e. with a classificatory father or classificatory elder brother. This pattern may be seen from Table 2.

The data here was given by twelve adult men (all *lutigi*) in Kamadugu Sukurela. It indicates the pattern of the dispersal of agnates, characterised today by a tendency for brothers or adult sons of the *lutigi* to seek their independence by migrating away from their home village altogether. The high rate of migration to diamond districts in Kono means that perhaps only one senior agnate will reside permanently in the home village, and that several of his dependents will be real or classificatory grandsons and women whose husbands are absent from the village. Several *luiye* also include 'strangers' or neighbours. And the higher ratio of females to males often results in households occupied solely by women and children. Of the total population of Kamadugu Sukurela, 158 were men, 202 were women, 176 were children.

The Household

In modern-day Kuranko villages two house structures predominate: the traditional thatched round house and the rectangular pan-roofed house. But this architectural difference in house types has not significantly altered the pattern of household composition or the symbolic organisation of space within and around the household area. The new style of house, with its greater number of rooms, simply means that more people can be accommodated under the same roof. Since the building of these modern houses requires considerable capital outlay, it is common that the owners of such houses have to meet requests and claims for help from distant kin, and even from 'strangers' and visitors.

		Same house	Same *luiye*	Another *luiye* (same village)	Another village (same chiefdom)	Another chiefdom			Diamond districts	Army or Police	Outside Sierra Leone
						Visiting	At school	Learning Arabic			
BROTHERS	Classificatory brothers		5						4		
	Real brothers		3	1		2				1	
SONS	Children		15			1	3	2			
	Adults		1	8					6	1	1
	TOTALS	0	24	9	0	3	3	2	10	2	1

Table 2. Residence of Agnates (Kamadugu Sukurela).

Wealthier households therefore comprise a greater number of distant dependent kin and outsiders. Nowadays it is customary for a visitor to be lodged in the house of a wealthy man; this is not always, as was the case in the past, the house of the chief.

Most households comprise a man and his wife (or wives) and unmarried dependent children. The household will often also include the house owner's elderly widowed mother or grandmother, grandsons, and visiting kin. Fostering patterns result in many households including classificatory sons and daughters, or dependent classificatory brothers and sisters. If a man has several wives then his senior wife will occupy a room in the house, but junior wives may have to occupy outhouses together with their children.

Abdul Mara's house in Firawa (see Diagram 2) will serve as an example in our discussion of household composition. It should first be noted that Abdul is, by local standards, a wealthy man (he is a trader and tailor). He has seven wives. Moreover, he is a member of the ruling 'house' in Barawa. His position of political responsibility, his wealth, the size of his house, and his sense of duty to *kebile* kin, have influenced the expansion of his household. Poorer families often do not have the resources to be as accommodating. Another factor influencing the composition of Abdul's household is the absence of his four brothers from Firawa; Abdul has incorporated younger classificatory brothers into the household, not only as a charitable gesture but in order to maintain a viable farming unit. The members of the household and their relationships to Abdul are shown in Figure 2.

Morowa (Moresuri) lives in a one-roomed house next to the main house. He is in effect a member of the household, working for Abdul, eating with the household, and subject to Abdul's authority as the house owner (*bontigi*). Morowa is Abdul's younger *kebile* brother, who, as a result of domestic difficulties at home, has chosen to live with Abdul. Konkuru is Abdul's *kebile* sister's son. Konkuru's father is dead and his father's younger brother was somewhat lacking in fulfilling his obligations as Konkuru's 'younger father' (he was, for example, unwilling to pay the expenses for Konkuru's initiation). Abdul took this responsibility himself and Konkuru now lives and works with Abdul (who is Konkuru's mother's classificatory brother). Yandi is the son of Abdul's father's *kebile* brother. When Abdul's father died the *kebile* brother married one of his widows who bore him a son (Yandi). The mother died when Yandi was six months old and Abdul's mother raised the child. Yandi now lives and works with Abdul and is a permanent member of the household. Abdul was responsible for finding Yandi a wife and for paying the bridewealth involved in the marriage.

Tilkolo is a legacy wife (*che musu*), inherited by Abdul after the death of an elder *kebile* brother. Her eldest son is the child of her late husband. At the time I made this survey three of Abdul's children were living away from home: his eldest daughter was living in Kabala with his

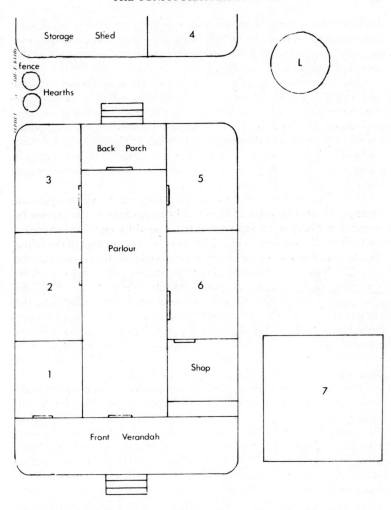

Diagram 2. Abdul Marah's House (Firawa)

1. Guest room; 2. Ferema and another wife; 3. Tilkolo and another wife; 4. Yandi and his wife; 5. Kamumba and another wife; 6. Abdul and his 'sleeping wife'; 7. Morowa's house; L. Lavatory.

youngest brother, his second eldest daughter was living with his sister in Kondembaia, and Mantene's infant daughter was living temporarily with Mantene's mother at Bandakarafaia (Mantene had returned home to Bandakarafaia to wean her child).

A study of this particular household reveals patterns and tendencies which are of general significance. A man and his wife (or wives) and

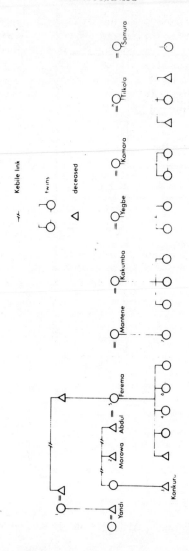

Figure 2. Abdul Marah's Household (Firawa)

Key

1. See text. This woman was inherited by the husband shown when her previous husband (Abdul's father) died.

2,3,4. See text.

5. Ferema's sister's son eats with the household but sleeps elsewhere in the village.

6, 7, 8. See text.

dependent children form the nucleus of the household or family (*dembaiye*). Attached to the household there may be *kebile* brothers who have chosen to take up residence as a result of strained relationships at home or as a result of a father's death. At any time, other kinsmen may be living in the household. Children especially sons, are usually sent to live with their father's brothers for a year or more to become familiar with their classificatory fathers so that, should their real father die, they will be accustomed to another home. Fostering (*kerifa*, literally 'safekeeping') is also common with grandparents (maternal and paternal) 'because the grandchild is the favoured child of the grandparents'. Fostering children with their grandparents affirms the continuity of the lineage through three generations. Fostering with the father's sister or mother's brother is less common, but should a child's fathers be dead or unable to care for him, the child will be fostered with the real sibling of one of its parents rather than be sent to live with its father's classificatory brothers. The idea of fostering a child with a half-brother is treated with amusement: 'It never happens.' But it is clear that a young man will sometimes seek the guardianship of a classificatory father of classificatory elder brother if there has always been amity and mutuality in the *kebile*.

Other kinsmen attached to the household may be sister's sons whose fathers are dead (or who cannot meet their obligations to their sons), elderly widowed mothers, grandmothers and classificatory mothers (women never return to their natal group in old age). Occasionally the household will also include 'strangers' or non-kinsmen who have sought the protection of a senior respected man in the village in a time of personal misfortune.

The house owner (*dembaiyetigi*) regards as his family 'everyone in his care, especially his own wife and children'. In fact the word for family—*dembaiye*—means 'motherhood' (from *demba:* a mother who is breast feeding her child). The household is the basic corporate unit in Kuranko social life: it forms the primary farming group, shares the food produced as a result of its collective labour and recognises the authority of the household head who is responsible for finding bridewealth for the marriages of dependent brothers and sons. He is also responsible for looking after the interests of daughters and sisters of the household after they have married and gone to reside in the households of their respective husbands. The household also forms the basic group for domestic sacrifice.

The variability in patterns of household composition reflects the degree to which Kuranko men are free to choose their place of residence. Data on geographical mobility is presented in the following table.

Has never resided outside village	Born elsewhere in chiefdom and resided there		In Colonial Army		In Colonial Service		In Diamond districts			At School 2-3 years	At Koranic School 3 or more years	In Guinea or Freetown		Residing with kin in other chiefdoms	Total Number of men
	5-10 years	more than 10 years	2-3 years	3-4 years	3-4 years	more than 4 years	1-2 years	2-3 years	more than years			1-5 years	more than 5 years		
4	3	1	1	1	4	1	3	3	9	1	1	1	1	1	36

Table 3. Geographical mobility of adult men (aged 35-65) —Kamadugu Sukurela.

I have already related this factor to other factors: land is not owned by the kinship group, property or inheritance considerations do not bind a man to his senior agnates, bridewealth can be amassed by seeking the assistance of a maternal uncle or by working abroad for wages, married sons can easily find land for farming and so quickly terminate the period of their dependence on their father or elder brothers. Other factors, related to the stresses and rivalries within the field of agnatic kinship, are also involved in the developmental cycle of household and *luiye*; these will be discussed in detail in chapter 8. It is, however, important to note that the Kuranko make a distinction between children of the same mother (*na keli meenu*) and children of the same father (*fa keli meenu*). Household composition reflects this distinction. Individual wives and their children will occupy different rooms in the house or subsidiary huts within the household complex. Sometimes a man will build a small one-roomed hut for himself (especially if he is old) and his wives will occupy the main house or other houses in the *luiye*. Moreover, as sons come of age and enter into competition for their father's inheritance (or office), the line of separation and tension tends to reflect latent rivalries between half-brothers and ortho-cousins (*fa dennu*, literally 'father's children'). Once the inheritance is decided, non-inheriting brothers or sons will often cut themselves off from the original *luiye*. Residential propinquity and the quality of kinship mutuality or amity are closely linked; even within the *luiye*, lines of potential competition or opposition among agnates are marked by spatial distance.

Finally, it should be noted that the multi-lineal composition of the Kuranko village is not accompanied by any overall integration, theoretical or actual, in terms of descent. There exists several locality-based groupings which cut across descent, household, and *luiye* boundaries. Although labour cooperatives (based on age-set and friendship ties) and various cult associations are only occasional groups, they confirm village identity and solidarity. Residential groupings reflect an interplay between two principles of identification: locality and descent. Although the ideology of agnatic descent plays an important part in influencing the composition of household and *luiye*, mutuality and friendship are the factors which ultimately determine the constitution of residential units. Actual social groupings beyond (and sometimes at) the domestic level are best described as 'strategic' or 'compromise' groupings, characterised by a high degree of choice and manipulation. The agnatic dogma may be transformed at the level of actual social organisation by matrilateral and bilateral kinship affiliations. This underlies the general usage of the term *nakelinyorgoye* (kinship) and enables people to say 'everyone in the village is related, except strangers; and this relatedness (*nakelinyorgoye*) extends throughout the chiefdom'.

Notes

1. See Littlejohn (1963) for a comparable analysis of the Temne *ankanta*.
2. Hubert and Mauss 1968.
3. In Kuranko thought, weak-willed and malevolent women are often blamed for men's misfortunes; they may be witches, they may betray a husband's secrets of invincibility in time of war, they may spread rumours about faults in a husband's character, or, by instigating adulterous affairs or declaring divorce, set men against each other in feuds that may lead to acts of sorcery. For further discussion see Jackson 1975.
4. I have published an account of Kuranko witchcraft beliefs elsewhere (Jackson 1975).
5. Refer Jackson 1974.
6. Cf. Tauxier (on the Bambara) 1927:280; Paques 1954:69.
7. Informants explained that red is the colour of danger, that the bones of the *kole* fish are dangerous because they often stick in children's throats, and that the 'stone pole' *nyenne* is dangerous because one can sustain an injury if a stone falls on one or if one falls on a stone (*morgo buira fara ma magba, fara buira morgo ma magba*—'person falls stone on injury, stone falls person on injury').
8. The crocodile (*bambe*) is the totem of the Sise and the Kargbo clans.
9. Plants and animals are classified according to whether or not they are domestic or wild, e.g. *yimbe* (bush yam)—*kwiye* (garden yam); *nyenkume* (domestic cat)—*fera nyenkume* (wild cat); *fera ninki* (bush cow)—*ninki* (cow); *fera ro bonde* (wild okra)—*sue tema bonde* (garden okra).
10. *Sundu* is also the name given to a child which survives after its mother has already lost many children in childbirth, infancy, or through miscarriage. An infant, buried in the *sundu kon*, may be reincarnated; the spirits of the children who die in infancy are thought to inhabit the bodies of the Sengalese fire finches (*tintinburuwe*) which feed on rice husks, nest in the eaves of houses, and are the tamest of all town birds.
11. The mediatory significance of *dege* (raw rice flour) and kola in household sacrifices is discussed in Jackson 1977a.
12. Sierra Leone Population Census 1963.
13. See Leach 1971:57.
14. Gamble notes that Mandinka villages in Gambia comprises several *kabilo* (n.d. page 1); these are comparable to both the Kuranko *kebile* and *luiye*. Among the Mandinka of Western Mali, *kabila* is translatable as lineage or sub-clan, while *lu* (cf. *luiye*) and *lutigi* designate household and household head respectively (Hopkins 1971:101-2).

15.   Although the Kuranko distinguish between 'down town' (*sue dugu ma*) and 'up town' (*sue kanto*)—connoting 'west' and 'east'—the east-west orientation of Firawa is fortuitous and the cardinal points of the compass are not significant in the laying-out of houses or villages. East and west are generally called *teli boi* ('sun come from') and *teli yige* ('sun go down'). The north-south axis is referred to as *teli kankan file* ('sun crossing between'). It is said that if one faces the east, then the south is to one's left, the north to one's right. Men are buried with the head towards the east and the face turned to the north (the right is associated with men); women are buried with the head towards the east and the face turned towards the south (the left is associated with women). At sacrifices, animals to be slaughters are oriented towards the east, and prayers are directed to the east.

4. Life and Death

Lenke a ta a koro bi namfa (The *lenke* tree does not benefit those beneath it)
—Kuranko proverb[1]

In the previous two chapters I have shown how the Kuranko structure their world in terms of cultural categories which are ordered along both temporal and spatial axes. This arrangement or configuration of cultural categories provides an epistemology, a cognitive map, which enables Kuranko to conceptualise all social relations, literally and figuratively, in terms of nearness or distance in space and time.

The discontinuities that mark off one category from another are, from one point of view, significant variations in the pattern of reciprocity which at one extreme is 'generalised' and at the other 'negative '.[2]

For the Kuranko, life was created by God (*Ala* or *Altala*) and the basic principles of social organisation were laid down by the ancestors or 'first people'. In Kuranko charter myths which make reference to *m'bimba Adama* and *m'mama Hawa* ('our ancestor Adam and our ancestress Eve'), disobedience of divine decrees leads to the separation of God and man. Thereafter, emphasis is placed upon the ancestors as mediators between an otiose high God and the world of man. Man must strive to respect the words and customs of the ancestors, through sacrifice and through conformity to the patterns of the past. Filial piety and respect for elders are replications or extensions of principles of social relationship which ramify beyond the world of the living.

The omnipotence of God and the authority vested in ancestors and elders also involve and entail responsibility for those under their protection. Ideally, this responsibility to protect and care for dependents is a reciprocal of the respect (*gbiliye*) which subordinates accord their elders. Respect is rewarded by blessings (*duwe*) and a state of blessedness (*baraka*)—food in abundance, success, long life, prosperity, good luck. The curse (*danka*) is the exact opposite of *duwe;* it leads to *fuguriye*— hunger, misfortune, poverty, illness, weakness, death. If a person suffers misfortune in life then he or she is said to 'have *danka*', to be accursed. An ill-behaved child may be referred to as *danka dan* ('accursed child'), and a person who abuses parents, elders or ancestors is said to 'have *danka*' (*danka toe*). It is not that the ancestors are conceived to be actively malevolent, rather that a failure to respect them leads to their withholding of *duwe;* they cease to mediate the flow of blessings which derives ultimately from God.

57

Fuguriye or *baraka* may be inherited, and a family which has suffered no serious misfortunes among its members may be called *baraka me* ('blessed'); similarly, a woman who has borne many children who have all survived into adulthood may be called *barake a kone ro* ('blessed womb').

The Gift (die *or* dimale)

One of my most valued memories is of the goodwill and hospitality that Kuranko everywhere extended to me during the course of my fieldwork. Whenever I arrived in a village I was presented with gifts of rice, chickens, and kola. Speeches of welcome would be made. I would be lodged in the best room in the best house in the village, and for as long as I stayed there, I would be assured of food, companionship, respect and protection. If there were no chickens to give, then my hosts would apologise with an earnestness that I often found embarassing. This hospitality overwhelmed and disarmed me, but I quickly learned that it was customary to treat a 'stranger' in this way.[3] When one visits a neighbour's house, the host will always fetch kola and distribute it among his guests. It is a symbol of friendship, a way of bestowing blessings, an affirmation of goodwill.

A distinction between sacrificial gifts (offered to extra-social beings such as God, the ancestors, and the spirits of the wild) and ordinary gifts is not always easy to make. Nonetheless, the Kuranko say that a sacrificial gift is given in the name of a spirit category, while ordinary gifts are given in the name of persons or groups of persons. Thus, if one gives kola to another person in the name of God, then that kola is a sacrifice (*sarake*) and one is a sacrifice-giver. An elder explained this to me as follows:

N'tara a taran ke fila, musu fila. A na sarake bo a kebi a di ke keli ma; a kebi a wo di musu keli ma. Wolatu na sarake ke ar bira. An duwara an ko a l me sarake bira ra ('I went and met two men, two women. I took a sacrificial gift and gave part to one man, part to one woman. Therefore my sacrifice was accepted by them. They were blessed. They said may my sacrifice be blessed and accepted').

Three important principles, obtaining for both gift-giving and sacrifice, are alluded to here: (1) the gift must be accepted(it must be seen to be used), (2) although the gift is actually given to one person it is symbolically given to a category of persons, (3) the gift bestows blessings on the recipient and a state of blessedness on the relationship between the donor and the recipient (it is customary for the recipient of any gift to say *ko baraka baraka*—'I say blessedness'—as a sign that he has accepted the gift and recognised its symbolic value).

Gift-giving, like sacrifice, involves giving things which are highly valued as life-sustaining. A gift signifies one's love or respect for another person, group or being, as well as the value of the relationship between self and other.

On one occasion, shortly after I had arrived in Dankawali (a village which I visited frequently), my host—Fode Kargbo— presented me

with a chicken and some kola. I thanked him for the gift and he replied
that it symbolised the respect with which they regarded me. Fode then
elaborated on the reasons why kola is given to 'strangers'. He began by
saying that kola is 'the most blessed fruit'.

'When a child is born they will say "find kola". It is brought and chewed. The
kola is then put in the child's mouth. When you are a grown man and you enter
a country where you are a stranger, people will give you kola before anything
else because it is the first food in life. When a woman is full grown and you want
to bring her into your *kebile* from another *kebile* (i.e. marry her), then your own
kebile will say "let us tie kola and send it to her *kebile*".'

Fode added that the tree of life in Eden was the kola tree; 'it is a
symbol of respect'. 'If no respect is shown then you are not a person. If
you do not give kola you are not a person.'

Apart from this category of gifts which are given to 'strangers' (such
gifts are called *fandale*), the Kuranko distinguish burial gifts (*sakondole*),
unsolicited gifts from friends to assist in paying a court fine, arranging a
marriage or initiation (*magbenle*, from *magben*—'to ask for assistance'),
and marriage prestations. The first prestation is always known as 'four
kola' (*wore nani*), and usually signifies infant betrothal. The second
prestation includes all gifts and services given to the family of the bride-
to-be up to the time when she formally goes to live with her husband.
These gifts are known as *fure kelfan* ('marriage thing'). The third
prestation includes whatever is subsequently given by the bride-
receiving group; these gifts are known as *musu ma kelfan* ('woman call
thing').

All these gifts have a single symbolic meaning; they bestow and
sustain life. The Kuranko emphasise the importance of showing
sympathy (*hinantei*) to others, helping and respecting others.[4] Fode
expressed this view as follows:

When a man gives his daughter to your *kebile* (in marriage) it means that he
does not want your *kebile* to die out (*ban*); when a man gives you food it means
that he has respect for your life; when a person gives you clothing it means that
he does not want you to be disgraced (*yarabiye*—disgrace, impoverishment).

Conversely, if food or clothing are given and then refused, or not used
and appreciated, then it is said of the recipient 'leave him; if he cannot
appreciate the gift then he will never appreciate anything; there is
nothing more you can do for him'. This is why an invitation to share a
meal is never refused. If one has eaten already, one must still partake of
the meal before announcing the fact. Of food sharing, the Kuranko say
'it brings people closer together.'

Exchanging greetings and shaking hands connote the same principle
of sociability. One should never pass a person by without greeting them.
To snub or seem to ignore someone is considered to be tantamount to a
show of animosity, a denial of the person's existence. One greets people
anew in the morning, afternoon, and evening. Thus, *i keene* ('good
morning' or *tana ma si* ('sleep well?'), *i ni teli* ('good afternoon') or *tana ma
teli* ('nothing wrong with the afternoon?') and *in wura* ('good evening')

signify the three main periods of the day and the three kinds of informal greeting. *In woli* ('greetings') may be used to greet a person at any time of the day; it may also mean 'thank you'.

All these customary modes of communication and exchange make it possible to create at least a semblance of goodwill, even though one's personal feelings may belie it.[5] To relax these routines of greeting and gift-giving (as I sometimes did when preoccupied with work) is to invite good-humoured chiding from one's neighbours. 'Why don't you greet me. Don't you know who I am?' The significance of these apparently trivial communications in a closed community stems from the fact that hidden tensions and envies inevitably exist; a reluctance to comply with these routines might precipitate feuds or create schisms which would threaten the integrity of society itself. The customary formality that characterises so much of Kuranko community life is, in my view, a defense against varying individual sentiments and capricious personal moods. But we should also note that restraints on informality in communication (often manifest in avoidance relationships) may serve to demarcate social boundaries. Thus, a wife never addresses her husband by his personal name; when she greets him she must kneel momentarily before him, and husband and wife should never display affection in public. Children are also taught to maintain a deferential and formal attitude to their father in public. Commoners must address a chief as *Mansa* ('lord'), and *finas* and *jelis* must always greet a ruler with appropriate praise words and phrases. Equality and hierarchy are established through a contrast between informal (personalised) and formal (depersonalised) modes of address and communication. The contrast also implies a distinction between 'public' life (*kenema*) and 'private' life (*duworon*) and we shall see later how the Kuranko concern themselves with the discrepancies between the overt and covert dimensions of social relations.

Misdemeanour

Various aspects of what the Kuranko call 'bad behaviour' (*son yuguye*) can be closely related to the foregoing account of respect, reciprocity and patterns of communication.

I once asked Bundo Mansaray to tell me what the word *korindiye* meant. He told me that a *morgo korindiye* (a mean, miserly, greedy or selfish person) is 'someone who does not give at all. Therefore he will not prosper, he will not get any children'. Bundo went on to say that 'Kuranko fear the whiteman (*tubabu*) and the European way of life because Europeans are *korindiye;* why you (i.e. myself) are welcome here is because you give and show respect.' In fact I had given presents to Bundo and his wives that very morning (Bundo was my host in Sukurela). The general Kuranko attitude towards Europeans is that they are unsympathetic and condescending. They entertained no direct or reciprocal relationships with Kuranko people. It is often felt that literacy and education will create a similar class of persons who will 'look low upon their brothers' and regard them as 'bush people' undeserving of sympathy and unworthy of respect.

When Bundo listed other kinds of 'bad behaviour' he stressed that disrespect for another individual is at the same time disregard for the whole society. Breaking a promise (*baiya*)—so called because of the way *baiya* beads fall from a broken string— may cause serious setbacks in a collective enterprise. Abandoning a person or failing to fulfill one's part of a bargain (*togetoge*) may imperil a person's safety. Theft (*kankanye*) robs a person of property necessary for farming, cooking, house-building, marrying, or self-defence. Betraying secrets or 'scandalising a person's name' (*minanfogeye, bulseye,* or *torgotinye*) likewise endanger the safety or life of others and bring them into false disrepute. Rudeness and disrespect (*darogbuye,* literally 'mouth foul') signify utter disregard for the authority of parents, elders, and ancestors. Disobedience is considered to be a corruption of traditional codes; *ka kuma tinya* (to disobey) means literally 'to word spoil'. Telling tales (*damaiye,* literally 'having a big mouth'), and gossiping (*korofole*) spread false rumours and may create discord within the community. A boaster (*morgo wasine*) or 'haughty' person is condemned for similar reasons. Boasting (*yunke*) implies aloofness, setting oneself outside the law.

It is said that all these infringements of customary codes of conduct will bring misfortune (*fuguriye*) and Kuranko parents, in raising their children (*ma kolo tine*—'to bring up or mould'), emphasise the virtues of caution, restraint, forebearance, fortitude, reserve, and respect for others. The following proverbial sayings illustrate this.

a to, n'ta to, i sa ye (you stop, I will not stop, you will see). As the speaker utters the words he successively points to the three main creases in the palm of his hand. The saying means 'you have received a warning; if you do not desist from what you are doing then you will regret it'.

ni dugu ma fan ma a dogon, a time (if ground-on-thing (i.e. snake) not hide, it will not stay long). This means that 'if one is not careful and respectful, then one will not stay alive for very long'.

hali morgo ma tuli ke sonso ro a to ala wulan la a bolo (if you cannot cook the river crayfish in oil, then leave it with its redness). This implies that 'if you meet a person you can't respect, don't disgrace him, but leave him the way he is'.

bamba ka ta n'kul la sise sa m'bolo (the crocodile will not molest you if you have no chickens). The saying means that 'you should not gossip about other people's affairs'.

in sa ro a for ma di, koni la fere ha yi la (to say no to temptation is difficult, but liberation comes from it). This implies that 'equivocation and deceitfulness always lead to trouble'.

It is, however, noteworthy that children are considered to be 'outside the law' until they have been initiated. A tattletale or petty thief, if a mere child, is often a figure of fun and the butt of jokes even though such misdemeanours are punished by thrashing the child (either parent may administer the punishment).[6] But a child has no jural status in the community. If a child steals food from a neighbour's garden, an altercation or palaver will inevitably follow, but the matter will be settled by the child's parents and not be considered a matter for a court or moot hearing. If a grown man behaves badly it is often said that the initiation process failed to make him a true adult, and his behaviour is labelled infantile. This is illustrated by the following account of a tattletale (*dame*).

'My younger brother was a *dame*. Once, when we were children, we caught a wildfowl (*sensere*) on the farm, and ate it. My younger brother came to town and told everybody what we had done. He was always doing this. One day we caught another wildfowl. We went and placed it in a fishing weir; then we caught a catfish and placed it in a trap on the farm. We did this when my younger brother, the tattletale, was absent. Then we told him to go and look in the trap, then in the weir. He went and found the bird in the weir and the catfish in the trap. Then we ate them. The tattletale returned to town and told his father, "Father, today I went and found a catfish in the tràp and a bird in the fishing weir." His father seized him and thrashed him for telling lies (*funye fole*—a liar). He held his tongue then. On another occasion we caught a cutting grass in the farm trap and cooked it and shared it amongst ourselves, and gave the tattletale his share saying "You are the *nyenne* of this place, so here is your share." The tattletale refused it. We threatened to beat him up if he did not accept his share. He became confused and protested that he could not see any nyenne. He pleaded with us and said that he would never tell tales again. Three days later we caught another cutting grass and ate it on the farm. The tattletale returned to town in the evening and wanted to tell people what had happened, but he was afraid of the thrashing which his brothers had promised to give him if he informed on them. So he said to his mother, "Let me sit here cutting grass (*kuyan*)?" His father demanded to know why he had said this and asked "Did you eat *kuyan* today?" The tattletale said, "I cannot say; they made me keep quiet about it, and promised to thrash me if I spoke up." His father assured the tattletale that his brothers would not beat him. So the tattletale told his father about the *kuyan*. His father told him that he would not tell his brothers about the incident.

'The tattletale still lives in this town . . . over there . . . His bad habits have never left him. Not even the *fafei* (initiation house) could change him.'

Similar gossip, told for amusement or to point a moral lesson, is typical of informal conversations among friends. But the levity of an account such as this stands in marked contrast to the manner in which people discuss more serious offences, in which formal rather than diffuse sanctions become operative.

Sectors of Authority

The worst crimes are those which, in Kuranko thought, endanger life in a direct way. Witchcraft is a heinous crime, punishable by death, because witches kill people or ruin the crops and property upon which people's livelihood depends.[7] Sibling incest (*tersan koe*) is regarded as a form of greed or theft, since to keep one's sisters within the family is to deprive another family of a wife and childbearer. Adultery (*yelenye*, or *kemine koiye* if a man is held responsible and *musu koiye* if a woman is held responsible) leads to a disastrous breakdown in the affinal network of ties that binds a community together. Gluttony, lust and the refusal to share scarce resources with others (the word *meeye* denotes overweening and selfish desire as in *musuko meeye* [lust] and *nunfulu ko meeye* [avarice]) are severely censured because they deny life to others.

Homicide (*morgo fagale*—'person killing') was, in the past, punishable by death; the *kebile* of the victim would seek a vengeance killing. Sexual intercourse with a pregnant woman or with a woman who is breast-feeding a child (when the relationship was adulterous) was also considered to be a form of murder (*nie koiye*, literally 'life taking').[8] In the former case, a miscarriage would be induced, and in the latter case the child would grow sickly and die.

The right to pronounce sentence on these crimes in which life was taken was the prerogative of a Paramount chief; killing endangered the safety of the entire country or chiefdom. Other disputes or delicts, involving two or more families, are settled by the town chief (*sutigi*) and his council of elders (*manse l morgobannu*). This category of delicts includes debt cases (*yuli ko kele*), adultery cases and other disputes concerning women (*musu ko kele*), inheritance disputes (*che ko kele*), disputes over land boundaries (*dugu ko kele*), cases of sorcery and cursing (*gborle ko kele*), theft (*kankanye*), and witchcraft. Table 4 is a compilation of data, based on Native Court records for the amalgamated Sengbe chiefdom 1946-67, and indicates the numbers and kinds of cases heard.

Before the Native Court system was instituted (and even after) there was another sector of politico-jural authority, centered upon the cult associations. In every village there is a 'master of the young men' (*keminetigi*) and a 'mistress of the young women' (*dimusukuntigi*). The *keminetigi* is usually a master of one of the male cults and his position involves responsibility for the organisation of male initiations and the moral supervision of young initiates. Offenses which are regarded as the result of weak will or childlike proclivities (disrespect of elders, rumour-mongering, breaking promises, divulging secrets) are commonly dealt with by the *keminetigi*. The *dimusukuntigi* acts in a similar capacity, supervising female initiations and settling disputes that arise from the refractory behaviour of a young bride or from male encroachments upon the female domain. Cases of witchcraft are often dealt with by a male cult association—*Gbangbe*. Further details of the politico-jural role of the cults will be given in Part III.

It can be noted at this point that killing enemies, witches and murderers, alienating the property of non-tribesmen, or depriving foreigners of land were, in the past, approved activities. Morality was thus relative to social distance and was frequently suspended altogether at the boundaries of the tribe. In many cases, this boundary between the diffuse community and outsiders was defined by the chiefdom itself. About sixty years ago a group of Barawa men from the now-abandoned

Year	Abuse	Theft	Divorce	Obstructing Police	Contempt of Court	Witchcraft	Sorcery	Breach of Contract	Debts	Abduction	Land Disputes	Adultery	Assault	Inheritance Disputes	Breaking Local By-Laws and Chief's Orders	Paternity
May 1946 Dec. 1946	1	2	21	–	–	–	–	–	6	–	2	1	2	1	3	–
1947	–	4	28	–	–	–	2	–	15	–	1	2	4	1	19	–
1948	1	2	38	–	–	–	–	–	14	–	1	3	3	–	26	–
1949	1	6	19	–	–	–	–	–	9	–	–	1	4	2	5	–
1950	2	1	20	–	2	–	–	–	10	–	–	2	1	–	4	–
Jan. 1951 Sept. 1951	1	3	29	–		–	–	–	13	–	1	1	1	2	–	1
Nov-Dec. 1957	–	–	10	–	–	–	–	–	2	1	2	–	–	1	–	–
1958	2	5	26	–	18	–	–	–	10	3	3	3	5	–	–	–
1959	–	3	39	–	10	1	–	–	21	4	12	7	2	4	3	–
June-Oct. 1965	4	5	21	–	2	1	–	2	12	1	6	6	5	–	–	–
1966	4	7	24	1	1	–	2	–	20	1	9	8	2	–	–	3
(3 months only) 1967	1	2	4	–	–	–	–	–	6	–	4	2	–	–	–	–
TOTALS	17	42	279	1	33	2	4	2	138	10	42	36	29	11	60	4

Table 4. Cases heard in Sengbe chiefdom Native Court (Kabala) 1946-67.

village of Kurekoro discovered that some men from the neighbouring chiefdom (Woli) had destroyed a kola grove near the Merimeri river. The Woli men attacked the group from Kurekoro, tying them up and beating them. War broke out. Farmhouses were burned, hostages were taken. The war ended when the Woli chief sent a message of apology to Barawa; peace was confirmed by the offering of a sacrifice. A curse was

placed on the liver of the beast; *kebile* elders from both Barawa and Woli
ate some of the liver, thus assuring one another that should the quarrel
flare up again they would all be equally accursed. This feud illustrates
the tensions which formerly prevailed between chiefdoms, even
between those linked by common ancestry and clanship.[9]

Even within the chiefdom or the village the ideals of reciprocity and
respect for law and order are often disrupted: respect is not accorded;
those in authority fail to protect their dependents; there may be an
inrequivalence between the value of bridewealth or bride-service given
and the value of the bride received; not everyone in a family is equally
favoured; envies and tensions develop in interpersonal relationships and
at times God and the ancestors seem partial or capricious in their
bestowal of favours. Such discrepancies within the ideal system of
reciprocity have to be rationalised intellectually or made good by
concrete action. It is to questions like these that I shall turn now.

Sectors of Reciprocity

Diagram 3 illustrates the configuration of the major Kuranko social
categories, schematised in terms of spatial and temporal dimensions.
Ideally, descent-based categories coincide with residence-based
categories so that genealogical and territorial distance are congruent.
In actuality this congruence rarely exists. No concept of common
descent links the ancestors of the various clans in the local community—
although fictive kinship links may sometimes be said to relate joking-
linked clans. The village is multi-lineal and 'Village unity is conceived
in terms of values strongly contrasted with those that underpin the
lineage.'[10]

The primary local group—the household—invariably includes
distant kin and occasionally accommodates strangers. The secondary
local group—the *luiye*—seldom comprises agnates alone. Fragmentation of the subclan (*kebile*) leads to a dispersal of kin throughout the
chiefdom. Clans are likewise scattered throughout Kuranko country
and are represented disproportionately in various villages and
chiefdoms. Moreover, migration tends to weaken the effectiveness of
kinship ties. In short, even though genealogically-close kin ought to
live together, they in fact often live apart. Conversely, genealogically-
distant kin or persons unrelated by kinship often live together. This
implies an ambiguity in both authority relations and in the pattern of
reciprocity.

One problem that arises is: to what extent can paternal authority be
exercised over sons who no longer live with their father and who are no
longer dependent upon him for their means of livelihood. Or, does one
behave towards kinsmen who live in the same household in the same
way as one behaves towards kinsmen who live in another household,
luiye, or village, when all are equally close genealogically.

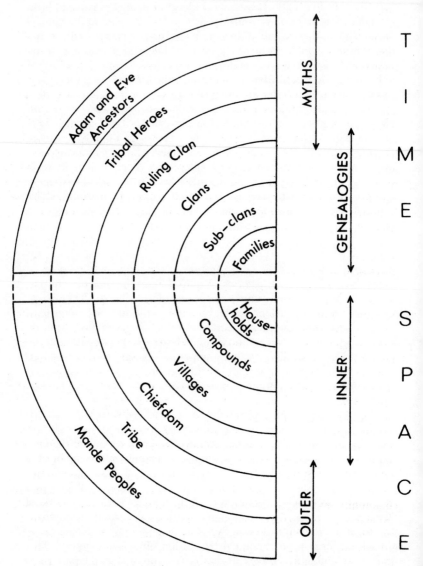

Diagram 3. Paradigm of Kuranko Social Structure

A closely-related problem concerns the ambiguity in authority relations and in the pattern of reciprocity at the margins of the group. At what point does one cease to regard persons as close kin and regard them as distant? Among the Kuranko there is evidence of tension and incongruity between groupings defined in terms of residential propinquity and groupings defined in terms of descent. Descent offers an ideology of identities; locality and residence determine the actual and effective constitution of groupings. The disparity between these two dimensions of social reality often creates problems which are not easily resolved.

The Ideology of Kinship

The Kuranko word which most nearly translates the English word 'kinship' is *nakelinyongoye*. The word literally means 'mother one partnership/relationship' and the metaphor of maternal attachment indicates that the term connotes the ethic of kinship rather than the jural system of rights and obligations which is associated with patrilineal descent. The Kuranko apply the term to all kin reckoned by agnatic or uterine affiliations, and to all affines. This cognatic emphasis is also indicated by another term—*bonson* (literally 'coming from')—which denotes all the descendants of one man, and in some cases, of one woman. *Bonson* is a cognatic descent category which consists nominally of all descendants through both male and female links of an apical ancestor or ancestress.[11] From the individual's point of view all cognatic descent categories to which he belongs converge upon him to form his *bonson*, or kinship circle. It is necessary to add, however, that the Kuranko use the term *bonson* to refer to a category of persons; *bonson* never describes an actual group.

Although the terms *bonson* and *nakelinyorgoye* seem to belie the strictly agnatic principle of descent in Kuranko society, it must be remembered that the strong sense of community identity among Kuranko villagers inclines them to use descent terms and kinship terms qualitatively or in a general and metaphorical way.[12] For example, age-mates and friends often address each other as *biranke* (male affine), and I have heard young men refer to a respected contemporary as *berin* (maternal uncle). These usages indicate how relationship terms may be strategically employed to emphasise values based on co-residence. They also indicate the manner in which affinal relationships develop out of friendship and neighbourhood bonds, drawing people within the local community into a network of quasi-kinship links.

The word which actually denotes agnatic kinship is *mui nyorgoye* (from *mui*, 'to deliver a child') and *mui* kinsmen are those who have the same father. However, there is considerable ambiguity in the use of this word: some informants regard it as synonymous with *nakelinyorgoye*; others associate it with close agnates; others use it to refer to cross-cousins. In the latter sense, cross-cousin marriage is sometimes spoken of as *mu l fure* (*mui* marriage).

Although there is no unequivocal term to denote the group of close agnates who trace their descent to the same father or paternal grandfather, the Kuranko do make a clear distinction between one's close agnatic kinsmen and other kinsmen. Thus, a man might say:

n'nakelinyorgoye kela pati pati ('this is my real kinsman') to refer to his real siblings. Similarly, a person might refer to his or her half-siblings (including *kebile* siblings) by using the term *fadennu* ('father's children'). The importance of this distinction between uterine and agnatic kin is shown in the following proverb:

Barana n'dama na keli ma koni katara min bi birindi kela ma ('All bananas on a single stalk are one (of one kind) but especially those on a single bunch')

Noah translated the proverb on the basis of Orwell's lines: 'All relatives are equal but some are more equal than others.' The agnatic nucleus is therefore made up of husband and wives and their children. Even though kinship terminology extends throughout the *kebile* and clan, Kuranko attitudes and behaviour indicate the overriding importance of the unity and solidarity of this agnatic nucleus. Yet the polygynous household is in reality made up of several matricentric cells. In some cases one refers to uterine kin as *na keli meenu*, by contrast with *fa keli meenu* (siblings of the same mother and same father, by contrast with siblings of the same father but different mothers). The same kind of distinction is made between *na ware* ('mother's side/place/domicile') and *fa ware*. The fundamental importance of the father's place is expressed by a saying: *bei fa ware l tirina* ('everyone is aspiring to their father's place/position'). This means that a man's sons are always striving to assure the prosperity of the father's 'place', fighting to boost paternal prestige and to guarantee the continuity and honour of the father's lineage and name. Yet most Kuranko stress that one should know 'both sides' and be able to call the names of both paternal and maternal ancestors at a domestic rice-flour sacrifice (*dege sarake*). As Chief Sinkari Keli Kargbo expressed it, 'If you do not know the names of your ancestors on the father's side and on the mother's side, it means that you do not know where you are from.'

The complementarity of *na ware* and *fa ware* is also exemplified by Kuranko naming conventions. The first child is customarily named after a predecessor on the father's side; he or she 'goes to the father's side'. The second-born 'goes to the mother's side', and successive children are named alternatively for the father's side and for the mother's side. Variations do, of course, exist: Koranic names are widely-used, notably by Muslims, and some names commemorate the unusual circumstances of a child's birth. One rather apocryphal example of the latter is as follows. A house caught fire while the woman of the house was away at the streamside. Her baby boy was in the house, unbeknownst to her neighbours who busied themselves getting the furniture from the house. Luckily the house-owner's dog had wrapped the baby in a lapa and dragged it out of the house. The child's parents named the child for the event: *Nyawule* ('prosperity-bringing dog').

A person's complete name is therefore made up as follows: first, the mother's name (this differentiates full siblings from half siblings; the father's name would, it is pointed out, not have this differentiating function), second, the derived personal name (from the father's side or from the mother's side), third, the clan name (inherited patrilineally).

When collecting genealogies I would first ask an informant to name his *nakelinyorgonu*. Almost invariably he would name his real siblings. In seeking to gather more extensive genealogical information I constantly found that informants had forgotten the names of kin who lived elsewhere. One informant confessed, 'I do not know the names of my father's brother's children because they don't live here'. Residential separation not only weakens the effectiveness of kinship relations, it also produces lacunae in genealogical knowledge. Ties between dispersed or distant kin become abstract, matters of principle rather than rules of practice. As we shall see, the field of classificatory kinship describes neither a system of automatic or operative rights and obligations nor a realm of actual face-to-face relationships. It is a domain characterised by abstract principles and recurrent problems.

Morowa's Family

Morowa's family (*dembaiye*) consists of himself and five dependents: his elder brother, who is a dwarf and therefore not the family head, his younger brother, his two wives, and an unmarried sister. Morowa's father is dead and even though his father's brother theoretically has full authority over him and his labour, Morowa lives in another *luiye* and is practically independent. After harvest he divides his crop as follows: a token payment to his father's brother, the remainder for himself, his dependents and for hospitality to friends and visitors. Morowa has also spent some time working in Kono and he has made token gifts to his father's brother out of his earnings. Morowa relies on his dependents for labour in making his farm (although his elder brother is a dwarf and therefore 'useless and cannot work'), but he relies on assistance from his *kere* for the heavier farm work. His *kere* is a friendship group, comprising five men, three of whom Morowa describes as friends, two of whom he calls neighbours.

The household constitutes the primary production and consumption unit in Kuranko society. Genealogical or residential separation not only reduce the ties of cooperation and mutual assistance in farming, they also weaken a persons rights to make claims on the scarce resources of distant kin. The boundary line between the household and the wider community marks the point at which a transition occurs from operative kinship to symbolic or token kinship. This disjunction can be better understood if we examine the system of property-holding and inheritance.

Since the *dembaiye* is the primary production and consumption unit it is not surprising to find that it is also the effective property-holding group. The household head (*dembaiyetigi*) 'owns' the house as well as the household members. When he dies, most his property is distributed among near kin and only token gifts are given to distant (i.e. *kebile*) kin. But close kin who have lived apart from the family for some time seldom in fact share a significant portion of the inheritance because living apart implies either a lack of amicability or an absence of economic cooperation. Although the inheritance ideally belongs to the *kebile*, it is actually thought to be the property of those who have shared in its production. This implicit distinction between closeness in kinship and distance in affection, or between actual cooperation and theoretical involvement in productive activity, is one of the commonest causes of legal disputes over the inheritance of property. A conflict often arises between the claims of an elder son (who has been living and working with his father) and a younger brother (who has been living apart and may indeed have 'cut his mouth off' from his elder brother's *luiye*). Let us examine an actual inheritance case.

When Fina Yira Kargbo's father died the following property was left:

(1.) Two wives;
(2.) Four sons and two daughters;
(3.) Shirts, trousers, underwear: 22 pieces;
(4.) Three caps;
(5.) Two pairs of shoes;
(6.) One trunk;
(7.) One house;
(8.) One farm, brushed, hoed, and ready for sowing.

On the 'day of the inheritance division' (*che fare lon*), the property (*che*) was distributed as follows:

(1.) The senior wife was inherited by a younger real brother of the deceased; the junior wife was inherited by a classificatory brother of the deceased. But the junior wife refused to marry this man and she asked if she could remain with her co-wife (who was a *kebile* sister). Her plea was discussed and her request granted.[13]
(2.) The children remained with their mothers.
(3.) The clothes were distributed among *kebile* brothers of the deceased: a pair of shorts was given to one section of the *kebile*, and other articles were distributed among classificatory brothers in the *kebile* section of the deceased.
(4.) The caps were inherited within the *kebile* section.
(5.) Same.
(6.) The trunk was inherited by the eldest son.
(7.) The house was inherited by the younger real brother of the deceased.
(8.) Same.

In this case, which conforms to general principles, the most valuable property (the farm, farm produce, house, widows and children) was inherited by the younger brother of the deceased. But the levirate applies, in principle, to the wider category of *kebile* brothers. Thus, token gifts which had little material value were given to *kebile* kin. Fina Yira stressed that it was not the actual value of the articles that mattered, rather the symbolic value of the gift, for 'it was not given to any one person; it was given to all.' The giving of these token gifts to *kebile* kin indicates the operational diffuseness of *kebile* ties, but it also emphasises the conceptual importance of them. Even though the Kuranko say that '*kebile* kin should help one another', this does not mean that this moral injunction is always recognised in practice. In fact, we shall see that *kebile* ties are notoriously unstable and equivocal. A person's livelihood depends far more on his near kin and upon the bonds of friendship which are spontaneously generated within the local community. Thus, although classificatory kinship terms appear to signify the unity of the *kebile*, *kebile* relationships are in reality qualitatively different from the relationships which link members of the family or household. Moreover, the Kuranko tend to regard near kin who live apart as like *kebile* kin, and to regard *kebile* kin who live and work together as members of the same household as like near kin. Conceptually, *kebile* relationships refer not only to genealogical distance but also to spatial distance. Classificatory kinship should not be regarded as an extension of nuclear kinship relations because there is an implicit recognition that *kebile* or clanship ties are abstract while the ties of kinship within the minimal lineage or co-residential group are real. Abstract moral principles such as the principle of clan brotherhood or the principle that *kebile* kin should help one another can, paradoxically, hold true only when the principles remain unrealised at the level of action. The ideal is intolerant of the real, the abstract rejects the particular, principles eclipse persons. The problem with *kebile* relationships is that they constitute an ambiguous and indeterminate category, standing between the fictional, unactivated bonds of clanship and the real, operational bonds of nuclear kinship. When *kebile* relationships are forced into practice they become problematic; they then involve a contradiction between ideals and realities.[14]

Ambiguities in Kinship

When distant clanspeople do not live in one's own community one is reckoned to have no real obligation to them. In this case kinship bonds are purely theoretical. Variations in modes of reciprocity are determined by both genealogical distance and territorial separation. But as this distance and separation increases, the greater is the likelihood that people will be related to each other in more than one way. Choices often must be made between alternative and contradictory terms of reference and address, and this gives the impression only that there is, at any one time, a real 'fit' between cultural patternings and the complexity of actual interpersonal kinship relationships. The following example illustrates some aspects of the problems, choices and strategies that can occur.

When I first arrived in Firawa, Noah was accorded the respect due to him as a member of the ruling Mara clan. Praise-singers and xylophonists met us on the path into the village, and as we proceeded to

Noah's brother's house (where we were to lodge), various women came
to greet Noah, bowing in the customary manner, shaking his hand,
paying him their respects. Noah clearly enjoyed the prestige of being
what he called 'a prince of the ruling house' and he was keen to impress
upon me his status in Firawa. Not long after we had settled in, one of
Noah's classificatory sister's sons paid us a call. But when he gave Noah
some kola, Noah refused the gift on the grounds that the young man had
not come out to greet him when he arrived. The man protested that
Noah had not sent for him. Noah argued that the man was (1.) his elder
sister's husband, (2.) his sister's son, (3.) a subordinate to a ruler;
therefore the man had no right to be annoyed that Noah had not sent for
him as it was his duty to come and greet his 'master' (*tigi*). At this point
an elder was summoned to arbitrate. Noah and his nephew addressed
the elder in turns and the argument was settled in Noah's favour. Two of
his classificatory sisters who were present, clapped their hands in
approval of the decision. Noah gave them some of the kola, then he ate
kola himself, but not so much in the spirit of a gift received as an
argument won. In this case the nephew felt that Noah had no right to
demand respect in such a self-righteous manner. Although the elder's
judgement had formally upheld the privileges and rights of a ruler, the
conflict remained unresolved. When we were leaving Firawa two weeks
later Noah's nephew used his privileges as sister's son and stole Noah's
cap. If Noah or his nephew had chosen to emphasise their affinal
relationship (the young man was also Noah's elder sister's husband),
then no such licensed disrespect would have been possible.

A second example illustrates the extent to which complications,
ambiguities, and mutually-contradictory frames of reference can
develop within the field of kinship.

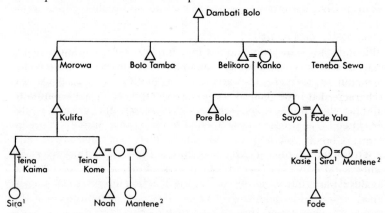

Figure 3. Ambiguities in kinship terminology.

Notes: 1. Sira (Teina Kaima's daughter) is also Kasie's wife
          2. Mantene (Teina Kcme's daughter) is also Kasie's wife

When Kanko's husband (the Firawa chief Belikoro) died, Kanko was inherited by Belikoro's grandson—Teina Kaima. Teina Kaima should have called Pore Bolo 'father', but because of the marriage of Pore Bolo's mother (Kanko) to Teina Kaima, Pore Bolo called Teina Kaima 'father'. In practice Teina Kaima reciprocated, calling Pore Bolo 'son'. Pore Bolo's sister (Sayo) followed her brother's usage, calling Teina Kaima 'father'. The second ambiguity in this genealogy arises from the fact that Sira is both Noah's sister (his father's brother's daughter) and his classificatory mother. In practice Noah regards her as a sister.

As a general rule, operative relationships are established on the basis of the priority of genealogical links in the two previous generations; links which can be traced further back tend to be forgotten or disregarded when they are discrepant with more recent connections.

Terminological ambiguities may also arise when affinal ties contradict kinship ties. Matrilateral cross-cousin marriage may be mentioned in this context, because it transforms the mother's brother into a father-in-law. In the case above we should also note the ways in which status determined by age position may contradict status determined by genealogical position. These matters will be discussed further in chapter 6.

Giving and Lending

Every community is interlinked by a complex network of credit and debt (*yuli*) which generates a continuing circulation of goods and services within it. A person can borrow (*dondole*) from anyone except a close kinsman 'because he would be duty bound to give you something if you were in need'. Borrowing from one's wife's father or brothers is rare 'because they are recipients of one's bridewealth payments'. Borrowing from one's mother's brother is more common 'because only some of the things given by your maternal uncle are free gifts'. Borrowing from *kebile* kin is not uncommon, and this is an indication of the effective difference between close kin and distant kin. Yet, *kebile* kinship defines a category mid-way between the field of close kinship (characterised by 'generalised reciprocity') and the field of neighbourhood ties (characterised by 'balanced reciprocity'). There is often considerable ambiguity about whether or not *kebile* kin have claims upon one another or, like non-kinsmen, transactions with them must be formalised in terms of credit and debt.

The socio-economic reasons for borrowing and lending become clear when we consider the precariousness of the Kuranko economy. When food is in short supply or when a villager is in need of money (for paying fines, debts, bridewealth etc.) he can either ask kinsmen for help or borrow from a non-kinsman. The problem with asking help from kinsmen is twofold: first, close kin (members of the same household and/or production-consumption unit) are likely to be also in need at the same time (e.g. during the 'rainy season hunger'); second, distant kin

Creditor	Relationship	Provenance	Debt
Pore Mara	*kebile* brother	Sukurela	1 cow
Konde Kargbo	wife	Sukurela	Le. 3

Debtor	Relationship	Provenance	Debt
Sinkari Sise	friend	Sukurela	Le. 8
Karifa Mara	*kebile* brother	Sukurela	7 *lankono* of rice (value Le. 14)
Kusan Koroma	friend	Diang	Le. 7
Konkoru Mara	*kebile* brother	Sukurela	Le. 28
Momodu Fula	friend	Sukurela	Le. 8
Karifa Sano	friend	Firawa	Le. 4
Nyale Mara	*kebile* sister	Sukurela	gold
Mantene Kargbo	wife's sister	Sukurela	gown
Sundukon Sise	no relationship	Sukurela	rice
Fore Sise	wife's father	Sukurela	gown (value Le. 6)
Nyindaiye Thoronka	hunter and teacher	Sukurela	1lb. of gunpowder
Thoronka Sise	no relationship	Sukurela	4 *lankono* of rice (value Le. 12)
Kumba Kargbo	mother's sister	Sangbamba	Le. 10
Damba Kargbo	wife	Sukurela	Le. 6
Mantene Sise	no relationship	Sukurela	2 lapas
Tigire Sise	no relationship	Sukurela	Le. 2
Namfa	wife's mother	Sukurela	goat and Le. 2

Table 5. Morowa's Creditors and Debtors.

may be unwilling to offer help on a purely altruistic basis and the person requesting help may be unwilling to receive assistance in the form of a loan. Asking non-kinsmen for help circumvents these problems. A formal credit-debt arrangement is consistent with the definition of social relations in this sector, and moreover it is probable that at any one time there is someone in the community with a surplus of rice or some money saved which he can lend. Because different varieties of rice mature at different times, farmers of a *kere* group often plan their sowing so that they will exchange surpluses in order to have a steady supply over a longer period than if they worked alone.

Reasons

Morowa gave her money to buy rice; it has not all been repaid.
The money was given to Morowa for safekeeping; it was then stolen.

Reasons

Morowa gave her money to buy rice; it has not all been repaid.
When Karifa returned from Kono he had no money; he borrowed rice to make his farm.

Morowa lent him rice (value Le. 7).
Morowa gave his brother his radio to sell for him; the brother spent the money.
Momodu went bankrupt and Morowa helped him set up another trade store in Sukurela.
Karifa's wife's family wanted bridewealth (one cow was unpaid).
Morowa lent him what he had at the time (Le. 4).
Nyale wanted some gold to have jewellery made.
Mantene asked Morowa for the gown because 'she had no clothes'.
Morowa harvested his rice early and lent some to Sundukon.
Fore asked Morowa for a gown.
Asked Morowa for it.

Asked for it.

She wanted money to buy seed rice for her farm.
She needed rice from Morowa's farm to make her own farm.
Morowa sold them to Mantene on credit.
Money needed to pay wages to farm workers.
When her younger brother sued for refund of bridewealth Namfa requested help from Morowa.

Table 5 (*contd.*)

In 1971, members of Bundo's cooperative planned their sowing as follows:

Bundo planted *bako* (a 'sweet' variety of rice which is readily marketed). *Mamudiake* was planted by another man, because he had no help in scaring birds from the farm. This variety of rice is the last to mature and by the time it is ripe the birds are eating the seeds of wild grasses (i.e. it is well into the dry season). He also planted a variety called *gborokuli* because it matures quickly and is ready to harvest towards the end of the rainy season when food is scarce; his wives helped him scaring birds from the crop. A third man planted *gborokuli*, for harvest at the end of the rainy season, and another variety—*bako*—for storing in the granary. His wives planted *yaka* (swamp rice) which is a slow-maturing variety. A fourth man planted *fosa*, a very slow-growing variety, so that he would be free to do other farm work (cultivating cassava and bananas). He also planted some *gborokuli*, and his wives planted *yaka*.

Members of this *kere* lend rice to other members when supplies are short and the loan is repaid in terms of customary units of measurement.[15]

In order to elucidate further the pattern of credit and debt (*yuli*) let us examine Table 15 which lists Morowa Mara's creditors and debtors. Several significant facts emerge from the study of this particular (and typical) case.

(1)   The social concomitant of the system of 'staggered' rice production is that everyone in the community is at some time indebted to everyone else. The traditional barter system had similar implications: blacksmiths would exchange hoes, cutlasses and axes for rice, hunters would exchange meat for rice, and weavers and dyers would supplement their own farm production by exchanging cloth for foodstuffs (*don fan*, literally 'eat thing'). In short, a person's livelihood depended upon others; the kinship group was neither socially nor economically viable on its own.

(2)   Goods given to *kebile* kin are usually considered to be formal loans, though Morowa pointed out that these were the most difficult to reclaim. I have no evidence to support the assertion, but informants often told me that most of the debt cases which are taken to court involve loans to *kebile* kin. Of the total number of court cases listed in Table 4 (710), 18% were debt cases and there is evidence that such cases have become more numerous during the twenty year period which is covered. It is also noteworthy that a man will not be held liable for a *kebile* brother's debt, nor will he feel obliged to repay it if requested. Many Kuranko say that a debt is never 'written off'; a debt can be inherited and there are instances of people inherited their grandfather's debts and being requested to repay them.

(3)   Morowa will, in time, 'write off' two of his debts. He would not seek court action to reclaim a gown which he 'lent' to his wife's younger sister, nor would he ask the hunter (to whom Morowa is apprenticed) to give back the 1lb. of gunpowder which he lent him some months before. In the first case, Morowa's joking relationship with his wife's younger sister precludes a formal claim; in the second case the hunter is 'like a father' to Morowa and he would not claim from him.

(4)   Morowa does not consider his gift of rice to his classificatory mother as a real loan, even though it was asked for and given as such. 'I will not give her a loan next time she asks for something', Morowa told me, 'I'll only give her things as free gifts'.

(5) Morowa will not ask his wives to repay what he gave them. 'What a wife has, her husband owns', and Morowa considers it his responsibility to give to them and look after them.

(6) Morowa only intends claiming debts that have been outstanding for more than one year. He was adamant that it would be improper to embarass his debtors if they were not in a position to pay off their debts to him.

Creditor-debtor relationships characterise and even signify the nature of inter-clan relationships. They indicate the point at which reciprocity undergoes a transformation from being altruistically motivated to being a system of formal calculation and economic exchange. Yet, as the example above shows, all transactions (even between close kin) are remembered. Of particular importance are transactions between affines, because if divorce is ever declared the *furufa* (bridewealth) must be refunded and every article given and the occasion on which it was given must be specified in a court hearing. The wife-giving group, who will also have kept an accurate record of all transactions, will confirm or correct the account.

Today, more and more transactions tend to be calculated in terms of credit and debt or evaluated in terms of money. In many villages the *kere* system has declined in importance and it is not uncommon for young men to offer their labour for immediate cash rewards; the *kere* system is often based on formal contract rather than reciprocal cooperation among a group of friends. One reason for this change is the introduction of markets. Many farmers grow rice for sale on the Kabala or Kono markets, as in Bundo's case, and then use the money received to pay for farm labour and to purchase imported commodities.[16] Such changes have weakened cooperative ties and brought economic hardship to villagers. For instance, the price of imported commodities is higher in a Kuranko village than in Freetown. And because money is needed to purchase them, Kuranko are obliged to calculate labour and capital investment far more in terms of financial profit than in terms of social relationships. As the Kuranko move towards a market-dominated peasant economy they become less and less the subjects of their own social destiny, more and more objects in a national or international economy whose vacillations they cannot comprehend. The sources of life and death become relocated. One ceases to depend on members of one's own community for one's well-being, and one's very existence seems to depend upon an outside world that one cannot communicate with, understand, or control. The dilemma of the anthropologist in the third world is very much a part of this. How can we treat the people whom we study as subjects and not as objects when the world with which we are identified and associated has in fact reversed this equation?

Summary

The principle of reciprocity which the Kuranko apply to relationships among co-villagers is summed up in the frequently-quoted metaphor: *nyendan bin to kile a wa ta an segi*. This refers to the manner in which a particular kind of grass (also used for thatching roofs) bends one way as you pass through it and then bends back the other way as you return through it. The idea of affinal ties being like a pathway is again expressed in a phrase which is often used to explain why and how marriages bind different *kebile* together: *kile ka na faga* ('so that the pathway does not die').

In this chapter I have outlined the ideology of kinship and communitas in terms of reciprocity and shown how this ideology is in many ways problematic. The realisation of kinship principles often depends on whether or not genealogically close kin actually live together and constitute a single production-consumption unit. There is a tension in Kuranko social life between the given, inescapable ties of nuclear kinship and the chosen, manipulatable ties of distant kinship and neighbourhood. Co-residence implies, for Kuranko, onerous and problematic relationships even if they are conceived to be governed by cooperation, altruism, amity and reciprocity. Informants often commented upon this by using two similar proverbs: *morgon' be morgon mi sigine, wo'n den den bi kela* ('people who are neighbours—sit/live together—they are the ones that quarrel'), and *morgon be i siginyorgoye le kela* ('people quarrel with their neighbours').

Residential separation (while it may reflect original conflicts) enables a person to decide whether or not he will extend genuine, rather than token, respect to others. Every young man looks forward to the day when he will achieve independence from his father, yet he also aspires to his father's position. In every sector of Kuranko social life people strive to achieve some balance between freedom and constraint, between duty and desire. I have endeavoured to draw a distinction between those bonds—like friendship, joking relationships, clanship, neighbourhood—which are potential bonds, developed on the basis of choice and able to be realised or allowed to lapse at will, and other bonds—like the ties of nuclear kinship, affinity, co-residence—which, once established, are 'givens' and allow for little flexibility.

In Part II I will discuss kinship and affinity in greater detail, paying close attention to kinship and interpersonal relations rather than to kinship groups. The ideological constructs, problems, transformations and variations which have been sketched out in the preceding chapters will be explored in depth. But Part II is related to Part I in a more specific way. We have already noted that the prevailing oppositions—male/female and elder/younger—indicate even more profound oppositions between discrete socio-spatial and socio-temporal categories. In studying male-female relations and elder-younger relations constant reference to Kuranko concepts of space and time are therefore necessary.

Notes

1. The *lenke* tree seeds itself with exploding pods; the ground beneath the tree thus does not receive any seeds from the parent tree. If a person gives to distant kinsmen rather than fulfilling his primary obligations to close kin, then this proverb may be used to describe and censure his behaviour.

2. Sahlins 1968: 145-9.

3. The word *sundan* is used to describe a stranger, visitor or guest; imported varieties of rice are also called *sundan*.

4. *Hinantei* means 'full of sympathy, compassionate', by contrast with *hinantei ma* or *hinan sa ro* ('unsympathetic, harsh, lacking in compassion'). Towards the conclusion of a court hearing an elder may make a plea for sympathy or leniency on behalf of the defendant, saying '*a ra seria tinya, koni ma kinikini a ma*' ('he has spoiled the law but let us be sorry for him/be lenient with him').

5. In discussing the disparity between surface and deep reality (social form and private sentiment) among the Kissi, Denise Paulme makes a comment that is no less true for Kuranko society. ' . . . sourire, patience, accueil généreux dissimulant leurs sentiments profonds. A les mieux connaître, l'observateur est frappé par l'état de tension ou vivent ces êtres d'apparence si paisable.' (1949:969).

6. Among the Temne, children are punished by severe flogging; Mende parents often prefer to punish misbehaviour in other ways—withdrawing food and similar deprivations. These factors have been related to patterns of personality disturbance in these societies (Dawson 1964:309). Other writers (e.g. Fortes 1969:234) have related ancestor images and beliefs to child-parent relations. It is possible to conjecture that the passive role of paternal ancestors among the Kuranko and the belief that ancestors punish misbehaviour by withdrawing blessings and protection are related to the fact that fathers play no active part in raising children and that punishment by withdrawing food is not uncommon.

7. I have published a complete account of witchcraft beliefs and confessions among the Kuranko elsewhere (Jackson 1975)

8. I observed a court case in December 1969 in which a man was tried for the crime of adultery with a woman who was breast-feeding her child. The case followed the woman's confession to adultery and her husband took the case to court. The adulterer was fined Le. 100 (£50) and a cow. The cow was sacrificed and the meat shared among the villagers. The adulterer was also ordered to pay additional compensation to the family of the women's husband.

9. The Barawa people (Mara) are said to be older than the Mara in Woli, although both have the same ancestor. A special term— *borsingbi yamusa* ('elder part—younger part of the relationship')—is used (but only in this particular context) to signify the relative seniority of the Barawa Mara.

10. Horton (on the Kalabari) 1962:198.

11. Among the Temne, *bonshaw* is the name for composite lineage groups, made up of the *makas* (exogamous patrilineal lineages) and the *makara* on the mother's side (see Dawson, citing Littlejohn, 1964:307).

12.   See Bloch 1971:79-87. The Diang Koroma sometimes speak of the
      Barawa Mara and the Kamadugu Kargbo as their kinsmen
      (*nakelinyorgonu*). But as one informant put it 'this does not mean that we
      are from the same mother, but that we have some relationship'. He
      referred, in this instance, to the fact that these three chiefly lines used to
      intermarry in order to create a system of political alliances among them.
      Today, recollecting these alliances through marriage, men will comment
      'if we are giving a sacrificial gift it will be given to *Diang n Barawa* (Diang
      and Barawa) because they go together'.

13.   If a woman wants to remarry a man who is not a member of her late
      husband's lineage then the matter may be more problematic. In one case
      which I observed, two of a woman's husbands (both brothers) had died;
      after the death of her last husband she wanted to remarry a man of her
      own choice rather than become the legacy wife (*che musu*) of a third
      brother. The court elders heard the case from her point of view and from
      her father-in-law's point of view; they decided that her paramour should
      'beg' her father-in-law to release her. Within hours of the court hearing,
      the man agreed that his daughter-in-law should marry the man of her
      choice.

14.   For further discussion see chapters 8 and 10.

15.   The Kuranko traditionally used a unit of value —*lankone*—in barter
      exchange. One *lankone* was equivalent to 10 mats, 10 rattan containers of
      rice, 10 *gbalgbalan* of cloth (each *gbalgbalan* was 4 lengths of cloth
      measured from elbow to finger tip), or 10 bunches of tobacco leaf. A cow
      was valued at 5 *lankone*. Individual mats or containers of rice were valued
      at I *bolfa* ('handfull').

16.   In 1970 a government decree forbad trucking rice south for sale except by
      government permission. The decree was annulled in 1973 as a result of
      protests in the northern region.

PART II

5.   Male and Female

In Kuranko thought and social life the category distinction between male and female is so fundamental and pervasive that most Kuranko regard it as 'natural' or divinely decreed. Margaret Mead refers to sex differentiation as 'one theme in the plot of social life'.[1] My concern in the following four chapters is with Kuranko variations on this theme and with the symbolic ramifications of the male-female dichotomy in Kuranko social life. As we shall see, this dichotomy pertains not only to the field of kinship and marriage; it serves as one of the basic armatures for structuring all social relations.

Male and Female Domains
The Kuranko frequently express the division of the sexes in terms of a contrast between *ke dugu* ('male place/domain') and *musu dugu* ('female place/domain'). Supernatural sanctions, in the forms of protective fetishes and medicines, swears, and cults objects, are used to maintain the boundaries between these domains. Secular sanctions also preserve the exclusive rights of men and women. The separation and complementarity of the sexes is said to be achieved by mutual distance and respect; to resist hearing, seeing or speaking of certain hidden aspects of the domain of the opposite sex is thought to maintain a kind of pact of secrecy which is important for the preservation of life itself.

Every Kuranko village is sited near a stream, one part of which is reserved for men and banned to women (usually upstream), another part of which is reserved for women and banned to men. Women fetch water from the women's part of the stream; they also bathe and launder there. The prohibitions against a person of the opposite sex trespassing in the vicinity of these river pools are based on the notion that adults should never see the nakedness of the other sex in public. This privacy is necessary for other reasons too because the same river pools are used for ritual bathing and purification, notably during initiations and after funerals. When neophytes are washed and divested of their pre-initiation dress they enter that phase of initiation ritual which is concerned with sexual differentiation. When widows are washed and purified forty days after their husband's death, they are ritually dissociated from their former marriage. In these cases the transition from one status to another involves streamside rites which are doubly significant: the location of the rite part-way between town and bush serves to objectify the dual aspect of a confused or transient identity which must be separated and polarised, while the washing away of the

81

'dirt' associated with the previous state serves to free the neophyte or widow so that they can proceed to assume a new identity.

Infringements of the prohibitions which maintain these exclusive domains are serious matters which may be taken to the chief's court. In the case of women, the female cult association—*Segere*—may take up the issue since it is here, as we shall see, that the ultimate sanctioning powers of women are located. Women may also swear (*gborle*) their part of the stream so that men who trespass there will be afflicted by some disease (usually said to be *kee*—elephantiasis of the testicles).

The Kuranko house is also divided into male and female areas. Women never sit with the men on the front verandah of the house and whenever I invited a woman to join a group of men for conversation on some subject of interest to me she would invariably indicate embarrassment. Only rarely do women participate in men's conversations and at court hearings or moots women remain silent and deferential even when the proceedings fail to represent or reflect their personal points of view.

Men spend little time in the women's domestic area at the back of the house; women have the right to abuse intruders or to throw scalding water over them. Although I spent a great deal of time in the cooking compounds (talking to women or preparing food for myself) I paid the penalty for these intrusions; men would often mock me and women would either scornfully ignore my presence or deride my avowed interest in their domestic activities. Within the house, men may not enter the women's rooms, may not tamper with women's trinket boxes or use women's kitchen equipment without prior permission. Men protect their own privacy with an almost obsessive concern since their protective fetishes and medicines should never be seen by women. It is feared that if a wife or woman sees these personal medicines then she will gossip about them or deliberately divulge the secret of their whereabouts, so endangering a man's safety.

During a woman's confinement her husband and other men are forbidden to trespass in the vicinity of the house. The custom of sending a woman to her natal group for the birth of her first child is said to be a way of guaranteeing a strict separation from her husband during this critical period. Birth is an event which allegedly concerns and involves women only. During confinement, a woman's mother and sisters act as guardians as much as attendants and nurses.

If a man transgresses any of these rules then legal action may be sought. The penalty is usually a fine (a cow must be given to the women of the community for sacrifice), but if the women are not satisfied with the court's judgement they may have recourse to the mystical powers of *Segere*, the most powerful of their cult associations. In other words, if men fail to uphold women's rights in court then the women can call into operation sanctions which depend upon forces which lie outside the jural control and knowledge of men. Yet even within the bounds of secular jurisdiction women may be represented by the *dimusukuntigi* (the elected leader of the women). She acts as a spokeswoman and mediator in court cases which concern women's rights and privileges in the collective sense. When the newly-elected *dimusukuntigi* was installed in Firawa in January 1970 one of her first pronouncements was that men should not go anywhere near a house where a woman was giving birth. For the most part this rule is respected. As one man told me 'No man would dare go there; the thought would not enter his head'. The fact is that both men and women willingly respect the secrets of the opposite sex; it is a matter of active cooperation and deliberate collusion rather than of mere submission or fear. This generates a relationship of complementarity between the sexes which, at the level of mystical or cult activity, leads to a 'horizontal' equality of male and female domains that transcends the everyday hierarchical relationship between the superordinate male and the subordinate female.

As a general rule men should not associate with women when the latter are, so to speak, in a state of physiological abnormality, i.e. during a woman's menses, confinement, illness or death. Nor should a man have sexual intercourse with a woman who is breast-feeding a child. Sexual intercourse with a menstruating woman is said to be 'dirty'; it may make the woman ill or affect her ability to bear children since 'some of her waste will be pushed back into contact with the new seed'. Sexual intercourse with a mother who is breast-feeding her child is banned because it is said that the sperm will contaminate the mother's milk (*kinyi*, literally 'breast water') and so cause the child to become weak, sickly, contract diarrhoea, and die. Sexual intercourse in the bush, in the rice fields, or during the daytime is allegedly prohibited; in the former cases it 'spoils' the protective fetishes in the chiefdom. But many married couples treat these restrictions lightly and there is considerable variability from person to person in beliefs about sexual pollution. However, most Kuranko are quite adamant that intimate association with the opposite sex during sickness is dangerous—it actually jeopardises the life of the invalid. Women prefer their daughters to nurse them in sickness, and men their sons. As one woman expressed it, 'Although God made men and women for each other, a man does not know how to care for a sick woman. Men should not see women when they are indisposed (i.e. should not see their sexual organs or see them suffering from fever, diarrhoea or vomiting). Men should never boast that they know women; they do not.' Men are reluctant to call upon brothers or other men to attend them during sickness because, if the other man has had adulterous relations with the invalid's wife, then his administrations will only exacerbate the illness. One man commented, 'A son is all right because he would never interfere with your wife.'

These events are all characterised by irregularity or periodicity. They indicate disorder, an interruption of normal routines. They therefore occasion the imposition of strict rules which serve to isolate or mark off the domain of irregularity from the domain of regularity. Since 'dirt' is commonly associated with disorder and 'purity' (*gbe*) with order, it is considered important that unclean things do not defile the clean. Usually this process involves some kind of sexual segregation, because the Kuranko regard sexual intercourse at the wrong time, in the wrong place, or with the wrong person as being inimical to order and life (*nie*).[2] Sexual intercourse with the wrong person (adultery or incest) is thus censured because it causes tensions and 'darkness' between men; in the case of a divorce which follows from an adulterous affair one could say 'he/she has spoiled the marriage' (*a ra na fure tinyan*). Adulteries can also 'spoil' (*ka tinya*) sacrifices for it is an offense to God and the ancestors to offer gifts in a state of impurity. When I asked Chief Dambi Lai Mara of Bandakarafaia why the sacrifices to the land (*dugumasarake*) had been discontinued he told me that 'people were pure in those days', meaning that the frequency of adultery has now made it impossible for men to sacrifice together without offending the ancestors. Kuranko men consider it imperative that recreational sex (which is based on free choice and random or transient liasons between individuals) should be subjugated to procreative sex (based on male decisions and a system of affinal contracts between groups in the local community). At first glance it seems ironic that although men are often willing partners in clandestine love affairs, women are blamed for instigating them and for causing the breakdown of goodwill between affines which often results. But given the fact that women are not contractually committed to each other as the men are, it is inevitable that women should be considered irresponsible and dangerous.

It is possible to relate the complex of beliefs concerning male-female differences and the rules governing sexual contact to the sexual division of labour in economic life and in child-rearing. Yet, as we shall see in the next chapter, the Kuranko concern with the segregation of the sexes is an indication of more far-reaching intellectual interests than the domestic and economic complementarity of paternal-maternal and husband-wife roles.

Women perform practically all the domestic and household chores (sweeping, cooking, fetching water and firewood) and a Kuranko man will consider it degrading to do such work. For this reason it is rare to find Kuranko 'house boys' in Sierra Leone and I have often heard Kuranko men speak slightingly of men from other tribes who derogate manhood by taking such employment. Although Kuranko men say that child-rearing is the joint responsibility of both parents, observation makes it clear that it is the mother who plays the major role in child care. From this point of view the father is practically superfluous or expendable. The emotional bond or primary attachment to the mother is expressed in terms of the importance of the mother's breast and the mother's milk. Even after weaning, a crying child is often comforted by being given the breast. And I have often observed an adult man seeking succour or moral support from his mother when an argument with his father has reached an impasse. The Kuranko say that 'the head of the breast [nipple] may be turned downward but the milk never spills [is never wasted] on the ground' (*kinye kunye yegbe n'done ama kori ama sorn tintin koye ma*). The emotional primacy of uterine bonds is also suggested by the terms which define kinship or the kinship group: *dembaiye* (household or nuclear family, from *demba* 'a suckling mother'), *nakelinyorgoye* (kinship, from *na* 'mother'), *mui nyorgoye* (from *mui*, 'to give birth'). It is also noteworthy that when the curse (*danka*) is used by a person against a close kinsman, it will always be prefaced by the words 'if we did not suckle at the same breast' or 'if we were not born of the same mother'; in other words, uterine bonds are referred to when expressing the ultimate values of kinship. To repudiate these values is to be accursed.

Secondary attachments are gradually rather than 'traumatically introduced, as in the quasi-parental care given by elder siblings or grandparents, and in the custom of fostering children (*kerifa* or *ma kolo tine*) with their father's uterine brothers or their father's parents. In many cases, boys do not stop sleeping with their mothers until they are ten years of age, but it is extremely rare for young children to sleep with their fathers. The paternal role and the maternal role are different and complementary: the former connotes jural authority, provision of food, ownership and control of property, descent relations and ancestral blessings; the latter connotes emotional attachment and security, personal care and nurturance.

The heavy labour of rice farming is done by men, and control and management of rice production, storage and allocation are the men's responsibility. Men offer sacrifices connected with planting and harvesting, men always sow the seed and build and control access to the granaries. It is because rice is the 'senior' and staple food (Kuranko say that the word for rice—*kore*—is cognate with the term for elder brother—*koro*) that upland rice cultivation is primarily the concern of men. Women cultivate some swamp rice, but it is of secondary importance and men consider it as inferior in taste and quality. With rice, kola is thought to be the most important mainstay of life and therefore kola trees are always 'owned' by men and inherited patrilineally.

Apart from playing a subsidiary role in upland rice farming, women are concerned with gardening and the cultivation of supplementary crops. The sexual division of labour implies a distinction between primary and secondary production, the former being the preserve of man and the latter being the preserve of women, children and old men. Where men, women and children cooperate in the cultivation of a single crop (particularly rice) there is a division between primary and secondary tasks. Thus men prepare the farmsite and sow the seed while women and children tend the maturing crop and work at weeding it and scaring birds away from it.

The metaphorical possibilities which these divisions in economic life suggest are certainly developed by the Kuranko themselves. They compare rice cultivation with the raising of children. When a young woman is ready for initiation they say 'her breasts are ripe' *(a kinye ara moi)*; a pregnant woman is 'well fed' *(ara fa)*. The seed or grain *(kuli)* is compared with the bones in the body or with the potency or substance of a man's words *(i la kume wo kuli sa ɫo*, 'your words are without substance').

The manner in which maleness is correlated with order, life, seed, primary production, control, and the supervision of the most difficult tasks, while femaleness is correlated with secondary, nurturant, and mediatory roles leads us at once to the foundations of Kuranko thought. The economic system is logically consistent with the intellectual system and the same criteria of differentiation underline both. But before we go into further detail it is important to note other role distinctions based on sex.

Among various craft and occupational specialisations women are never hunters, blacksmiths, weavers or leather workers. Fishing is, however, always done by women. The making and mastery of powerful medicines is the preserve of men, although certain knowledgeable old women may acquire a reputation as herbalists. Legitimate magic, or sorcery, is associated with men *(besetigi*, 'medicine-owners' or sorcerers'), but illegitimate magic is associated with women, particularly the use of poisons *(daberi)* and witchcraft *(suwa'ye)*. Certain ritual professions are also divided into male and female activities. Among the *jelis*, women *(jelimusu)* play the triangle while the men *(jeliba*, literally 'big *jelis'*) are always the xylophonists. Drummers are always men. Women are never diviners *(bolomafelne)* and sacrifices are never offered by women.

Legally, property cannot be owned by women although most women do in fact accumulate wealth in the form of domestic utensils, trinkets and heirlooms which they can 'will' to a daughter before they die. In other words, objects and valuables which a woman receives from her mother (heirlooms and clothes) or from her brother (occasional gifts of money or domestic equipment) cannot be appropriated by her husband. Morowa's wife explained that a woman 'feels that these things belong to her personally'. She then commented upon certain changes in property-holding which have occured during her own lifetime: 'If a woman gets something and she says that it is hers and that she has control over it, then that is a lie. The husband is the owner [*tigi*], though in some cases some women do not regard the husband as the owner. But this is because of the present day. In the past women never owned property, but nowadays they feel that they do own their household things. But what the elders told me about the past is that whatever a woman possessed in those days, it all belonged to the husband; but we, the children of today, say that whatever a woman has the husband should not have control over it—it belongs to her.'

The Ideology of Procreation

Kuranko ideas about conception and procreation are built around the unshakeable conviction (shared by both men and women) that it is the male who makes the child, the woman being simply the passive vessel in which the foetus grows and from which the child is born.

I was discussing these ideas with Lamina Kalokko and his wife, endeavouring to get Lamina to elaborate on what he meant when he said that the 'man owns the child'. His wife was shelling groundnuts in one corner of the room. Lamina took a groundnut from her winnowing tray and cracked open the shell, indicating that the shell is like the woman while the seed *(kuli)* 'which belongs to the man' is like the child. To convince me further he pointed out that unless a woman receives the male seed then her ovum is just wasted and is shed during menstruation. Lamina's wife gave her support to the argument: 'A man without sperm [*koiyi*][3], even if he is married, will not get a child. But as soon as the woman takes another man who has got sperm, she will conceive.' Rather the same comments came from Fode Kargbo at Dankawali. He told me that 'the man owns the child' and added that 'a child belongs to the father because women cannot bear children without men.' I asked him if the reverse would not also be the case: that a man without a woman could not have a child. He replied: 'Even if a man gets a wife and he is impotent, the woman cannot bear a child without a man. The woman will say that this man cannot give her children and so she will find another man to have sex with; then she will bear a child.'[4]

The Kuranko consider that the identity of the child is determined, both biologically and jurally, by the father. By contrast, the mother influences the destiny *(latege)* of the child in the ways in which she raises it and in the ways in which she honours and respects her husband. The blessings of the child's paternal ancestors, which are thought to play such an important part in the child's destiny, are, as we shall see, actually mediated by the child's mother. In both its mystical and practical aspects, the patrilineal ideology thus depends upon a harmony between husband-wife and paternal-maternal roles.

Threat and Danger

The contrast between uterine and agnatic affiliations has already been alluded to: *fa ware* (father's side/place) is contrasted with *na ware* (mother's side/place); *fa keli meenu* ('father-one-kin') is contrasted with *na keli meenu* ('mother-one-kin'). Uterine ties connote emotional attachments while agnatic ties are based upon formal jural codifications. This contrast can be viewed as one aspect of a wider system of oppositions between male and female attributes, activities and symbolic identifications. In order to elucidate this system of oppositions the following set of contrasts is presented.

MALE	FEMALE
agnatic descent	uterine affiliations
role	personality
determination	influence
duty	desire
strong	weak
even	odd

In chapter 1 I described briefly the impact on Kuranko society of the raids of Samory's Sofas during the 1880s. The memory of these decimating incursions lives on in legend and anecdote. It gives definition to the feeling of insecurity, distrust and threat which is noticeable among the Kuranko when they are confronted by outsiders. Erstwhile tribal enemies are known as *morgo fian'* ('black people'), and this is one instance of the more general association of ideas (outsider-black-sinister) which has been discussed in Chapter 3. We have also noted how the Kuranko concern for containment and for maintaining boundaries is expressed in various protective rites, in the use of protective medicines, and in social values which stress reserve, caution and self-restraint.

The outsider who penetrates the boundaries of the group and becomes a 'stranger within' symbolises and personifies the idea of threat and danger. But the Kuranko obsession with protection, containment and concealment is at first glance baffling, given the social controls that curb the misuse of powerful medicines[5], the absence of warfare throughout the twentieth century, and the lack of empirical evidence for people seeking to harm others. Kuranko beliefs about mystical threat are concerned with internal rather than external dangers and, as I shall show, these beliefs are articulated in such a way that women personify these dangers. In order to elucidate the Kuranko notion that women are generally weak-willed or malevolent let us first look at the mythological explanation for male-female differences. The text recorded below was given in answer to the question: 'Why the male-female antagonism in Kuranko life?'[6]

You know, if you see women showing treachery *(monekoe)* towards men it is for no other reason but that all men in this world are in the hands of the women. We say that we are in the hands of the women because women bore us. Before this time it would have been good for God to say let women be ahead and let we the men be behind. If you see that the women are behind it is because the power that God gave to men was not given to women. We did not have anything to do with that.

From our ancestor Adam and our ancestress Eve—those were the two first people in this world and they were the ones who bore us all. According to what we have been told they went and found a fruit tree and that fruit was not good to eat. Nobody in this world was supposed to eat that fruit. But Adam and Eve were sitting under that tree and they were very hungry. They were told that they should watch over the tree but that they should not eat the fruit on it. No sooner had they been told that than Satan came. He said to Eve, 'Wa, you are a stupid person, you are hungry and this fruit is very sweet—why don't you eat it?' He picked one and gave it to Eve. He picked another and gave it to Adam. Had Adam swallowed his first we should have been under the women. He put the fruit in his mouth and she put the fruit in her mouth. But Eve was too quick. She swallowed hers. As Adam was about to swallow his, the one who had left them to watch over the tree came and said, 'Don't swallow it!' Then Eve was asked, 'Where is your fruit?' She said, 'I have swallowed it.' Then they said, 'Eh, women cannot resist anything.'

Now, to know why we say that women are under us it is because when a baby girl is born it is a man that goes and pays bridewealth for her. She becomes a wife, inferior in status to that man. Now, when women consider the fact that they bore us but yet we pay bridewealth for them and they become our wives, they become angry.[7] Therefore they use all kinds of treachery in order to ruin us. Women are treacherous towards men because they want to rule the men. But there is no way in which this is possible because we pay bridewealth for them. And because they swallowed the fruit.

This account passes from the mythological to the sociological frame of reference , both rationalising and seeking to explain the male-female opposition and the view that women are inimical to men. The narrative emphasises the difference between female control over the birth and raising of children and male jural control. We are told that women are envious of this male jural hegemony (particularly in the context of marriage). What we are not told, but what I will later show to be similarly significant, is that men are envious of female powers, especially the emotional bonds between mother and child. The systematic yet impersonal character of jural ties stands in contrast to the less predictable and more personal nature of emotional bonds and voluntary affiliations. Kuranko men disavow such bonds, when they occur in male-female relationships, because they are considered to be capricious and because they weaken the jural order. Ideally, men are associated with the activity principle, women with the passivity principle.

In Kuranko numerology, women are associated with the number 3, men with 4. This reverses the usual Mande pattern (c.f. Bambara and Dogon) but it makes reference to different facts. Men are associated with the higher number because they can withstand greater hardships than women, endure insults longer without losing their tempers, and maintain political and jural control more competently than women.[8] Men have a reserve of strength (referred to in the myth) which makes them 'one better' than women. This really means that men are more even tempered, able to resist temptations or curb their personal impulses better than women. It is generally believed that women are malevolent without necessarily intending to be so; their natural weakness of will or moral fibre makes them easy victims of satanic impulses.[9] Men who were happily married would speak of women's weakness in a rather bemused way ('they cannot help being as they are'), but other men, less happily married, would often elaborate on the vindictive and perfidious proclivities of women.

The significance of Kuranko number symbolism also depends upon the distinction between odd and even. In divination the diviner lays out cowrie shells or river pebbles and then assesses the degree of threat or danger in any forthcoming enterprise by noting the distribution of odd and even numbers (usually threes and fours). If odd numbers appear at the ends of the rows (sometimes referred to as gates—*geti*) then something is amiss and sacrifice is directed as a way of restoring harmony. But in directing a sacrifice and explaining the causes of disharmony a diviner frequently instructs a male client to question his wife about her behaviour. It may be suggested by innuendo to a hunter that his bad luck is caused by the infidelity of one of his wives[10]; a farmer whose harvest has been poor may be told that his sacrifice before sowing has been 'spoiled' by a wife's mischievous thoughts or deeds. Sudden deaths or violent afflictions may be explained by allusions to witchcraft—the most sinister expression of nefarious and active female influence.[11]

These beliefs about the weakness and danger of women must be given a structural explanation. In the first place, the notion that women are dangerous seems, in a society with a strongly agnatic ideology, to be an inevitable concomitant of that ideology. Virilocal residence means that women from outside the compound (and in some cases from outside the village) come as relative strangers into a group whose cohesion depends upon a clear disjunction between insiders and outsiders. Although the in-marrying woman relinquishes all jural rights in her natal group, she retains sentimental links with it; in particular her active influence over her brother contrasts markedly with ideally passive role as wife.

In former times men jealously guarded the secrets of their warrior strength, yet a woman might marry into the group or seduce a man and then act as a spy for another group with whom hostile relations existed. The following anecdote has value, not so much as evidence of actual betrayal but rather as an indication of a manner of thinking. During the wars against the Sofas, Konkuru's grandfather used to bathe himself ritually in the dead of night in order to secure protection against fatal injury on the battlefield. The Sofas bribed one of his wives to confide the secret bathing place to them. She did so, and he was captured one night in a raid, without his sword or wargown, and taken away and executed.

Despite the fact that this kind of explanatory anecdote is typical, the threat associated with the in-marrying woman is not solely a consequence of their position as interlopers or of their structural role as mediators of relations between discrete groups. It is in part a consequence of beliefs which precede or anticipate these facts, which indeed force Kuranko men to fulfil their own prophecies about the threat of women. Because men think of women as potential seductresses or traducers, the maintainance of jural control and social order is thought to depend upon men resisting the allures and schemes of women. This idea finds its simplest expression in the injunction that a man should marry a woman for her behaviour, not for her appearance.[12] But the obsessive secrecy and social distance that men strive to maintain in the face of female influence means that women always remain outsiders, and given this role, men's fears about the dangers of women can only be corroborated.

A paradoxical or double-bind situation arises from the fact that while women are ideally passive and submissive (serving the husband by raising his children), women have the primary responsibility for bringing children into the world and raising them. In this sense, women as mothers, are active, while men play a marginal and passive role. This situation, I suggest, may account in part for the male conviction that women are active intriguers. There is also a paradox of a more sociological kind, arising from a conflict between the ideological necessity of maintaining the kinship, group as a closed integral unit and the demands of exogamy and matrimonial exchange which will, by bringing outsiders into the group and by articulating matrilateral relationships, actually open up a breach in that ideally closed unit.[13]

In summary, the agnatic ideology postulates connections of a jural kind through males, but it also implies connections through females. As wives, women mediate relationships between different *kebile*. Within the nuclear family, women, as mothers, mediate the spiritual relations between the father (and the paternal ancestors) and his children. And a man's relationship with his matrilateral kin is conceived to 'go through' the mother.

At this point we should remark the qualitative difference between a man's attitude to his real mother *(na gbere)* and his attitude to other women: the former is characteristically an attitude of reciprocal trust and affection while the latter is often modulated by a sense of distrust and potential threat. In many Kuranko folktales it is a man's mother who rescues him from the hands of a malevolent female (often in the guise of a bush spirit or wild animal). A mother will often urge her son to be on his guard against the seductive wiles of strangers, not to trust other women. By contrast, a father will adjure his sons never to trust anyone.

The dogma of agnatic descent refers to property relations and jural status; as we shall see, this field of kinship relations is often characterised by competitiveness and disjunctions. This may be why the unique bond between mother and child, expressed in terms of uterine kinship, is the primary idiom for emphasising the values and ideals of kinship amity. Although men often scorn publically the female as virago, the image of the mother dominates the cultural unconscious. And though the importance of the patriline is emphasised in the Kuranko dogma of descent, the complete elucidation of Kuranko social structure requires us to explore the complementary aspects of its implicitly bilineal character.

Notes

1. Mead 1935: xvii.
2. The right hand (*bolinyeme*, literally 'hand good') is inauspicious while the left hand (*bolimaran*, literally 'hand not good') is inauspicious. The left hand is never used for eating because 'it is awkward' *(kankane)* and because it is used for blowing the nose, holding the penis to urinate, and in sexual intercourse. It is believed that if a man touches a woman's vagina with the hand and then brings the hand into contact with the mouth it will 'poison' him.
3. *Koiyi* means literally 'base of spine water'; men say that spermatazoa are not secreted by the testicles because ejaculation 'comes from the base of the spine'.
4. It is often alleged that a man and a woman must be biologically compatible (to have the same blood—*yile kelan*) in order to have children. Although male impotency is considered a just cause for a wife to divorce her husband, a man will not divorce his wife simply because she is barren; 'he will keep hoping that one day she will bear him a child', i.e. unlike male impotence, female barreness is thought to be temporary. A contemporary way of alluding to male impotence is to say 'his matches (fire) have fallen in the water'.
5. If sorcery is used without justification then it will rebound and afflict the malefactor. Sorcery can also be deflected back onto the sorcerer if his victim is well protected by anti-sorcery medicines.
6. The narrator was Keti Ferenke Koroma of Kondembaia.
7. This explanation of female recalcitrance is often given by women as well (see Sinkari Yegbe's remarks in chapter 6).
8. It is said that a man is able to endure insults hurled against him four times before he retaliates. Often, in justification of retaliative action, a Kuranko man will declare: 'He did it to me once, twice, thrice, and I forgave him each time, but when he did it a fourth time I took action'. Men are said to be able to withstand pain and hardship better than women. The significance of the number four is also borne out by the idea that persons with superior insight or vision have 'four eyes'; such a person is called *yalme* ('eye owner').
9. In the myth, Eve eats the forbidden fruit. She disrupts the initial order and harmony of the world. God withdraws from the world of man and thereafter all women are 'cursed'. Other myths make it clear that periodicity (which involves a continual oscillation between order and disorder) is connected with the menstrual cycle which signifies both fertility (potential life) and waste (the loss of potential life). Kuranko often say that the pain of childbirth and the hardships of raising children are consequences of Eve's original sin. A comparable Limba myth tells how pain in childbirth and subordinate social position are likewise the outcome of Eve's original disobedience (Finnegan 1967 : 267-70).
10. The number 3 is associated with bad luck, 4 with good luck.
11. Refer Jackson 1975 for further details.
12. The Kuranko words *yugi* (personality or temperament) and *kin* ('good' or 'beautiful') are used to describe behaviour rather than appearance, e.g. *ke yugi kin* ('this person has a good *yugi*'—is well-behaved), *ke yugi ma kin* ('this person's *yugi* is not good').

13.   It is also worth emphasising here that 'any form of virilocal marriage,
        whether it be patrilocal or avunculocal, involves the recognition of the
        matriline, and not accidentally, as a secondary by-product of the
        marriage transaction, but as a structural condition of virilocal marriage
        as such. The relation between mother's brother and sister's son is not a
        matter of matrifiliation. . . but a relation ineluctably included in this type
        of marriage. The recognition of the matriline—whether implicit or
        explicit—is the reification of the brother's debt to his sister' (Van Baal
        1970 : 300).

6. Marriage

The Kuranko distinguish three kinds of marriage: (1) Betrothal or endowed marriages—*musune me bire* (literally 'little woman held' (2) God-gift marriages—*ala ma die*, (3) Bride-service marriages. Each of these kinds of marriage implies basic differences in the kinds of things exchanged by wife-giving and wife-receiving groups. In God-gift marriages no bridewealth is given. Instead the parents of the girl prepare a 'dowry' for her (comprising pots, pans, rice, kola or money) and when she is initiated she is given in marriage to a wealthy Muslim 'in the name of God'. In this way a Muslim can demonstrate his appreciation to God for his good fortune. If any bridewealth were to be given then misfortune would follow. Such marriages are rare among the Kuranko and occur only between Muslim clans. I recorded no cases during my fieldwork. Bride-service marriages are invariably avunculate or matrilateral cross-cousin marriages. If a young man lives with and works for his mother's brother for some time then his uncle may give him one of his daughters in marriage. Male concubinage is known among the Mende and Kpelle, but it is never approved of (although it sometimes does occur) among the Kuranko. Secondary marriage is never found as a formal institution and trial marriage (known among the Temne) is also absent among the Kuranko.

The commonest kind of marriage, even today, is betrothal or endowed marriage. A girl is usually betrothed before she is born or in early infancy. A betrothed girl wears a red thread (*fen wulan*— 'thing red') around her wrist to signify betrothal. The first prestation is called *woro nani* ('four kola') although the betrothal gifts may comprise mats, money, domestic animals, kola and rice. Bridewealth is called *furufa* ('marriage thing') to distinguish it from ordinary wealth (*nunfule*) which is held, accumulated and inherited within a group. *Furufa* is a form of circulating wealth, which is immediately exchanged when it is received. Contributions are received irregularly throughout the betrothal period, at the giving-in-marriage ceremony, and throughout the period of marriage itself. *Furufa* also includes bride-service.

During late girlhood the betrothed child visits her prospective husband's home for stays of up to one month to adjust to her forthcoming marriage and to meet and accustom herself to her husband's kin. This custom is known as *sinkale* (borrowing or lending) and if the girl decides that the marriage will be insufferable she may,

95

after these trial periods, declare her disinclinations to her father. But, traditionally at least, marriages were made by the father of the girl and the father of the man to whom she was betrothed in infancy. Considerations of friendship between men and mutual assessments of the conduct and reputation of the respective families are of overriding importance. It is only when this evaluation proves wrong (for example, if the son-in-law mistreats the girl after she has been given in marriage to him) that the girl's father will contemplate divorce and demanding refund of bridewealth. But the high value of bridewealth given (valued at between £50 and £150 depending upon the relative wealth of the groom's family) makes divorce difficult (see Appendix A for details).[1] Besides, the bridewealth, once received, will have been passed on in making another marriage contract. And it is also difficult to calculate bride-service and assess the value of different kinds of goods given. When refunds of bridewealth do occur the wrangling and claims may continue to prepossess the affines long after a court settlement has been decided. Today, this issue is complicated by a Ministry of the Interior Memorandum (P3/5 of April 1963) which directs that in cases of divorce the only legal claim in refund of bridewealth is on property given on the marriage day together with initiation expenses. All other prestations, including bride-service, must be reckoned as civil debts and claimed independently. Although this facilitates easy divorce (refunds involve relatively small amounts of money) it also engenders disputes over debts which can completely alienate former affines.

A girl's prospective husband is also responsible for contributing to the expenses of her initiation. He must lend assistance to his prospective father-in-law during the preceding farm season and he must acquire large amounts of kola and money for gift-giving during the initiation rites. On the morning of the Operation Day, he fires his gun to signal that there is no impediment to the marriage and during the dance associated with this rite he gives away snuff and kola (100 to the mother-in-law, 120 to the father-in-law, 20 to the bride, 20 to her co-initiates). After the dance his relatives pound 10 kola nuts and ginger which is given to a close female kinswoman to take to the bride. This is yet another test of the bride's virginity; if she becomes ill after eating the concoction she is obliged to nominate her lover. If her virginity is proven, her husband sends her some country cloth or a piece of blue baft in acknowledgement, together with two mats, one for her and one for the woman who attends her during the clitoridectomy.

On the evening of the last day of the initiation rites, the prospective husband takes kola, tobacco and mats to the house where his bride-to-be is secluded. Next morning, he has a meal of rice, four chickens and a sheep or goat prepared. He then sends the girl's kin four lapas, four headkerchiefs, and the red berries for her new coiffure. The girl assents to the marriage by accepting the food and eating it. After this the husband sends 100 kola and 20 cents to the girl's mother, 50 cents to her father, and 50 cents to the woman who attend and nurse the girl after her clitoridectomy.

Many of these customs are recorded in Kamara and Drummond's paper on Kuranko marriage.[2] During my own researches (forty years later) I discovered less complexity in the sytem of marriage prestations; money is given instead of kola and many exchanges between affines during initiation no longer take place. It seems, however, that the giving-in-marriage cermeony remains very much as it was when Kamara and Drummond described it.

At the end of the dry season, the initiated girl goes to live with her husband. Some girls cry or hesitate at this time, and this may explain why the parents of the girl do not accompany her to her husband's house (although the husband's parents receive her). It is her maternal and paternal aunts and uncles who usually supervise the marriage transfer. On this occasion, money, mats, kola, domestic animals and clothes are given by the husband's group to the bride's father's group; in return the bride's father's delegate declares that the husband's family now assume complete control over the bride: jural rights over her labour, her sexual and procreative capacities, her children-to-be-born, and her person. This transfer of rights *in genetricem* and *in uxorem* is considered to be absolute and in perpetuity. Thus, the girl's agnates declare: 'Now we have come with your wife. She is your thief, your witch, your daughter, your everything. We have come to give her to you alive, but even when she is dead she remains your wife. You can flog her, abuse her, she is yours.' The bride should never return to her natal family, except on visits approved by her husband. When she dies, her husband (or a man delegated by him) must attend her burial; she is never buried by her natal family. Not only is the bride the wife of her husband's *group;* her very personality, perfect or imperfect, is made over to that group.

On the first night that the bride sleeps with her husband, women representing both groups may sometimes remain at the house until the marriage is consummated. The bloodstained sheet from the bridal bed is then displayed as final proof of the girl's pre-marital chastity. In order to express his gratitude the husband gives a cow to his father-in-law. He may sometimes add some money or kola, called the 'cow tether' (*ninki yule*) to confirm the affinal bond, or present his bride with a white chicken (a symbol of her purity). These gifts are all known as *koin nunfule* ('virgin wealth/price'). If the bride is not a virgin when she marries then her husband may demand compensation from her family and from her lover, whom she must nominate. In the Kuranko view, chastity before marriage indicates that a girl will probably be faithful after marriage.

The Dissolution of Marriage
Divorce is most frequent and conjugal difficulties greatest during the

first years of marriage—before a woman has borne children, before she has fully adjusted to life in her husband's household, before the amounts of bridewealth and bride-service become too high to allow easy severance of affinal ties. Divorce ratios and other pertinent data are set out in Table 6.

77% of all divorces in this sample were a result of the wife 'going on a *sumburi*'. i.e. eloping with a lover who then paid bridewealth to the estranged husband, thus compensating him for the loss of a wife. It is also noteworthy that 77% of the divorces involved a wife who originally came either from another village or from another chiefdom.

Since infant betrothal means that girls marry men much older than themselves and because a girl often marries a man who already has other wives, personal adjustment to marriage and residence in her husband's household is understandably difficult. Kuranko men often say that prospective wives and affines may often be inclined to dissimulate by feigning faultless characters so that marriage arrangements will not be impeded. One informant commented on the adage: *bolo kunde mera kure koro nyaonya a si bo* (however hard you try to dissimulate, you will be found out one day). He distinguished between behaviour before and after marriage, noting that before marriage potential spouses and affines sometimes deceive each other. The shock of recognition—when a wife sees her husband as he really is, or when a husband realises that his wife is quite different from the woman he so ardently courted—is given as a reason for divorce and marital difficulties during the first year of marriage. Moreover, during the early stages of marriage young wives often become involved in adulterous affairs with young men in the village. This custom (for it is admitted and tolerated, at least for young men) may lead to the girl eloping with her lover and to the lover persuading his father to find the necessary bridewealth to secure the girl's divorce. The term *sumburi* means both elopement and divorce. Most adulterous affairs, however, do not lead to divorce and rarely will a man divorce his wife because of sexual jealousy or on the grounds of adultery alone. Instead, the husband demands that his wife nominate her lover; he is then likely to be fined by the local court. But to preserve amicable relations among men of the community, adultery cases are often settled out of court. Many men told me that they would never go in search of an errant wife; but it was notable that these men had many wives.

The following case illustrates the tensions and antagonisms that can be generated if the various tacit and formal conventions for settling an adultery case are not respected.

When I first arrived in Kamadugu Sukurela it became quickly apparent that something was amiss, but the elders, who had welcomed my arrival, were reluctant to tell me what had brought about the atmosphere of subdued panic and depression among the villagers. On the day after my arrival I accompanied a friend to a house where a

No. of marriages	No. of marriages extant	No. of marriages ended with death of wife	No. of marriages ended in divorce	No. of marriages ended in divorce expressed as % of all marriages	Year after marriages in which divorce occurred			
					1st	2nd	3rd	4th	Other
49	28	12	9	18.3%	2	3	1	1	2

Table 6. Divorce Ratios (total marriage experience of living male informants Kamadugu Sukurela).

young man was lying on a mat on the floor, seriously ill. In the fetid gloom of the house many of the village elders were gathered in silence. Outside the house about twenty women kept anxious vigil. I discovered that the young man was dying of a curse (*danka*); months later, when I described the symptoms to a W.H.O. doctor in Freetown, I learned that he had been suffering, in all probability, from a form of encephalitis.[3]

He had eloped with the wife of a man from a nearby village. A few weeks after the woman had come to Sukurela to live with him, her husband came to demand her return. She refused to leave. Then the woman's father-in-law came to Sukurela and made the same demand, again with no success. The husband and father-in-law of the woman then took the case to court in Kabala but the court president referred the case back to the chief at Sukurela. The young man and the woman returned to Sukurela and ignored the chief's decision that the woman be sent back to her husband. At this stage the woman's father-in-law travelled to Kunya (in Sambaia Bendugu chiefdom) to seek the services of a renowned sorcerer (*besetigi*). A curse was uttered against the young man and the following day, while working on his farm, he was taken ill. His elder brother went to Kunya to have the curse lifted, but the *besetigi* said that the young man should come himself; in any case, the curse could only be lifted on the approval of the Paramount chief of Sambaia Bendugu. When the brother returned to Sukurela, the young man was dead. During the next few days people avoided the house where he had died, for fear of being contaminated by the curse. His kinsmen remained to supervise the burial; normally, however, the curse is lifted from the family before the burial rites take place. No one in Sukurela attended the burial or gave any sympathy gifts. It is considered imperative that no sympathy should be shown to a person who has died in this way, or to his family, lest this indicate identification with the state of sin in which all members of the family are implicated. After the burial, the dead man's wives, children and property (including grain stores) were taken to Kunya in order to have the curse lifted from them. A fee of Le. 14 was also demanded. No part of the inheritance could be shared out until the curse had been revoked; otherwise the inheritors of the property would also inherit the curse.

The people of Sukurela observed that it is not usual for a husband or his father to refuse to grant divorce in the event of a wife's elopement; nonetheless, in this case, the men were completely within their rights. When the young man had sent friends to 'beg' the woman's husband and father-in-law to release her and agree to a divorce, the requests were denied. It was said that the young man should have heeded the decision of the Sukurela chief's court. His refusal to send the woman back to her husband had led to a tragedy which had implicated the entire community.

The second kind of 'woman palaver', which is far more common, arises when a wife runs away from her husband and returns to her natal family. In such cases, the husband will again often attempt to secure his wife's return. It is noteworthy that such cases occur most often when the wife hails from another village. The following case illustrates some of the strategies and problems involved in securing the return of an errant wife.

A man from the village of Fasewoia (Sengbe chiefdom) arrived in Sukurela one morning to reclaim his wife; she had quarrelled with her husband, refusing to prepare food for him, and run away to Sukurela where her mother lived (her father was dead). The woman had been married previously to a Firawa man (Barawa chiefdom), but the marriage had ended in divorce. At a court hearing which lasted about two and a half hours, the Fasewoia man requested that his wife be ordered to return to him. Appeals to the woman's brothers and mother's brothers had been ignored. The court decided that the woman should return to her husband, a decision which was diplomatically necessary because the husband was the town chief at Fasewoia and much depended upon maintaining goodwill between these different ruling clans in the two neighbouring chiefdoms. But an implicit disagreement with the decision was evident when the woman's brothers and maternal uncles refused to accept responsibility for guaranteeing her return. It happened that some weeks afterward, the woman was still living with her mother. Her husband had asserted his rights and 'saved face' by bringing the matter to the court at Sukurela; this achieved, he accepted his wife's decision to leave him, and he spoke of the matter no more.

Any children of an adulterous union belong to the woman's husband. There is seldom any stigma attached to the adulterine child. But should a woman marry her lover and bear a child before the refunding of bridewealth (*yilboi*) and the legal declaration of divorce, then that child will be in an invidious position. It will remain in the custody of the former husband but it will be motherless and therefore disadvantaged. Such children are called *nye'morgodan* (literally 'self-person-child') or *nyere woli* (literally 'self child-bearing/bringing forth') and they are often victimised by their siblings and ill-cared for by their mother's co-wives.

Adultery is thus more of an index of marital disharmony than a cause for divorce. Yet it indicates precisely where the causes of marital instability lie. Adultery and divorce both stem from problems associated with polygyny, infant betrothal and male jural control. In the first place, a young wife (*gberinye*) may be at an immediate disadvantage in her husband's household, dominated by and perhaps discriminated against by her husband's senior wife (*bare* or *baramuse*)[4]. In the second place, her husband is usually much older; he may be impotent or indifferent to her as a person. In the third place, women are completely subject to their husband's control and although they can confide their grievances to brothers, mothers or even fathers, they are invariably blamed as the cause of them. In reality, women have little redress if their husbands wrong them. Their marriages are arranged by men and they sometimes feel they are used as objects and accorded little or no respect as persons.

It is because women are treated as objects and expected to conform to male expectations that, in the words of one woman (Sinkari Yegbe), 'they take their revenge'—by eloping with another man, by instigating a love affair, by disobeying their husbands. Women are fully aware that such recalcitrance involves playing men off against each other. Women with whom I spoke on this subject gave support to the idea that refractory behaviour such as refusal to cook, fetch water or wood, etc., is often the only way in which a woman can answer the indifference or maltreatment of a boorish husband. When I asked Sinkari Yegbe to comment on the male view that women are treacherous, she replied:

'Men could say that of us, but we would not say it of ourselves. It is true we are, since we cannot beat the men. If a wife wrongs her husband he will beat her. But she could not do that, even if her husband wrongs her terribly. So we use tricks. We become reluctant to work, even when the husband is hungry. And we could pretend to be sick [i.e. menstruating] and make excuses for not preparing food for our husbands.'

In response, men speak of the importance of not taking women too seriously, of refusing to be jealous of their affairs, of tolerating their caprices. But these attitudes mask the real fear that a refractory wife can cause altercations and tensions between affines. In fact the word *murute* (refractory, rebellious, disobedient) which is applied to misbehaved wives was, in the 1890s, used to refer to mercenaries and rebels who formed bandit gangs in the northern provinces of Sierra Leone. The husband is distrustful of his wife, not only because she is a woman (and therefore, in Kuranko thought, a different and weaker person) but also because she remains always somewhat outside the sphere of his personal control. This is, as we shall see in the next chapter, an oblique reflection of her hold over her brothers. A husband is faced with the dilemma of playing down spontaneous affection for a beloved wife and assuming affection for a wife whom he may not love; it is only by retaining formality and constraint in conjugal relationships that harmony is established. This guardedness of men is especially obvious in the ways in which they keep personal medicines and fetishes secret. A Kuranko adage says *musu kai i gbundu lon*—'Don't ever let a woman know your secrets.' Men firmly believe that 'women do not have a second thought' and one reason why Kuranko men dislike divorce is that the divorced wife will, it is claimed, spread rumours about her ex-husband and no woman will subsequently want to marry him.

Neither adultery or refractoriness is a justification for men to divorce their wives. In fact, it is the girl's family who usually declare divorce, and in most cases which I recorded this involved *sumburi*, i.e. the girl simply divorced one man and remarried another. In theory, the girl's family can sue for divorce if the son-in-law is impotent (*takale ar bu yi ro*, literally 'the fire or matches have fallen in the water'). But problems may arise here. In one case I recorded, a young man got married but proved to be impotent. His wife eloped with his younger brother and later married him. The divorced brother left the village, was subsequently cured of impotence, and returned home to claim his wife. After weeks of wrangling he was told to leave the village. When he died soon after, his father blamed the younger son for his elder brother's death. The father quit his *luiye* and took up residence at the other end of the village. The breach between father and son was never healed.

Divorce may also occur if the husband mistreats his wife, and if the son-in-law renegues on his obligations to render bride-service to his father-in-law. If a girl returns to her natal group with complaints that her husband has ill-treated her, then her father or (more commonly) her brothers may threaten divorce and admonish the husband. But they will also encourage the girl to return to him. As Sinkari Yegbe remarked, these displays of sympathy belie the real imperative: that the girl remain married. 'The problem of refunding bridewealth is too great to permit divorce, just for these reasons.' Sinkari herself was once married to another man. He loved her but she did not love him. She had been born in Sukurela, he lived elsewhere. 'I did not like his place', she said, 'and that is why we prefer to marry with our neighbours.' She left her husband and returned home to Sukurela, even though her parents were against it. Her feet were put in stocks. When she was released she still refused to return to her husband. Finally, her parents decided to allow the divorce, though her mother was decidedly not in favour of it.

In circumstances where adultery is an inevitable concomitant of the marriage system, it is surprising that the Kuranko have not institutionalised some form of male concubinage or secondary marriage. For it is the clandestine element of love affairs and the conflict between personal choice or preference and marital obligations or duties that the Kuranko find so troublesome. One particular case, which occured in Sukurela, will illustrate this.

A young man from Guinea came to Sukurela and asked a certain old man if he could stay in his *luiye* as 'his stranger'. After some time the young man and one of the old man's young wives became lovers. They even farmed together, and they lived in the same house, almost as husband and wife. The old man tolerated this arrangement, but only on condition that the young man did not usurp his jural rights as husband.

One day, the old man summoned the young man to the chief's court.[5] He explained that he had sent his wife to Sangbamba (a nearby village in the same chiefdom) to collect a debt. A few days later he had sent her to Farandugu (another nearby village) to collect another debt. She went and returned. The young man had become angry about her coming and going and had berated her. The old man had told the young man that he had no right to control the woman, especially since he had sent her to collect his debts— it was no business of the young man to interfere. Following this altercation, the young man had taken his belongings from the house which he had built in the old man's *luiye*, and that evening he had slept in the house of a friend (also from Guinea). In the morning he had allegedly returned to the *luiye*, pulled some thatch from the house and then gone down the road out of the village and 'sworn' it, thus placing a curse on whoever entered the house which he had built.

The defendant explained that he had neither berated the woman nor shown jealousy. He claimed that the quarrel between himself and the woman had arisen because she had refused to launder for him, even though they were lovers. And when he had asked her for his share of the rice from the farm they had made together, she had become annoyed and abused him. In turn he had abused her. The old man had come when he heard this slanging match and he had also abused the young man and ordered him from the *luiye*. The young man said further that he had taken his belongings from his house and gone to stay with a friend. In the morning he had returned and repeated what he had said about leaving, for when he had declared his intentions the previous night, everyone had said that he was drunk. He had then said that nobody should enter his house, that he had laboured and built it—if anyone entered it 'they would know about it'. But he had not put a curse on the house; he had simply taken thatch from the roof in a pique of temper. He claimed that the old man had told the woman never to serve him food in that house again. To this he replied: if she fails to give me food, then I will eat some of her share. The woman had replied: that will be the time I will slap you. And he had rejoined: if you slap me then I will deal with you properly.

The woman was summoned to court. She said that the young man had scolded her for going to Sangbamba and Farandugu, saying that she was going to see her lovers, not to collect debts. On the day she went to Sangbamba he had wanted to follow her. She also claimed that he had cursed the house.

The woman's co-wife was summoned. She said that she had heard the woman quarrelling with her lover. He had abused her and she in turn had abused his mother. 'And they have been as husband and wife there for almost two years'. She had heard the old man say that he would drive the young man from his *luiye;* the young man had said that he would leave the next day. But in the evening he came back and took his belongings from the house and went to a friend's house. Next morning he had come back and put his hand on the house, saying 'Do not enter this house' (to the woman), 'I built it and now that I have been driven away from it, whoever enters it will suffer the consequences.' Then he had called another man to whom he told the same thing.

This witness was summoned, but he did not know whether or not the young man had actually gone out of the village and cursed the house.

In judging the case, the Sukurela chief invited the visiting town chief from Fasewoia to comment. He claimed that the young man was clearly in the wrong:

'He knows that *he* did not marry that woman, and that the woman's husband is living in the same *luiye*. Where there is no respect for a husband there is trouble.[6] If the woman offended the young man then they should have settled the matter between themselves and not involved the old man in their affairs. But even when the old man came, the young man brashly ignored his presence. That was bad, and indiscrete. Moreover, he had no right to take the thatch from the house roof, whether to curse the house or not. Taking the grass signifies intent, therefore he was wrong.'

The section chief endorsed these remarks and added, addressing the woman and the young man:

'This is not the first time you have quarrelled and that I have had to rebuke you. On a previous occasion we told you that you did not marry this woman. If you are lovers, then you must respect this old man. It is not your right to control this woman. And you promised us that you would not cause trouble again. Since you have broken this promise I will agree with the words of the Fasewoia chief. You have been in the wrong.'

I have recorded this case in some detail because it illustrates some of the 'imponderabilia' that must be taken into account when examining specific instances of marital disharmony or of male-female relationships. The young man from Guinea was a 'stranger', a transient, and it is doubtful whether a local man would have so flagrantly set up house with another man's wife. The ambivalence of people's attitudes to the stranger is shown by their wariness of his use of 'foreign' mystical powers (the curse) and by the fact that although he was given hospitality in Sukurela, people felt that he and his Guinea companions had no real respect for local custom. When the court fined the young man, it was his companions from Guinea who assisted him in paying the fine; the consensus of opinion among the people of Sukurela was that it would have been prefereable if he had left the village altogether.[7]

When a marriage is dissolved either by divorce or the death of a spouse, the children of that marriage always remain in the husband's *kebile*. In cases where a widow remarries a man outside her husband's *kebile* (so contravening the levirate), bridewealth must be refunded, but the children remain in the husband's *kebile*.[8] Like divorce, the remarriage of widows outside their late husband's group is only tolerated in exceptional circumstances. For the woman must relinquish custody of her children and so make them motherless and disadvantaged in their father's group. Not only does adultery and divorce rupture affinal ties between *kebile;* it jeopardises the future of the children whose mother is crucial in mediating the blessings of their paternal ancestors.

Affinal Relationships
Biranye (affinity) denotes all relationships through marriage. Female

affines are all called *biran musu*, male affines *biran ke*. In theory, these terms classify together all members of another *kebile* or clan, related to one's own *kebile* or clan by any marriage link in the same or any descending generation. A man could refer to his *kebile* brothers' wives as *ma l musenu* ('our wives') and children of his kebile brothers as *ma l dannu* ('our children'). Here *mal* denotes 'ownership', unlike *ma* which signifies relationship. Thus, *ma tersannu* ('our sisters') means that *kebile* sisters are not 'owned' in the same sense that one 'owns' or 'controls' wives and children.[9]

In practice, there is an important distinction between relatives of the same family *(dembaiye)* and relatives of the same *kebile*. Because bridewealth is given and received by the *dembaiye,* the primary rights and duties of affinity refer to relationships between *dembaiye*. As the Kuranko put it, 'Marriage is *dembaiye* business'. Although affinal relationships are conceptualised in terms of exchange between *kebile*, they are operationally significant only at the level of *dembaiye* organisation.

All formal transactions between affines are mediated by a go-between *(furusonkolon*—'marriage go-between') who is never a kinsman of either party but must be friendly with both. He is nominated by the husband's family and then approved by the in-laws. All bridewealth transactions must pass through him, for in the event of divorce or dispute between the two parties he acts as a key witness in the court case. His reckoning of the total prestations is considered final.

Affinal relationships are characterised by reserve, formality and a complex of reciprocal rights and obligations which many Kuranko find onerous. In some respects, the formalities of affinal relationships can be understood as an elaborate measure aimed at strengthening the stability of the conjugal tie itself. But they are also necessitated by the fact that affinity is one of the most important aspects of network-cohesion in the local community. In the Kuranko view, affinity presupposes friendship and creates kinship. Fode Kargbo explained this idea as follows. 'If I marry the daughter of another man, then his family become my kinsmen *(n'nakelinyorgonu)*; if I give my daughter to you in marriage, then I will not do any evil to you because I would not wrong my kinsman. At the same time, you would not do me any evil because I have given you my daughter. Marriage makes people kinsmen.' When Kuranko say that 'affines should respect one another' they refer to the gifts, help, brideservice and sympathy which unite them in an unending cycle of reciprocal interaction. This reciprocity is described by the phrase, *nyendan bin to kile, a wa ta an segi* which implies that the gifts and assistance given by a son-in-law to his father-in-law are signs of his gratitude for the wife that he has received. If a wife fails to fulfil her marital obligations, then this reciprocity is weakened. If a father-in-law fails to receive periodic gifts from his son-in-law or if the son-in-law fails to render brideservice to his father-in-law during the farming season, then he will assume that his daughter is not behaving herself and the marriage mediator may be called upon to investigate the matter. Respect and friendship between affines is thought to depend upon the behaviour of women. Adultery or intransigent behaviour in the household may make a woman's husband feel unwilling to show much respect or gratitude to his affines. This is the message of the Kuranko adages: *kele da ma si ban, koni musu ko kele ti ban* (quarrels or fights will all resolve themselves in the end, but never those caused by women), *yanfe da ma si no, koni musu yanfe wo ti fo* (conspiracies can all be overcome except those of women). Sexual infidelity (or marriage to a woman who is not a virgin) are negative reflections on the bride-giving group, a source of antagonism and distrust.

The reciprocal bonds of affinity are again expressed in terms of kinship in the following commentary (Fode Kargbo): 'A man should be closer to his wife's father than to his own brother; he will be to his wife's father as his wife is to him.' In jural terms, the woman passes from the control of her father to the control of her husband, who is then said to be 'a father to her'. The father-in-law's relationship with the son-in-law is considered to be the strongest because there is a *direct* link between them, in contradistinction to other affinal links which are *indirect*, i.e. they are all mediated by ('go through') the father-in-law. This is why relationships between brothers-in-law are considered to be secondary. Moreover, the bond between father-in-law and son-in-law is non-reciprocal; the son-in-law is obligated to his father-in-law but not vice versa.

Between brothers-in-law there is a degree of reciprocity and a man's claims on and influence over his sister's husband may be understood partly as forms of compensation for the constant claims that his father-in-law makes on him. In Kuranko terms, the bond between a man and his sister's husband is indirect; it 'goes through the sister'. Thus, any help given by the sister's husband is help given through the sister to her brother. Conversely, if a man helps his sister's husband, it is regarded as help given to the sister, or to the sister's husband 'through the sister'. Assistance given to one's sister will indirectly benefit her husband. The reciprocity which is basic to the brother-sister relationship is, as I shall show in the next chapter, derived from the fact that a brother marries with the bridewealth received from his sister's marriage. A man's claims upon his sister's husband expand the field of reciprocity in affinal relationships. If a brother gives his sister in marriage then he expects in return assistance from the sister's husband in finding himself a wife. Such claims must, however, be made through the marriage mediator. If they are met, then whatever is given is reckoned as part of the total bridewealth presentations. It should also be noted that a man only has the right to make claims on his sister's husband when his father is dead. Theoretically, while the father is alive all claims on the sister's husband must 'go through him'.

A man's relationship with his mother-in-law is highly formalised. He cannot sit on his mother-in-law's bed or use a chair which she has just vacated. Such prohibitions are meant to make any sexual association impossible. Sexual intercourse or marriage with the wife's brother's wife is banned for a similar reason; in fact, the Kuranko regard such a union as incestuous. As Duwa Mara expressed it, 'She is equal to your totem; you cannot eat her and you cannot eat it.' Another informant explained that such a union 'would bring your wife and her brother into sexual contact'. The mother-in-law and the wife's brother's wife are structurally identified; to marry either would nullify the function of marriage as a way of setting up exchange relations between more than two groups.[10]

Although a man does not avoid speaking to his wife's mother, there is a prohibition against using her personal name. With one's affines familiarity is considered to be out of place. It would be unthinkable for a man to beat or upbraid his wife in the presence of her kinsmen; he is forever striving to make a favourable impression upon them. Yet these formalities often mask a conflict of interests between a man and his mother-in-law, a division between public and private attitudes or behaviour. These conflicts arise out of the emotional bond between mother and daughter, a bond which endures despite the separation of marriage. Although a girl's father arranges her marriage (the girl's mother must comply with his decision), it is commonly the mother who manipulates the breakdown of the marriage. This is not freely admitted, but I heard innumerable anecdotes and scraps of gossip which testify to the truth of a remark which Sinkari Yegbe once made: 'Mothers often help their daughters go on *sumburi*. And in these deceits, a woman's age-mates often play their part.' When Sinkari was married to a man from another village her age-mates chided her, saying 'You, a girl who was raised in a large town, will you accept living in that small village; if you accept living in that small village; if you accept that then it will be a burden that will kill you. When Sinkari did leave her husband her age-mates gave her moral support, even though, in this case, her mother disapproved.

Not only does the mother-daughter bond endure after the daughter's marriage: it is clear that women (granted no jural rights in deciding the choice of a spouse) command a position of considerable influence in reality. A man makes a marriage for his daughter on the basis of considerations of friendship with another man, but his wife often assists her daughter in breaking that marriage and remaking it according to choices more compatible with the interests of herself and her daughter. Not only do adulterous affairs bring mother and daughter or female age-mates together in an illicit pact which has the tone and manifest spirit of rebellion against male control, but they serve to create solidarity among women in the face of restricted mobility and jural disadvantages.

Rather similar problems arise as a result of parental complicity in the love affairs of their unmarried sons. During the seven years following initiation, a young man is not permitted to marry. But he is encouraged to have illicit affairs with married women 'to show that he is a man and capable of sex'.[11] The postponement of a young man's marriage may of course assist in supporting the polygynous system; delaying the marriages of young men is also necessitated by the fact that they cannot marry before their sisters' marriages have brought bridewealth into the family. Yet this double standard, which tolerates the love affairs of young men and which censures the '*liaisons dangéreuses*' of women, creates its own problems. It is as if the ideal of post-marital chastity and the subordinate status of women were threatened at every turn by conflicting imperatives. As we shall see, marriage may involve a complete transfer of jural rights to the husband's group, but the continuing attachments of a girl to her parents and brothers often challenge these rights.

Joking Relationships
In complete contrast to the formalities of affinity, a man's relationship with his wife's younger siblings and his elder siblings' spouses is characterised by joking (*tolon*).[12] From a woman's point of view, she jokes with her elder siblings' spouses and her husband's younger siblings. Where her joking partner is a woman, the term of address is *dinyon* and the relationship is known as *dinyoiya*. In all other cases the joking partner is known as *numorgo* (*morgo*—'person') and the relationship is known as *numorgoya*.[13]

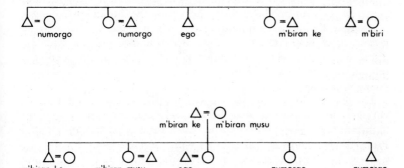

Figure 4. Joking relationships (man speaking).

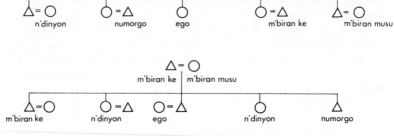

Figure 5. Joking Relationships (woman speaking)

The *numorgoya tolon* ('*nu* person relationship joking.) or *numorgo tolon* indicates the locii of authority in the bride-giving and bride-receiving groups.

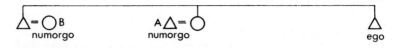

Because ego's elder brother receives bridewealth from A (ego's elder brother-in-law) ego has no claim on that bridewealth. In other words, ego is not directly involved in an in-law relationship with A, so the relationship is deformalised. On the other hand, ego's elder brother does not joke with A because he received bridewealth from him. Because ego's elder brother's wife (B) cannot joke with her husband (since he paid bridewealth for her and she is subject to his direct jural control), she jokes with ego 'to maintain a more affectionate relationship'. Informants sometimes mentioned that a woman could speak to her husband 'through her *numorgo*' (husband's younger brother) if she had a complaint against her husband; in this way the *numorgo tolon* helps retain formality between husband and wife by displacing the affective or informal elements of the conjugal relationship onto the relationship between a woman and her husband's younger brother.

The reason why a man can joke with his wife's younger siblings (not with her elder siblings) is that the wife's elder siblings will become his 'father-in-law' and 'mother-in-law' when his real parents-in-law die. Prohibitions against sexual contact with the mother-in-law and the demands of formal respect towards the father-in-law are quite unequivocal. But restrictions on sexual contact with the wife's younger sisters and the formal respect shown towards her younger brothers are more ambiguous. As with all joking relationships, their actualisation is always a matter of personal choice, although it is noticeable that people who joke together are related usually in a real rather than a classificatory sense. Sororal marriage means that a wife's younger sisters are potential wives. And the junior status of the wife's younger brothers in their own family makes it unlikely that they will ever become actual affines; the contractual arrangements of their eldest sister's marriage will not directly concern them. Thus, the wife's younger siblings are marginal affines and a symmetrical joking alliance expresses the 'social disjunction' between them and their elder sister's husband and elder brother's wife.

The Kuranko say that a man jokes with his elder brother's wife because he is only indirectly or marginally involved in the bridewealth transactions that connect the elder brother to his wife's parents or elder siblings. He is also a potential husband to this woman; according to the levirate he will marry her when his elder brother dies. Both leviratic and sororal marriages are anticipated in the joking relationships between men and women, which is one reason why the joking play includes sexual banter, teasing and flirting. The following exchange, which I once overheard, is typical.

Man to elder brother's wife: 'Come here to me, I'm going to touch your waist. We are going to sleep together tonight.'

Woman: 'Don't lock your door then, I'll be coming to you tonight.'

The next morning the banter continued. The man's elder brother's wives all gathered around him and threatened to strip the shirt from his back.

'Where did you sleep last night?', one woman taunted, 'you should have come to me. I was waiting for you!'

Such joking should, however, always be in public. It is considered imperative that it does not smack of illicitness or lead to real intimacy.

In most instances, joking relationships reflect a transient or confused situation. A man's female *numorgo* are not his wives, yet the sororate and levirate may make them so. This is why a man often refers to his female *numorgo as 'wife' (na musu)* and the woman reciprocates by calling her male *numorgo* 'husband' (*m'buin*). A man's male *numorgo* are only marginal or indirect affines, yet the death of his father or elder brothers may bring him into a direct contractual relationship with them. The privileged abuse and licensed disrespect which characterise the *numorgoya* indicate ambiguous relationships in which informality and imminent formality are commingled. The contradiction between the constraints of an obligatory or contractual alliance (affinity) and the freedom from constraint (friendship) is resolved through cathartic exchanges which contain elements of and allusions to both modes of relationship. For the Kuranko, the crucial factor in understanding this contrast between the formality of recognised affinity and the informality of friendship is property and wealth. They say that it is because a man pays bridewealth to his wife's father and wife's elder brother that he treats them with the full formality and respect demanded by in-lawship. It is because his wife's younger brothers are not *directly* involved in these transactions that he can joke with them. In the words of one informant, 'they are only shadow in-laws; your relationship with them goes through their elder brother'. Between men and women, the *numorgo tolon* connotes ultimate or possible marriage; a man's female *numorgo* are 'shadow wives'. In Radcliffe-Brown's words, 'The joking relationship is in some ways the exact opposite of a contractual relation.'[14] Joking connotes a juxtaposing of alternative and often mutually-exclusive patterns of behaviour.[15] One interesting exemplification of this principle is the manner in which Kuranko women explain the joking relationship with the husband's sisters. A convention of the joking play is for a woman to address her brother's wife as 'our wife'; reciprocally a woman may address her husband's sisters as 'our husbands'. In the former instance, the explanation given by the Kuranko is that if the sisters were men then they would regard their brothers' wives as their wives. One man elaborated on this general explanation by pointing out that 'if I die, my wives would be inherited by my sisters if they were men, therefore my wives are also their wives.' Furthermore, it is often said that a man's sister feels that the family has paid bridewealth for her brothers' wives; 'therefore, she will call them "our wives" (*ma l musenu*, '*ma*' being used in a proprietary sense) because what belongs to one belongs to all.' This 'residual claim' of a woman to the property (which includes the wives) of her natal group indicates an ambiguous status, deriving perhaps from the fact that she remains emotionally attached to her natal group even when jurally bound to her husband's group. This particular ambiguity is expressed by a joking play where a women acts as if she were in her brother's position.

For example, a woman might say to her elder brother's wife (her *dinyon*) 'Where were you last night; you should have slept with me; did you go and sleep with your lover instead?'

Marriage Types and Strategies

A review of Kuranko marriage preferences and strategies reveals the ways in which problems of affinity and problems arising from instabilities of the conjugal tie are resolved.

Most Kuranko express a preference for village endogamy and, in the past, marriage outside the chiefdom was proscribed except in the case of marriages arranged for purposes of political alliances between rulers.[16] A person refers to all other clans in the same community as *furunyorgonu*, literally 'the people we mix with', although *furu* can mean both 'marriage' and 'mixing'. The only exception is in the case of ruling clans who prohibit marriages with *finas*. Clans are all exogamous, except again in the case of the *finas* who are divided into two classes which may intermarry.

In Table 8, 92 marriages are analysed. 61.9% of the marriages were contracted in the same village (Kamadugu Sukurela). Of the 29.3% of marriages contracted outside the chiefdom (most involved a neighbouring chiefdom), 39.1% of these were kinship marriages.

Same village	Another village in chiefdom	A neighbouring chiefdom	Another chiefdom	Total number of marriages
57	8	23	4	92

Table 8. Provenance of Spouses.

12.5% of the marriages contracted outside the village but within the same chiefdom were kinship marriages. It is therefore clear that the preference for village endogamy is also a statistical norm and that where marriages occur outside the village they often tend to follow from previous marriages. The number of marriages contracted outside the chiefdom should be commented upon. Most Kuranko men have spent several years away from their village, in the diamond districts of Kono or (in the case of older men) in the army or colonial administration. This geographical mobility sometimes means that men marry when they are living away from home.

It is also noteworthy that village endogamy contributes to marital stability. Of the ten divorces in this sample, 60% involved marriages contracted outside the chiefdom and a total of 80% involved marriages with women outside the village. Village endogamy is preferred because of the great emphasis which the Kuranko place upon neighbourliness and friendship. Duwa Mara once asked me, 'If someone is far away and does not often see you, how could he like you?' A conventional saying makes the same point: *morgo min bi wulai yan la, i sai yena, a si yena, wu bi wo si dia kama* (literally 'person that is far away for a long time, you don't sing, he does not sing, how could you and he be friends'). Arranging marriages within the local community is thus based upon residential contiguity ('People that are not neighbours do not give their daughters in marriage to one another'), firsthand observations of the prospective bride's conduct, the friendships which develop between men in the various labour cooperatives and cult associations, the ease with which bridewealth committments can be met within the framework of community activity, and on the idea that if previous marriages have been successful then the families so related should continue to intermarry. Affinal ties (*biranye*) are regarded as ways in which the integrity and unity of the village can be maintained and strengthened. Marriage symbolises the values of reciprocity upon which good community relations depend. To give a sister or daughter is to give the means of life and continuity. And when a man helps his affines in their farm work, he enlists the support of his labour cooperative. In this way, reciprocal help among villagers is frequently related to affinal obligations and duties.

But if marriages forge alliances and contribute to village solidarity, they can just as easily cause rifts and antagonisms between families if they end in divorce or are plagued by marital problems. The friendships that lead to marriages being made may in fact be destroyed if the marriages break down. It is also true that the formal rights and obligations that link affines are often incompatible with the informalities of friendsip. These problems are partially resolved by arranging marriages on the basis or friendship *and* kinship. Kinship marriages are often preferred because they allow friendship, kinship (in fact siblingship) and affinity to merge. In the following table I have listed the types of marriage in a sample of 92 marriages from Kamadugu Sukurela. 44.6% of all marriages (including leviratic marriages) are kinship marriages and classified as such by the Kuranko.

Avunculate		X-cousin (mat.)		X-cousin (pat.)		Sororal		Leviratic	Other
K	B	K	B	K	B	K	B		
5	0	4	14	2	3	3	2	8	51

Table 8. Marriage Types

K—*kebile*—related; B—blood-related

Cross-cousin marriages and the privileged unions of the avunculate and sororate are all called 'kinship marriages': *nakelinyorgo fure* or *mu l fure* (*mui*, in this context, connotes· a kinship connection). None are prescriptive forms and the Kuranko seldom generalise beyond their own preferences or prejudices in this case, so that marriages 'depend upon the friendship existing between the families'.

The Kuranko terms for different kinds of kinship marriages are figurative and illuminating. Thus, if one takes a wife from the same *kebile* that one's grandfather took a wife from, then the marriage will be known as *wore koro woro feran* (literally, 'small kola under a large kola tree'). This signifies a regeneration of the grandfather's marriage. Marriage with one's sister's daughter (avunculate marriage) is only allowed when the sister is a *kebile* sister. A familiar Kuranko adage is used to refer to the impropriety of intimacy between a man and his sororal neice: *morgo berinne nyanka ti ke i kun to* (literally, 'person's neice's lice should not be put on your head', i.e. a person will catch lice if he is too intimate with his sister's daughter). Nevertheless, the possibility of such marriages may explain why a girl often addresses her mother's brother's wife as 'my co-wife' (alternatively, just *m'berinnamuse*— 'my uncle's wife') and a man addresses his sororal niece as 'my wife'. These usages are considered as joking play. The term for an avunculate marriage is *dogoma sonke* (literally 'handful of rice and sauce-price'). The Kuranko explain such marriages in terms of the brother-sister bond. If a sister gives her daughter in marriage to her brother she says 'this is my *dogoma* price; I am paying for the *dogoma* that you have given me'. This signifies that the sister is respecting the fact that her brother has helped her, looked after her welfare, made her gifts of domestic utensils and never withheld favours from her. The sister's claims on her brother are often exemplified by her right to take food from his plate (before or after her marriage). Thus, the significance of the handful of rice and sauce— the *dogoma*. Women occasionally rationalise this custom in another way; in the words of one women (addressing her brother): 'If you die we won't inherit anything of yours so we will enjoy what you have while you are still alive.'

Cross-cousin marriages are sometimes referred to by the phrase: *sogei bora ka minto meeye 'n'yo* (literally, meat comes to a place where there is voracity for meat'). According to Kuranko exegesis, the phrase implies the enduring reciprocity between brother and sister: if. A gives something to B which B likes and approves—such as a good wife—then B will want to return some gift to A who, to continue the analogy, has no wife.

Similar reasoning is associated with sororal marriages which are known as *sole bambane* marriages. The *sole* is a small raffia basket, *bamban* means 'to put on the back'. It is explained that 'when one sister marries a man and then later goes to her parents and asks them for a younger *kebile* sister to be her junior co-wife, then that junior co-wife is called *sole bambane* because she helps her older sister take care of the children.' Formerly, it was not permitted for a man to marry two blood sisters but this does happen nowadays. *Sole bambane* marriages are regarded as means of preventing tensions among co-wives (sisters will cooperate more readily and the younger will respect the authority of the elder) and as a means of consolidating good relations between two families. Bokari Sise, himself married to two (*kebile*-related) sisters, commented: 'It is a sign of appreciation for good care. My first wife was well cared for and her *kebile* was pleased with this and so they decided to give a second wife to me.' Occasionally, when a man's wife dies soon after the marriage her family will offer him a 'replacement' wife—a sister of the deceased woman—and ask for only a nominal addition to the bridewealth.

The stability and continuity of affinal bonds clearly depends upon there being an equivalence or balance between the value of what is given (a sister or daughter) and the value of what is received (bridewealth and brideservice). The Kuranko express this metaphori-cally. For example, I was questioning Duwa Mara about why he had given his daughter in marriage to his sister's son. His reply was: 'If someone gives you, you in turn should give to him. My mother was given to my father and I was born. Now in turn I decided to give my daughter to the same *kebile* as my mother came from so that the path does not die. I wanted to keep open the way between the two *kebile*.' To my subsequent question, 'Why didn't the bridewealth serve to end the debt?', Duwa replied, 'That was just between my uncles and my father. My father and mother have passed. I wanted to make my own way back to my uncles.'

Marital discord, adultery and divorce are regarded as breakdowns in recprocity; they threaten to 'block the path' that unites, in a real as well as a figurative sense, the numerous *kebile* and *luiye* of the village. In brief, the life-giving value of that which is given is not commensurate with the life-giving value of that which is given in return. Thus, if a woman fails to bear a child for her husband, refuses to cook or work for him, rejects the authority of a senior co-wife, spends too much time in her natal group, or is involved in adulterous affairs, then her husband may feel disinclined to respect his affines or fulfil his bridewealth and brideservice committments. The severe consequences of a complete breakdown of affinal bonds can be estimated by the extent to which the Kuranko tolerate and try to accept the causes of these imbalances. If a woman is barren, her husband usually accepts this stoically and 'prays that some day she will bear him a child'. Domestic malingering is often overlooked, a wife's visits to her natal group may be regarded sympathetically or with indifference, and adulterous liasons are, in many instances, disregarded or taken lightly—indications of women's weakness of will. Yet, by blaming women for discord with one's affines, men displace the source of the tension and seek to affirm their solidarity in the face of women's mischiefs. As we will see in Part IV, the male cult groups give dramatic expression to this tendency.

No matter how formalised affinal relationships become they must ultimately rest upon the qualities of personal relationships—between husband and wife, between father-in-law and son-in-law, and so on. And the Kuranko are quite aware of the indeterminate character of the relationship between conventional social ascriptions and affect. Marriage and affinity involve two essentially incomparable (yet ideally comparable) kinds of value: the quantitative value of bridewealth and the qualitative value of the bride. It is as if a sophisticated system of control engineering ironically required, as an integral unit ot its operation, a piece of organic tissue, perishable, volatile, and with a mind of its own. While men regard women as objects to exchange (having value in exchange), women strive to be subjects. This dialectical movement between the constraints of the mechanical order and the imperatives of individual identity underlies, in my view, much of the male-female antagonism in Kuranko social life. Sinkari Yegbe commented that 'men pay too much bridewealth for us, therefore they have complete control over us and every right to command us.' When I asked Sinkari Yegbe what a woman could do if she felt unjustly opressed by men, she said: 'A woman could go on a *sumburi*, this is the reason for *sumburi* (elopement with another man) . . . it is sometimes just to avenge oneself for a husband's mistreatment, sometimes it is because of one's real love for another man. But if a woman has no love for a husband, then no matter how kind he is, she will go on a *sumburi*. If she loves her husband but he uses force to mistreat her then she will have no alternative but to go away. Love should go and come back.' In some cases where a woman is unhappily married, her separation will be effected more easily if a subsequent 'kinship marriage' can be arranged. Morowa's wife fell in love with Morowa when she first met him. But at that time she was married to a man from Farandugu (a village in the neighbouring chiefdom). Her husband's mother brought word to her parents that she wanted to be divorced. Her father was happy for her to remarry because Morowa was his classificatory sister's son.

I want now to summarise the Kuranko arguments in support of or against kinship marriages. First, by far the most common reason given in support of kinship marriages is that they prevent divorce. In the case of cross-cousin marriages, the bond between brother and sister is perpetuated in the marriage of their children. Chief Fakuli observed that 'it is good that one's child should marry one's sister's child because there will be an assurance of amity. The children will not squabble because they will think of the mother and father who are brother and sister.' Chief Fakuli's sister's son gave his daughter to Fakuli's son 'through Fakuli'. In this case Fakuli's relationship with his sister is remembered for two generations. From the point of view of the married cross-cousins, a great burden may be placed upon them if they find themselves temperamentally ill-suited to each other; the husband's mother and the wife's father (who are sister and brother) will not want them to divorce. As one man put it, 'a girl will suffer from the complicity of her father and father's sister to keep the marriage going even when it is no good.'

A second reason for arranging kinship marriages is that they counteract the effects of residential dispersal in a family. For example, Fode Yira of Kondembaia told me that two of his sisters had married outside the chiefdom; one resided in Lengekoro, the other in Firawa. In order to 'keep the path open' with his sisters' husbands, he gave two of his daughters in marriage to his sisters' sons. This, Fode argued, will prevent a geographical separation from leading to a social rift within the family.

A third argument in favour of kinship marriages is that they 'play down' the formalities of in-lawship. In the case of matrilateral cross-cousin marriage a man could approach his mother's brother (who is also his father-in-law) and say 'I am not thinking of you as an in-law but as a mother.' With the maternal uncle as father-in-law a man could even dispense with the services of the marriage-go-between and ignore the formal conventions for addressing affines. Of the advantages to be gained from patrilateral cross-cousin marriage, one informant noted, 'My father has rights over his sister's husband, so the *biranye* ['in-lawship'] will not be as strong; it will be weakened by the link between my father and his sister and, through her, to his sister's husband' (the informant's father-in-law). Some Kuranko argue that patrilateral cross-cousin marriages are 'too close'. Others argue that, if a kinship marriage ends in divorce, the good relations between the two families will be irreparably damaged. And many people do not accept the confusions of roles and terminology which follow from such marriages. For example, with matrilateral cross-cousin marriage, a man's rights as father-in-law are partially contravened by the claims which his sister's son has upon him. If a man marries his sister's daughter (avunculate union) then his brother-in-law is also his father-in-law. His claims on his brother-in-law, which 'go through his sister, are then counter to the claims which the sister's husband has upon him as his wife's father. In the avunculate union, moreover, a man's own sister is also his mother-in-law. However, in such instances of terminological ambiguity it is usally the case that in-law terms of address are abandoned; affinity is assimilated into kinship.

A fourth advantage of marriage with the mother's brother's daughter is that bridewealth contributions will be much reduced; one's mother's brother will demand brideservice instead. It is thus often the case that when a man's father is poor (he may have few daughters to bring bridewealth into the family), his mother will ask her brother to find a wife for her son. The young man will probably take up residence with his mother's brother (i.e. uxorilocally), partly in order to facilitate the discharge of his brideservice commitments.

Because kinship marriages may lead to a form of restricted exchange, many Kuranko specify that at least one generation should elapse before two families are rejoined in a marriage. Kinship marriages are regarded as means of preventing the path dying out (*kile ka na faga*) between two families, yet the strategies of marriage-making are to open up many paths throughout the village and so create the groundwork for transforming strangers into neighbours, neighbours into affines, and affines into kin. There is a definite tendency to balance an interest in restricted exchange (kinship marriages) against the advantages of generalised exchange (which interrelates the entire community). A continuing connubium between two families would divide those families off from the community. And where kinship marriages are arranged, it is considered important that classificatory and not real connections obtain between the parties concerned. These factors underlie the prohibition on sister-exchange (bilateral cross-cousin marriage). Not only would such marriages restrict the ramifications of affinity, they would (in the event of marital difficulties) have several negative consequences. Noah elucidated as follows.

At least three families (i.e. *kebile*) should be effectively inter-related through marriage.

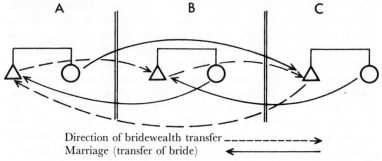

Figure 6. Marriage Exchange

If A marries B, B then uses the bridewealth received to marry C. Then, with the bridewealth received, C marries A. If only two families were involved then the exchange would be restricted and this would 'have too much of the brother-sister business in it'. So three families should be involved in order to mask the brother-sister linkages. 'Two families would simply give and return women and bridewealth to each other. This would be like receiving and giving nothing; it closes off the families and it could lead to antagonism between them. For, if I give my sister to you and you give me your sister in return, and your sister does not please me and we divorce, then you will mistreat my sister in return'.

In other words, sister-exchange would lead to a symmetrical but negative relationship between the two families in the event of marital difficulties or divorce. This is partly a function of the brother's obligation to defend his sister's interests and honour.

I have indicated why and how the Kuranko prevent kinship marriages from creating closed alliances within the community by requiring a generation or more to pass between one marriage and the next and by insisting upon classificatory rather than real connections between the parties concerned. The prohibition on sister-exchange is another example of these strategies that facilitate ramifying affinal interrelations within *multi*lineal communities. Why is it then that 19.5% of all marriages in the Sukurela sample (43.9% of all kinship marriages) are matrilateral cross-cousin marriages involving the children of uterine brothers and sisters?

The explanation lies in the operational difference between uterine and non-uterine siblingship. Matrilateral cross-cousin marriage usually occurs when a man's father is unable to provide bridewealth for his son's marriage. A sister's claims upon her brother allow her to approach him for help in finding a wife for her son. Fode Dabu of Kamadugu Sukurela explained: 'It is the same as a woman going to her people to get a *sole bambane* [a sister for a co-wife], to get someone to help her. When a man gives his daughter in marriage to his sister's son he will be able to get help from his sister's son when he needs it.' Referring specifically to the sister's son 'going to his mother's place', Fode used a very common Kuranko circumlocution: 'If people fail to give a wife to a dwarf because he is short, then he should be able to get a wife from his mother's brothers because they are all as short as he is' (*Komo kundune, nimor ma musu di ma, ha ke i wuru, i wa ti berin bare, i si anu dan keli sorundi, ha ke an da ma kode kode wonya la li*). In other words, if one fails to get a wife because one's father has no wealth, then one should always expect to get a wife from one's maternal uncles. But there is a difference in practice between a sister's claim upon her real brothers (the actual recipients of bridewealth from her marriage) and her claims upon her *kebile brothers*. If she wants a wife for her son, then she can only really ask her real brothers; they are actually indebted to her. On the other hand, if a sister wishes to show gratitude and appreciation to her brothers by giving a daughter in marriage to one of them, then she can do so just as effectively by giving the daughter to a *kebile* brother. In the Sukurela sample 5.5% of all marriages were of the avunculate type; all involved marriage with a *kebile*–related kinsman. In the same sample, 44.6% of all marriages (including leviratic marriages) were kinship marriages. Since these marriages are derived from the brother-sister bond or same sibling bonds the structural implications of siblingship require more detailed examination; this will be done in chapters 7, 8, and 10.

Kinship, Marriage, and Friendship

Kinship, marriage, and friendship imply different patterns and expectations of behaviour, but the significance of any one category must be understood in terms of its relations to the others. Kinship (*nakelinyorgoye*) and friendship signify two extremes, defined according to whether or not the relationships are given or chosen. The Kuranko regard kinship as a fact of nature, presented as an inescapable or immutable 'given' of social life. By contrast, friendship (*dienaye* or *dienamorgoye*, literally 'love/affection person relationship') is free of the inevitable constraints of kinship; it is an *ad hoc*, voluntary and optional relationship. While kinship makes reference to a pre-existing social order, friendship is subject to personal choice and influenced by temperament. Perhaps this is why problems pertaining to friendship pacts, promises and bargains figure so prominently in Kuranko oral narratives.

In Kuranko society, friendships may be formed with persons older or younger than oneself and the terms for friendship (*dienaye* and *kentiye*) can also be used to refer to friendships between men and women. This contrasts remarkably with kinship which, as we have seen, is structured strictly in terms of age and sex distinctions. Moreover, friendship transcends local group boundaries and even tribal identifications;

kinship remains specific and unique to a relatively closed, non-expanding social universe. Outside this context it becomes mere metaphor.[17]

Affinity (*biranye*) lies part way between these extremes. Marriages are arranged on the basis of the amity or friendship existing between families, yet the bonds of affinity which result are identified, in Kuranko thought, with kinship. Marriage, like friendship, opens up a wider field of social relations than kinship itself defines; yet affinal ties, like kinship ties, stand in a relation of contrast to neighbourhood or friendship bonds. Marriage also participates in both kinship and friendship since the woman is simultaneously an object of exchange between groups and a person. While marriage involves an alliance between groups it also rests upon the interpersonal relationships between husband and wife, brother and sister.

In Western societies marriage moves towards the friendship extreme and the interpersonal element in the conjugal relationship is emphasised. In Kuranko society marriage is assimilated into the world of rights and duties, the inescapable rules and constraints which characterise kinship. Love and friendship are not emphasised in Kuranko ideology; in fact they are often regarded as symbolically inimical to marriage. Personal preferences or random choices often conflict with social imperatives. Thus, should a woman take a lover she is in fact confusing marriage with friendship. In the same way we might say that incest tends to confuse marriage with kinship. This confusion of categories in which social prescriptions conflict with personal preferences is the source of many negative Kuranko attitudes about adultery and incest.

From another point of view we can regard adultery and divorce as the opposite of marriage: while marriage creates an alliance with or extends kinship to another group (mediating social and economic relations between men), adultery and divorce destroy the alliance and 'adulterate' the sacred quality of those life-giving bonds. Marriage involves a tension between male determination and female influence, objective necessities and subjective inclinations. The opposition of the dutiful wife and the lascivious mistress constitutes one of the major themes in Kuranko oral narratives; it is a theme which I shall return to in another work. But it is worth noting here that friendship offers the Kuranko an image of relationships which transcend the categories of normal social order. Friendship celebrates the fortuitous, kinship betokens necessity.

Finally, I should like to emphasise the importance of studying marriage as one modality of male-female relationships.[18] It is already clear that Kuranko marriage cannot be understood unless we relate it to the wider conceptual distinction between male and female. It may prove valuable to consider a man's affines (including his maternal kin) as 'feminine' and to examine attitudes to the mother's brother and to brothers-in-law in terms of two facts: (1.) in both cases the relationships are mediated by females (in the first case the mother, in the second case the wife or a sister), (2.) in both cases the relationship is with a male but the male belongs to a category which is 'feminine'. I shall take up these points in the next chapter.

Another aspect of this study which I will anticipate at this point is the manner in which the husband-wife relationship must be examined in relation to the brother-sister relationship. Then, since both these modalities of the male-female distinction refer to kinship and marriage, it becomes possible to relate them further to the system of male and female cult associations which elevate the sexual opposition to the level of local group organisation.

Notes

1. Divorce was, in the past, made even more difficult because the bridewealth would have had to be refunded in a single day. Noah's father was once obliged to refund bridewealth when one of his *kebile* sisters divorced her husband. At the time he had no brothers to help him amass the necessary wealth and his siter was not remarrying another man. His brothers-in-law arrived one day at his house and dispossessed him of everything he owned: they tore down the house, stripped him of the clothes he was wearing, and left him with nothing but a single cooking pot. Insulted and ruined, and without rice to live on during the forthcoming dry season, he left the village and walked 70 miles t (Makeni where he enlisted in the Frontier Police. This happened more than 50 years ago. But it indicates the problems of refunding bridewealth and the disruption of affinal ties which divorce entails.

2. Kamara and Drummond 1930 : 57-66.

3. Several other villagers died of the same disease during this period. From the point of view of local people, This was evidence of the way in which a cure on one person can endanger and contaminate everyone in the same community.

4. The word *bare* also means 'navel'. It is possible (though the Kuranko do not make this etymological connection) that the central role of the senior wife in the household is compared with the navel of the female belly.

.5. In a court case the plaintiff pays 40 cents to summon the defendent (this is called *sama sile fan*, 'summoning thing'). The defendant must pay the same amount, and this is called *sama sile koi yela ma fan* (literally 'summons back turn thing'). When the case is decided the guilty party forfeits his 40 cents; it is distributed among the council elders.

6. These remarks also reflect a case in which he himself was involved two days before; he had come to Sukurela to have an errant wife ordered to return to him.

7.   Another case, pending at this time, involved a Guinea storekeeper in the village who had cursed a local man after the latter's little girl had taken 10 cents to the store to buy kerosense. An altercation had arisen when the storekeeper claimed that the girl had given him only one cent. In this case the storekeeper had also disregarded local custom by cursing a man without first advising the local court of his intentions to do so.

8.   If a woman feels that her late husband and her new husband were antagonistic to each other (even if they were brothers) she may refuse marriage to the latter. This is because the spirit of her late husband may curse his usurper (in this case the curse is known as *fure koe*).

9.   A man's sisters can refer to his wives as 'our wives' because, as one informant put it 'if they were men they would be my brothers and my wives would be their wives'. Another informant commented that 'a man's sister feel that their family has paid for their brother's wives, so they say "our wives" because what belongs to one belongs to all' Furthermore, 'if I die, my wives would be inherited by my sisters if they were men; therefore my wives are also their wives, and my wife jokes with my sister, saying "Where were you last night? You should have come to sleep with me".' This evidence of a woman's 'residual claims' in her brother's group will be discussed further in chapter 7.

10. See Lévi-Strauss 1969a : 468.

11. If a man instigates the love affair then it is called *kemine koiye* ('young man action'); if a woman instigates it then it is called *musu koiye* ('woman action').

12. Apart from a general distinction between joking partners (*tolon nyorgonu*) and persons with whom no joking partnership exists (*tolon nyorgo ma*), there is a more specific distinction between joking (*tolon*) and serious exchanges (*sebe*—serious). Thus, before reacting to a statement, a person might inquire: *i tolon la wa ka sebe* (Are you in jest or in earnest?'). It is important to point out that joking relationships are not prescriptive; even with affines and sisters joking is possible—'it all depends on your relationship with the other person'.

13. If the *numorgo* is younger than oneself then he or she will be called *numorgone* ('little *numorgo*').

14. Radcliffe-Brown 1952 : 103.

15. Cf. Mary Douglas 1968.

16. About 1890 the Barawa people were driven from their country by the Koneke Temne. In 1907, D.C. Warren persuaded the Barawa chief, Belikoro, to return to Barawa with his people. Before leaving Kabala, Belikoro gave his daughter Sayo in marriage to Fode Yara Koroma; he also gave Fode Yara the town chief's drum (according to Barawa traditional lore) and told him to assume command of Kabala. When Fode Yara died, his eldest son—Kasi Koroma (now town chief of Kabala and called Alpha Amadu Koroma)—was very young and without resources. His mother, Sayo, journeyed to Barawa to ask her brothers for help. Two of her 'brothers', members of the ruling family of Barawa, each gave her son a wife. In this case the political alliance through marriage between Barawa and the town chiefs of Kabala (Sengbe chiefdom) has endured for over sixty years.

17. Cf. Jackson 1974 on idiomatic and metaphorical kinship usages.

18. This point of view has been outlined admirably by Rivière (1971 : 57-74).

7. Brother and Sister

Brothers call their sisters (real and classificatory) their *tersan* (plural: *tersannu*) and reciprocally, sisters call their brothers (real and classificatory) their *tersan*, a terminological equivalence which stresses the unique moral value of the brother-sister relationship. Brothers often refer to their sisters as *furu ke fannu* or *furu fannu* (literally 'marriage-do-things' or 'marriage means'), and, in some contexts, *mamusenu* ('our women'); these usages indicate that the bridewealth received from a sister's marriage is the primary means for a brother to get himself a wife. This bridewealth linking is regarded, by the Kuranko, as the basis of the brother-sister bond. The Kuranko often speak of marriage in terms of the exchange of sisters: 'Since a brother cannot marry his sister, he gives a sister in exchange for another man's sister'. Although marriages are in fact arranged by fathers, a girl's brothers are more directly and personally involved in her marriage since their own marriages depend upon it. Moreover, 'a father has many daughters by several wives, but a sister has only a few real brothers.' This kind of statement is often made by women, explaining why a brother will do more than a father to defend a woman's interests. It is also implied that there is a qualitative difference between the relationship of uterine brothers and sisters and non-uterine brothers and sisters. In the first instance the bridewealth linking is real, in the second it is theoretical. We should also note at this point that the bond between brother and sister has important implications for their children. As one informant put it, 'A brother behaves towards his sister's children as his sister does; a man is a mother to his sister's children.'

The spiritual indebtedness that a brother feels towards his sisters is emphasised by the Kuranko; they stress that a sister may often have to sacrifice her own personal happiness and endure hardships in her own marriage so that her brother's prospects of marriage (or his actual marriage) are not put in jeopardy. Similarly, a man's wives allegedly feel a special gratitude towards their husband's sister, since it was through the bridewealth received for her that their husband married them. And a man's children supposedly share this gratitude towards their father's sister. A man with many daughters is considered to be a wealthy man; his bridewealth receipts will be greater than his bridewealth commitments.

The spiritual indebtedness of a brother to his sister is supported and expressed by a formal system of rights and duties. A sister has the right to take food freely from a brother's plate (the *dogoma* or 'handful of rice and

125

sauce'), and she may justify this by saying 'If you die we won't inherit anything of yours so we will enjoy what you have while you are alive.' A sister also has the right to makes claims on her brother for material and moral support. A woman's domestic and household property is very often given to her by her brothers. And if her husband abuses or maltreats her then she may approach a brother for help. A man should sympathise with and support his sister in her marital difficulties, and he must continually make token gifts to her of rice, money, domestic equipment; he should always offer help in her gardening work. Men are so publicly solicitous towards their sisters that to an outsider the brother-sister bond seems to be the most important of all male-female relationships. This solicitude is, however, most evident between *kebile*-related brothers and sisters. In this case, geographical and genealogical distance means that the relationship is less personal than the relationship between brothers and sisters who have been raised together. During my fieldwork, the only occasions that I witnessed of men giving up seats in a vehicle to women were when the man and woman were brother and sister. Once, trekking to Firawa, we stopped at Komoia Badela—a hamlet on the banks of the Seli river. It was early morning and we were drinking some palm wine. As the sun began to break through the mist over the surrounding forest I signalled to Noah that we should push on. I knew that he, more than myself, disliked walking through open country in the heat of the day. Noah asked me to wait. A woman was sick. I went to the house where she was lying feverish and complaining on a mat. She was not seriously ill and I gave her some Paracetemol. When we finally left the hamlet I urged Noah to tell me why he had shown such concern for the woman; I mentioned that I had never seen him so concerned when members of his own family were sick. He told me that the woman was his sister, in fact a *kebile* sister, and that he was therefore obliged to look after her welfare. This obligation is reinforced by the fear of the sister's curse (*danka*).

The sister's curse is the negative side of a relationship which normally bestows blessings (*duwe*) on the brother: the bridewealth which enables him to marry, the help that his children can get from their mother's brother. As one informant expressed it, 'We fear and respect our *tersan* to secure their blessings and to avoid their curse; for us, the sister's blessings are more important than the mother's blessings. If your mother curses you then God will tend to ignore that, but if your sister curses you then the curse will really fall.' A sister's blessings are reciprocal to the way in which her brother treats her. Similarly, a father's blessings are reciprocal to the way in which one's mother behaves towards one's father; 'they come through the mother'. A mother might curse her child, but she is more likely to do so inadvertently and indirectly (by not fulfilling her duties towards her husband); she will, the Kuranko say, always recollect the pain she suffered in raising her child. 'But the sister will not have a second thought.' This last remark refers primarily to *kebile* sisters. They are not directly or emotionally bound to their classificatory brothers and they may exploit them at will.[1]

Because of the bridewealth linking between brother and sister and the indebtedness which a brother feels towards his sister, the sister's children also have a claim on their mother's brother which in a way repeats the sister's claim on her brother. But the direction of the claims is reversed in a man's relations with his sister's husband. This creates a reciprocal pattern of exchange and gift-giving between affines.

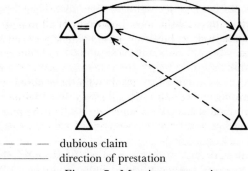

← — — — — dubious claim
←——————— direction of prestation

Figure 7. Marriage prestations.

Kuranko men 'look up to their elder sisters as if they were mothers, although this is for the sake of one's children more than for oneself; the sister's curse will bring poverty and bad luck which will mean that a man will not be able to get a wife and have children.' When the mother dies, the elder sister (*dimusu sire*) will 'become like a second mother to you'. In this case she may even be called 'mother' (*na*). Even while the mother is alive, a man treats his sister as a kind of surrogate mother. The sister could even suckle her baby brother if the child's mother is dead. Indeed, she is expected to do so, 'since she is closest to her brother'. Again, if the mother dies then her infant child may be sent to a sister of the dead mother to be looked after. This may be done if the father considers that the child's needs will not be properly met by the dead mother's co-wives. In these ways, the continuance of the brother-sister bond, expressed in terms of the spiritual and physical influence of the sister, gives to their children a field of extra-familial ties which are often used to compensate for deficiencies within the family itself.

Relations between brothers-in-law are often strained as a result of this enduring brother-sister bond and the claims which a man may make upon his sister's husband. A brother's guardianship of his sister's interests is often a thorn in the side of her husband, even if it is a source of security for her. There is always a subtle and difficult diplomacy involved here in which the relationships between brother and sister and between man and wife are tempered and balanced. A man must appear to side with and sympathise with his sister, yet not to the extent that he encourages her to divorce her husband or undermines the goodwill between himself and his sister's husband. As Sinkari observed, 'Men help their sisters because they received bridewealth from their sister's marriages. At times they make a great show of chastising their sister's husband and threatening divorce. But later they will advise their sister to return to her husband because of the problem of refunding bridewealth in the event of a divorce.'

Although a man has claims on his sister's husband that 'go through the sister' and a somewhat irksome influence over him, his sister's sons have counter-claims upon him. The privileged snatching that characterises the behaviour and attitude of a young man towards his mother's brother may be understood in terms of 'residual rights' of the mother in her brother's group.[2] But this customary privilege which 'imitates' the sister's claims on her brother should also be understood as a means of reciprocating and equalising the flow of gifts and services in a wider constellation of affinal relationships. The sister's son takes from his mother's brother because his mother's brother has taken from his father.

The sister's claims upon her brother may also be understood in more general terms: with regard to the rights of women and the constraints put upon men to respect women. The distinction between *ma tersannu* ('our related sisters') and *ma l musenu* ('our wives which we own') implies a contrast between 'women that marry in' who are sexually accessible and 'women that marry out' who are sexually prohibited. A man's respect for his sisters is therefore manifest in prohibitions against intimate contact with her. He must not touch her waist or neck, sit on her bed, make gestures towards her which have sexual overtones, or use language in her presence which makes reference to sex. A Kuranko myth explains why.

Once there were three children— two brothers and their sister. One brother was the sun. The other brother was the moon. One day their sister was bathing in the stream. It happened that the two brothers were passing that way. The moon came and stood there, looking at his sister. The sun turned his head away and called to the moon to cease looking at their sister's nakedness. The moon said 'no—our sister is beautiful to look at.' And he remained there, admiring her beauty and thinking about her.

When the sister had finished bathing she said to the moon: 'Now you can look at me as much as you wish. You have remained here to look at my nakedness despite the fact that we are brother and sister. Therefore, until the world ends everyone will look at you with no fear. They will admire you and be able to see you, just as you have admired and seen me.' Then she turned to the sun and told him 'You refused to look at me and you did not see my nakedness; therefore, until the world ends, nobody will be able to look at you or see your nakedness.'

Since that time it has been like that. When the moon is shining, everybody looks at it, admires it and sees it clearly. But when the sun is shining, nobody can look at it.'

In the myth, the moon was 'cursed by its sister; now people can look at it and see all its secrets. But the sun cannot be seen and it keeps its secrets from us.' The myth helps clarify the meaning of the sister's curse and the form which it takes in real life. The following case will serve as an example.

There is a man on our village (Benekoro) who had a wife and a sister. The sister and the wife lived together peacefully and liked each other. One day a quarrel developed between the man and his wife. The husband decided to drive his wife away. He beat her and then, when the sister came and tried to stop him, he fell on her and beat her as well. He paid no heed to her entreaties. So he drove his wife away.

Then the sister declared: '*Fonfende* (God forbid), did we not suckle the breast of the same mother, for if we did you have disgraced me by beating me and by sending your wife away. Therefore, from today until the day you die you will not marry another wife. Moreover, just as you have beaten me today, so you will be beaten and disgraced wherever you go and whatever you do.' As she said this she took off her lapa and stood naked before him.

Since that time the brother has not married again and wherever he goes and encounters other people, he will not leave before someone has given him two or three good slaps.

Such curses can only be lifted by the man making a public apology before the elders of the village. He must give his sister a *lapa* (symbolically re-covering her) and then, if the sister agrees to accept his apology, she lifts the curse by saying 'God forbid, did we not suckle the breast of the same mother, for if we did we are brother and sister. Should you disgrace me you yourself will be disgraced.' Water is then brought and a propitiatory sacrifice is offered to the ancestors.

The effect of a sister's curse is to deprive a man of the means of life— his rice crop may fail, birds may come in flocks and scavenge the mature grain, his marriage may be cursed with childlessness. In the case which I have recorded above it is clear that the sister's hold over her brothers is a powerful sanction for supporting women's rights. The sister's curse is a legitimate power which stands in direct contrast to the illegitimate powers which women (as wives) are thought to possess: witchcraft and poisons.

A sister's claim on her brother constitutes a kind of counterbalance to a husband's claims on his wife.[3] Although the agnatic ideology emphasises the male role as provider, as the focus of jural authority and control, and as the maintainer of the group's integrity, women (as sisters) are given a positive and active role in influencing social life. Sister and wife are terms which connote quite different positions:

SISTER Insider who has married out, bound to her brother by personal ties, separated (jurally) from her brother's group.

WIFE[4] Outsider who has married in, bound to her husband by jural ties, separated (sentimentally) from her husband.

I have already alluded to the ways in which the formalities of the conjugal relationship lead to the wife's disaffection, even though the

Kuranko regard such formalities as ways of strengthening the marriage compact. Cross-cousin marriage may be understood as one way out of this dilemma since the personalised bond between brother and sister can be made to support the conjugal relationship between their children. I have never known a Kuranko person to go as far as saying (as do the Dogon) that in theory 'brothers should always marry their sisters' or that a man steals from his mother's brother because he is angry that his mother did not marry her brother[5], but many Kuranko attitudes to marriage imply the ideal, if oblique, union of brother and sister. That is to say that the personal rapport between brother and sister can act obliquely to reinforce the conjugal tie between their children. If marriages are arranged on the strength of cross-sibling links in the previous generation then, in Kuranko thought, they will be 'safe'—they are contracted with kin rather than with strangers. More important, they will be characterised by altruism, and affinal transactions will tend to be calculated less in material or quantitative terms than in terms of quality of cross-sibling bonds. When marriages are arranged on the basis of friendship between men then they will be 'safe' in one sense, but prone to instability in another. The Kuranko point out that the bonds of friendship are not supported by mystical sanctions, which is the case with the brother-sister bond. The impersonal or calculated aspects of affinity may thus conflict with the personal or altruistic qualities of friendship. In the event of marital difficulties friendship between affines can be destroyed. Siblingship contains elements of personal affection *and* obligation. If affinal relationships are established on the strength of cross-sibling bonds then, in the Kuranko view, there is greater likelihood that they will be mutually compatible.

It is now possible to relate this contrast between the brother-sister relationship and the husband-wife relationship to Kuranko concepts of sexual relations. In the first place we have seen how there is a formal difference between these relationships. A wife is expected to be deferential towards her husband. She must bow when she approaches him and always refer to him as 'husband' (*m'buin* or *n'ke*), never by his personal name. On the other hand, a brother must always be deferential towards his sister. He must commiserate with her in times of trouble and assist her whenever she requests help. But perhaps the most marked difference lies in the fact that while sexual relations between husband and wife are 'natural', sexual relations between brother and sister are 'unnatural', indeed, in Kuranko terms 'unthinkable'. Just as conjugal relations militate against the ideal separateness of the sexes, the brother-sister relationship affirms that ideal. The conjugal relationship is sexual, the brother-sister relationship is chaste. And in Kuranko thought, virginity symbolises purity and order; it takes to its logical extreme the ideological demand for a strict separation of male and female. Inasmuch as the sister's blessings influence the fortunes of her brother's children, the sister signifies the 'virgin wife'. I will return to this theme when I examine the symbols of initiation ritual. For the time being however, it is important to emphasise once more that the complementarity of the husband-wife and brother-sister relationships reflects not only different patterns of behaviour but different symbolic transformations of the male-female opposition.

Matrilateral Kin

The most important extra-*kebile* relationship is that between a man and his mother's brother. This relationship has often been interpreted in three ways: Radcliffe-Brown regarded it as an 'extension' of a man's relationship with his mother; Van Baal has stressed that it is a 'reification' of the 'brother's debt to his sister'[6]; it can also be regarded as an 'extension' of a man's father's relationship with his wife's brother. In my opinion it is necessary to regard these three aspects of the relationship as simultaneous. The ambivalent attitudes of sister's son and mother's brother derive from the fact that they are related in several ways which imply contradictory frames of reference.

In Kuranko thought the mother's brother is 'like a mother'. The mother's sister is called *na* (mother) and *berin* (mother's brother) is, in the words of one informant, 'another word for mother'. When I asked people to say who their *berin* was the reply was often 'my mother'. The idea is that the mother's brother is regarded as a mother 'because he belongs to the mother's side (*na ware*). The uterine group represents femininity and maternity.[7] Reciprocally, a man calls his sister's children *berinne* ('little *berin*'). The sister's children are said to 'come from the mother's brother's side/place, maternally'.

A similar pattern can be described in the case of a person's relationship with his or her father's group. The father's sister is said to be 'like a father', and father's brother is called *fa* (father). As one informant put it, 'the father's sister (*tene*) is not called father because she is not a man, but she is really a father to you.' One of the reasons given for the rarity of patrilateral cross-cousin marriage is that 'although you can marry your father's sister's daughter, it is none the less true that your *tene* is a father to you; therefore her son or daughter is a brother or sister.' A woman calls her brother's children *tenne* ('little *tene*').

A person's relationship with these categories of *berin* and *tene* is largely determined by the nature of sibling bonds in the previous generation. If one's father and his brother failed to get on well together, then one will still call the father's brother 'father' but one's attitude towards him may not be one of 'filial piety'. The father's sister's hold over her brother determines indirectly her relationship with her brother's son. Just as a brother fears his sister's curse, so does his son. Moreover, a man regards his father's sister as a stern, demanding and distant person, i.e. as he would regard his father.

On one particular occasion I went with an informant to visit his father's sister. The visit was not prompted by any sense of duty or affection on the part of my friend; rather, he had suggested the visit in order to demonstrate what he had been telling me about the problematic aspects of the father's sister-brother's child relationship. When we arrived at her house, the old lady was sitting on the verandah. Upon seeing her nephew she began a long tirade, complaining about his negligence and indifference, his failure to visit her regularly, his failure to give her anything. This went on for about ten minutes. When my friend gave her 20 cents, she disdained to accept the gift, regarding it as poor compensation for his disregard. I asked her why she expected so much of her nephew, and she replied' I have every right to command respect and sympathy from him because I am his father's sister; I am a father to him.' She continued to explain that she was entitled to 'control' her brother's wife in the same way; 'I am senior to my brother's wife, just as the husband is senior to his wife.' In other words, her claims upon her brother's child were based on her claims over her brother and his wife, since they had married with the bridewealth received from her marriage.

Gradually our conversation got round to a discussion of the power to curse. Although she avowed that she had the power to curse her brother's child (if he was negligent, indifferent, abusive, etc.), she knew of no actual cases. 'Danka would only be used in very serious instances, such as: if I were hungry and my brother's son refused to share food with me; if someone beat me in the presence of my brother's son and he did not intervene; if someone abused me in the presence of my brother's son and he did nothing about it.' In her view, one should care for and respect the father's sister and 'behave towards her as one would behave towards one's own father, because the father is also the brother of the tene.'

The relationship between mother's brother and sister's son is considerably more informal, affectionate and free of obligation. Nevertheless, the maternal uncle should not withhold help from his sister's children—this would be tantamount to withholding help from his sister.[8] There is also a difference between a man's attitude towards his mother's real brothers and his attitudes towards his mother's kebile or non-uterine brothers. Although all one's mother's brothers are called berin, one feels less constrained in demanding favours from one's mother's real brothers. A man may call his maternal uncle's wife 'my wife' (na muse) but the Kuranko refer to a proverb which indicates that this is only a manner of speaking—i berin na muse i da musu lon, koni i sa musu ma ('your mother's brother's wife is your wife by word of mouth, but she is not your wife in fact'). A woman may also call her maternal uncle's wife 'my co-wife' (n'sina), but again, this is a manner of speaking. It indicates the possibility of marriage between mother's brother and sister's daughter (avunculate marriage).

Apart from occasionally snatching some article of clothing or taking rice from the mother's brother's plate and indulging in mischievous banter, the sister's children have certain ritual claims on the mother's brother. The general Kuranko explanation for this is that the mother's brother is *fisa* than (superior in status to) his sister, therefore he is also *fisa* than his sister's children. This implies a superiority of the wife-giving group over the wife-receiving group; the claims of the sister's sons on the property of their mother's brother are ways of restoring symbolically the bridewealth paid by the father to his wife's group. Keli Kargbo phrased it as follows: 'The father's bridewealth was given to your mother's group, so you feel that your mother's brothers owe you something. But if you go too far in taking things from your mother's brother, he will get angry. Then people might say "don't worry, you are *fisa* than your sister's son".'

At certain times, the sister's child may actually 'beg' the maternal uncle with the words, *m'berin, n'kan tele* 'uncle, put my neck/throat straight').[9] When a child is born, the maternal uncle must give his sister a token gift lest the child's throat be blocked and it will not be able to swallow food. And at sacrifices offered by the maternal uncle, the sister's child may come and snatch the neck of the butchered animal, saying *m'berin, a kan* ('uncle, your neck/throat'). At the same time the man's sister may snatch the rump, saying *ma musi sore* or *tersan sore* ('sister's rump'). In explaining why the neck is snatched in this way, one informant noted: 'It is because when the man's father went to marry the mother, he said that he wanted her as a wife and his words came from his throat. So whenever the mother's brother sacrifices an animal, his sister's child takes the neck in recollection of the time when his mother's brother took bridewealth and gave his sister in marriage to that child's father.' Clearly, this 'residual right' to take from the maternal uncle is related to the claims that the mother has on her brother, as well as to the fact that a man feels that his father is over-indebted to his wife's brothers. If a man snatches something from his mother's *kebile* brother (who was not a direct beneficiary of his sister's bridewealth), then the mother's brother may chide him saying 'Now look here, I did not receive your mother's bridewealth.'

At the funeral rites for a maternal uncle, the sister's son acts as a guardian of the widows and property of his dead uncle because 'he is the closest person to the dead man who is not also a member of his *kebile*'. He has no direct right to any part of the maternal uncle's inheritance. When a man calls his mother's brother's wife 'my wife' this anticipates the remote possibility that, if all the mother's brothers are dead, then a sister's son may, in theory inherit the widows. Since the widows will probably be considerably older than himself, such a 'marriage' does not imply sexual union; it is regarded more as a kind of custodianship. The sister's son customarily receives a token part of the maternal uncle's legacy (*che*) in return for guarding it during the forty-day period between death and property distribution. The Kuranko stress that the sister's son is chosen for this role because 'if the dead man's shade comes to haunt or trouble the widows, it will find the sister's son there and think of him as a sister. The dead man's sisters will also be in the house, protecting the widows'. It is also the sister's son who leads the widows through the village to the streamside when the time comes (after 40 days) for their ritual purification and remarriage.

It is noteworthy that when a man's maternal uncle dies, the mother's brother's son becomes his *berin* and the mother's brother's daughter becomes his 'wife by word of mouth'. The general principle of ascribing maternal attributes to all matrilateral kin is illustrated by the Kuranko adage which explains that *ni yi berin buye l ka i berin de bola* ('if you split open your uncle's belly, another uncle will come out'). One informant elaborated by saying that 'a goat produces a goat, a cow produces a cow, an uncle produces an uncle.' The mother's brother's eldest son in fact succeeds to his father's position when his father dies. Unlike one's patrilateral cross-cousins, one's matrilateral cross-cousins are only temporary siblings. One could marry one's mother's brother's daughter; one's mother's brother's son is a potential 'uncle'.

Matrilateral kinship is not constrained by the jural ties and obligations which characterise agnatic kinship. Relationships on the mother's side are thereby alternatives to and compensations for some of the limitations of agnatic kinship. If one's father cannot find bridewealth for one to marry, one can turn to one's mother or, through her, to one's mother's brother for help. If one's father is dead and one is at a disadvantage among his agnates, one can go and live with one's mother's brother. As Duwa Mara once told me, 'If a man is not in his father's home then you will find him in his mother's home.' For these reasons, matrilateral kinship is not 'treated lightly': *ma li ware yan morgo ti tolon berinya kwe la* ('we in this place do not joke about the mother's brother-sister's son business'). Chief Keli Kargbo of Sukurela emphasised that it is important for a man to know both maternal and paternal ancestors: 'If you do not know their names it means that you do not know where you come from.'

In the next chapter I turn to a closer consideration of the polygynous family structure and the matri-segmentation within the family which, like matrilateral kinship, are potential sources of division and dispersal in the field of agnatic kinship. While this chapter has been based upon an examination of the brother-sister bond, the next chapter concentrates on the relationship between mother and son. The focus of attention will be on the ways in which uterine ties are related to agnatic ties within a system of complementary functions.

Notes

1. In an analysis of eleven cases of witchcraft confessions and an examination of witchcraft beliefs among the Kuranko (Jackson 1975), I suggested that 'the witch can be defined as a woman who puts her role as wife and mother; she subverts the conjugal relationship by acting toward her husband as if he were a brother, i.e. someone she has a direct claim upon. This idea is obviously connected with the more general Kuranko concern with the conflict between women-as-objects and women-as-subjects.'

2. See Goody 1969: chapter 3.

3. Van Baal has noted that by 'consenting to being married off, the sister, physically the weaker, secures for herself a strong position. . .She avails herself of the weak position of her brother, who is her debtor, *vis-à-vis* herself, as well as of the weak position of her husband *vis-à-vis* her brother . . . By the simple act of agreeing to be given away in marriage to a man of another group the woman, has manoeuvered herself into an intermediary position allowing her to manipulate. Two men protect her' (1970 : 293–294).

4. In the past, sister and wife denoted two kinds of position, but a free-born wife was also distinguished from a slave-wife. The term *hore* or *horo* means free-born (by contrast with *yon* [slave] and *yonye* [slavery]) and a man might ask another man *i la hore le kela?* ('is this your free-born wife?'). .

5. See Griaule and Dieterlen 1970:93; Griaule 1973:13.

6. Van Baal 1970:300

7. Cf. the Dogon (Griaule 1973:15).

8. The Kuranko say that the sister's son could never curse his mother's brother 'because he could not curse his mother'. But if the sister's son abuses his mother's brother then the latter may invoke the curse (*danka*) with these words: 'Now look, if your mother and I were not born of the same woman then no matter, but if your mother and I were born of the same woman and you have disgraced me in public and before an assembly (*nyemaia la*), then God will disgrace you.'

    The curse is lifted by the sister's son apologising in front of witnesses and elders, stretching out on his belly on the ground and saying *m'berin i nyanti ma koto* ('my uncle, forgive me'). The phrasing of the curse indicates how the mother's brother-sister's son relationship is thought of as deriving from the bond between uterine brothers and sisters.

9. The word *kan* means 'neck, throat, and language'.

8. Same Father or Same Mother

Ke l dan sia, musı don den, ke l den wo bolo (a man has many children, a woman bears them; a man's children are in her hands)
—Kuranko proverb

'However much people may love you, your mother loves you more'
—Noah Marah

In the previous chapter I noted how the relative instability of the conjugal tie is often compensated for by the relative strength of the brother-sister bond; the Kuranko often emphasise this fact when justifying the desirability of matrilateral cross-cousin marriage. More generally, the perduring ties of siblingship, filiation and descent are contrasted with the often ambivalent, unstable and mutable ties of affinity. This is illustrated by the words which are customarily used in greeting a kinsman who has been away from the community for some time and, upon his return, fails to greet his relatives: 'Since the world began there have been people saying that one could say "my former wife" but never "my former child" [or kinsman].'

Because the brother-sister bond is in a sense the structural inverse of the husband-wife relationship[1] (it is based upon a prohibition against sexual intimacy, it signifies mystical influence rather than jural control), it has greater value for consolidating affinal ties; in fact, affinity becomes an extension of kinship relations already existing.

In Kuranko structure, women occupy crucial mediatory roles. A man's relationship with his maternal uncle is mediated by his mother. A man's relationship with his sister's husband's kin 'goes through the sister'. And a man's relationship with his father and with his paternal ancestors is mediated by the mother. In reality a man's destiny, luck, and fortune will therefore depend upon male-female relationships in the previous generation and be influenced by the cross-sibling bonds in his own generation. Despite the emphasis of the agnatic ideology on male-male connections (and an ostensible concern for the transmission of property and succession to positions of authority), this agnatic system is in fact mediated by male-female connections.

The Influence of the Mother
The Kuranko are quite emphatic about the distinction between 'real' (*gbere*) siblings and *kebile* siblings, between uterine and non-uterine kin. Of a sibling with the same father and same mother as himself, a Kuranko man will say *nakelinyorgoye le kela pati pati* ('this is my

proper/real kinsman'). In this context the term *nakelinyorgoye* ('kinship') or, alternatively, *mui nyorgoye* (literally 'parturition kinship') refers to the fact that two persons actually share the same mother. But siblings of the same father and different mothers are called *fadennu* (literally 'father's children'). Among the Kuranko this term is used primarily to denote the rivalry between non-uterine brothers. Whereas, among the Dogon, the father-son rivalry is the prototype of all *fadena* rivalries,[2] the Kuranko say that the *fadenye* is the consequence of rivalries between co-wives.

The importance of the mother in the destiny of her child is considerable since it is the mother who mediates between the child and its agnatic forbears. Although a child's fortune or destiny depends largely upon the blessings (*duwe*) of the father and the patrilineal ancestors, those blessings are mediated by the child's mother. The quality of her behaviour towards her husband is directly related to the fortunes of her child. Respect for one's mother is perhaps more important than respect for one's father. A Kuranko proverb makes the point: 'If you become annoyed with your mother, disaster will follow; if your mother becomes annoyed with you, disaster will follow.' In the past, a young man would make a garden for his mother. The former word for garden was *nakoe* ('mother gift'), because the garden produce would be given to the mother to secure her blessings.

The Kuranko firmly believe that when a wife works hard to please her husband, then her children will prosper. As one informant commented, 'We believe that the husband bestows blessings on the wife and these blessings pass on to the children. Therefore we say that the destiny (*latege*) and prosperity (*baraka*) of the child depends on the mother.' A Kuranko saying elaborates on this idea: *fe'e wa serine ne-e n'serine dan tei serine* ('if the father brays and the mother brays, the child will never bray'). This means that if a wife challenges her husband's authority in public then her child will always be subordinate to others.

These ideas are frequently expressed in *jeliba* praise-songs, which also celebrate the good fortunes of a person in terms of the mother's role. 'Your mother laboured for your father; you are the book (*kitabu koran*) of your mother' '*i i n'na le bolo*' ('you are in your mother's hands').

The mother raises the child, the father 'owns' it. This usually means that a person feels a greater personal debt to his or her mother and a greater sense of obligation or formal respect towards the father. This emotional division pervades the entire field of uterine kinship on the other hand, and the field of agnatic kinship on the other. A child's destiny depends both upon the father's *position* and upon the mother's *personality* or *disposition*. The father-child relationship is based upon filial piety, respect and formality. This is especially so in the case of the father-eldest son relationship; they must avoid each other in public and even feign mutual animosity. The mother-child relationship is based on maternal love and affection; it is more intimate, personalised and informal. An exception to this is the mother-eldest daughter relationship; although the Kuranko say that 'a woman is closest to her eldest daughter' the relationship is often one of subdued rivalry, probably because, if a woman dies, her eldest daughter will fulfill her role as 'mother' *vis-à-vis* her younger siblings.

Adultery, clandestine affairs, domestic recalcitrance, disrespectful behaviour towards her husband— all can interfere adversely with the fortunes of a woman's child. On the other hand, a mother who has endured the hardships of raising a child and who has shunned the temptations of infidelity will expect God and her husband's paternal ancestors to favour her child.

There is a saying: *dan-soron ma gbele koni a ma kole* ('a child's birth is not difficult but its raising is'). *Gbele* means 'difficult' or 'full of problems', *gbeleye* means 'hardship' or 'difficulty'. The Kuranko emphasise that the greatest hardship in motherhood is in caring for a sick child, in ensuring both the physical well-being and the spiritual good fortune of a child. By comparison, women say that childbirth is easy. If a mother admonishes her child, she will often recall these hardships and sacrifices in raising it. And when she prays for her child's prosperity, the same sentiments are echoed:

If I did not labour for my husband and if I caused my husband and any other man to quarrel (i.e. on account of the woman's infidelity), then may God ignore my prayer. But if I laboured for my husband and never caused a quarrel between him and another man, then may God answer my prayer'.

If a person suffers from misfortune in life, other people often allude to his or her mother's influence over that person's destiny: 'If a child becomes prosperous or useless, in either case he should ask his mother for the reason why.' A woman is always urged to 'bear up for the sake of her children' because the children's destinies depend upon her fortitude and upon her behaviour towards her husband. This is one of the principles inculcated during a girl's initiation. She must learn to suppress her personal desires when they run counter to the requirements of motherhood.

Noah's mother bore five sons. All have grown to manhood and become successful in the world. Their success is attributed to their mother's behaviour and qualities. She has been a faithful and dutiful wife, and she has worked hard and stinted herself for the sake of her children. Noah recollected that once his father was obliged to 'beat' her to discourage her from working too hard during the building of a new house in their home village of Korekoro. At sacrifices, it is customary for xylophonists to sing the praises of a man's mother, emphasising that all prosperity is ultimately conditional on the mother's behaviour towards her husband.

From Table 9 it can be seen that almost 60% of married men have more than one wife. In the polygynous family not all children prosper to the same extent, and not every inequality in endowment or fortune can

Age of men	Married men					Unmarried men	Total men
	Number of wives						
	1	2	3	4	5		
18 – 45	18	17	6	1	0	9	51
45 and over	1	2	0	1	1	0	5
Totals	19	19	6	2	1	9	56
Totals as percentages of whole sample	33.33	33.33	10.71	3.57	1.78		16.07% unmarried 83.93% married
Totals as percentages of married men	40.42	40.42	12.76	4.25	2.18		

Table 9. Polygyny Rates (Kamadugu Sukurela)

be convincingly explained in terms of the mother's behaviour towards her husband. Infant mortality (up to age 3) is extremely high. In a sample from Sukurela which included 145 births, infant mortality was 54.43%. Moreover, it is random. Considered together with the seemingly random or fortuitous distribution of factors such as intelligence (*hankili*) and personality (*miran*), this fact sometimes creates contradictions in Kuranko ideology. A person's birthright determines his social role or position, but at the same time certain individuals are born with talents or capabilities which are not commensurate with their assigned social role or position. Where personality or disposition is not commensurate with role or position an element of unpredictability challenges the ideal order (in which a relation of determinacy is supposed to exist between social position and individual disposition). A younger son may be endowed with talents which enable him to rise above his subordinate status and so challenge his elders or compete for political office. A father may be irresponsibile or incapable of fulfilling his obligations to his dependants. Jealousies and tensions often arise in such cases. And women often bear the brunt of them.

In the first place, a woman may blame herself for her child's misfortunes, or she may assume guilt for the misfortunes of a co-wife's child. The most tragic and dramatic examples of this kind of self-indictment are witchcraft confessions when a woman, afflicted by some unbearable illness, acknowledges guilt for the death of a child in the family.[3] The high infant mortality rate and the high incidence of sickness in young children is terrible enough. But when considered in relation to a husband's expectations that his wife will bear him many children and in relation to the importance attached to women as mediators of blessings, it becomes understandable that Kuranko women can sometimes be overburdened by the weight of personal responsibility. In this way, witchcraft confessions can be rationalisations of essentially inexplicable or arbitrary catastrophes. Among the Kuranko, women tend to be introspective in the face of misfortune; men tend to be extrospective. It is not so much the pressure of public opinion which inspires these nightmarish declarations of witchcraft guilt, but rather the system of Kuranko thought itself. Quite simply, women tend to get blamed for men's misfortunes; women take the blame. This syndrome indicates the extent to which extraordinary events which have negative consequences for the social structure are explained in terms of interference by uncontrolled personal powers. Men personify structure, women symbolise anti-structure.

In the second place, women often harbour grudges against a co-wife or actually blame a co-wife for the misfortunes of their own child. This displacement of guilt sometimes means that a woman will privately blame a co-wife for the miseries and handicaps which she suffers in the household. Quite commonly, the scapegoat is the senior co-wife (*baramuse*) who has authority over the junior wives in domestic affairs and who is often favoured by the husband. The *bare* is often addressed as 'elder sister' or 'mother' and we could conjecture that these tensions between senior and subordinate wives are displacements of unresolved rivalries in the natal group between daughter and co-mother or a girl and her elder sister. Sinkari Yegbe once told me that one of the things that sometimes makes a woman 'regret her womanhood' is that 'in the [polygynous] household, if the husband gives anything to his wives it always passes through the senior wife to the junior wife. You cannot cook unless he gives you rice. You cannot go to market unless he tells you to go and gives you money to buy things with. You cannot wear clothes without them first going to the older wife. The husband cannot give you anything except through the *baramuse*.' Literate Kuranko often translate *baramuse* as 'best loved wife', so indicating that their privileged status often implies preferential treatment. In order to mitigate the tensions between successive wives, Kuranko men frequently consult their first wife about the choice of a second wife. This may lead to sororal polygyny, since if the co-wives are sisters they 'will help each other and not quarrel'. I have also known men place an imminent curse on their wives so that should one of them gossip maliciously about another, then her children will die. Noah explained that 'since jealousies among half-brothers [*fadennu*] are mostly created by the wives, this curse will keep those jealousies out of the family.'

Despite the ostensible formality between husband and wife, personal preferences, favouritism and love may cause disaffections among co-wives. Cooking is shared among the wives on a three-day roster system. Wives each sleep with their husband in turns. But sometimes a man may favour one wife, or his senior wife may delegate work to her junior co-wives and do little herself. Many dissensions among co-wives reflect deviations from the proper division of labour.

I was conversing with Keti Ferenke Koroma one day at Kondembaia when we were interrupted by the arrival of his senior wife who wanted him to come and settle an argument. The altercation lasted for about an hour. The senior wife explained that the younger wife had fetched some firewood from the bush which she (the senior wife) had then used to make her cooking fire. The junior wife had become angry and berated the senior wife for using the firewood which she had brought. Ferenke listened patiently to the views of each wife. Then he began to explain the rights and privileges of the senior wife, how the junior wife should fetch wood and water, how she had no right to buck against the authority of her 'elder sister'. All the while, the younger woman stood apart, sullenly muttering under her breath. When the argument was settled, she left the cooking compound and came out to the front verandah of the house where she began ranting about the injustice of it all, blaming her husband for all the petty palavers which occured in the household. It seemed that Ferenke had encouraged or approved the senior wife's decision to go to the *dimusukuntigi* about the matter. The junior wife avowed that she didn't care one way or the other—'let them go', she said. At that moment another woman (a neighbour) arrived. She started moralising about the importance of domestic harmony, saying that co-wives should not quarrel, that they are sisters, how if one dies then her domestic property will go to none other but the junior wife. She went on to say that a woman should always remember that the husband paid bridewealth for her, that she is therefore pledged to him and must conform to his wishes. 'My husband gave £166.12 for me', she proudly declared.

Kuranko folktales about conflicts between co-wives are numerous. They censure wives to never gossip about their co-wives, they caution men to be on their guard against being captivated by a woman's beauty and thereby causing jealousy among his wives. They warn senior wives not to exploit the advantages of their superordinate position, they encourage women to show fortitude in order that their children will prosper.

Folktales about orphan children indicate, with some force, the disadvantages of being without a mother. Indeed, when the Kuranko speak of an orphan (*kelne*, 'single, solitary, all-alone') they mean a child which is motherless, not fatherless. Even though a person refers to his mother's co-wives and mother's sisters as 'mothers' (*na kura*, literally 'new mother') there is a considerable difference between the quality of the relationship with a proxy mother and a real mother. A mother's sister cannot mediate the paternal blessings to her adopted child. And a mother's co-wife may favour, deliberately or inadvertently, her own children to the detriment of her adopted child. In both cases an orphan child is alienated from the source of its prosperity, both materially and spiritually. I once asked Morowa's wife to tell me why there were so many Kuranko folktales concerning the plight of orphan children. She said: 'In some instances, when the co-wife is very cruel she maltreats the child and at times beats it. When she prepares food she will give a larger portion to her own children and then give the leftovers to the orphan child; they will continue to live like that until God comes to their assistance.'

I asked why the child's father could not intervene if one of his children was being victimised. At times, if the orphan cries and the father hears it crying, he will call to his wife to feed it. But the woman may grumble at that and feel that her husband is blaming her for not taking good care of the child. If she is not feeding the child properly, and the father asks why the child is crying, she may say that it is just because the child wants to cry. The man may accept her word and say nothing more. This could continue until the child grows very thin. It could even die.' These comments indicate the strength of the primary bond between the child and its real mother, and how secondary attachments between child and father or between child and co-mother are often tenuous and unsatisfactory despite 'official' or ideological statements to the contrary. A woman is expected to be a good mother to any of her husband's children; this is understood in terms of the husband having paid bridewealth for her and in the terms of his role as the 'family provider'.[4]

Fadenye

In Kuranko thought the rivalries and tensions between non-uterine brothers (including *kebile* 'brothers' but excluding clan 'brothers') are directly connected with the rivalries and tensions between co-wives. There is no one word that denotes 'blood brotherhood', but the Kuranko usually specify a uterine brother by the phrase *n'na kele kore* ('my mother-one-elder brother'). A uterine younger brother is one's *na kele doge,* and a uterine elder sister is one's *na kele koremusi*. Non-uterine siblingship may be denoted by the phrase *mai na kele n'da ma, koni ma sa fa kele ma* ('we mother ones are, but we are not father-ones'). Rivalries for political position, conflicts over the distribution of the inheritance, and envies arising from the unequal fortunes of various half-brothers are cited as some of the reasons for hostility among *fadennu*. In the words of one man, 'Your *fa dan* will not want you to be more prosperous than he is.' *Fadenye* is said to exist between non-uterine sisters too; 'in some instances one sister is more fortunate than the others and she looks low on her sisters and so they do not get on well together.'

This contrast between the amity among uterine brothers and the hostility and rivalry among non-uterine brothers belies the fact that tensions do exist among uterine brothers. The Kuranko emphasis on *fadenye* as the only area of fraternal rivalry and tension is undoubtedly a way of displacing conflicts from the domain of nuclear kinship onto functionally less important relationships. In Kuranko politics, offices such as the speakership and town chieftaincy are fervently and often bitterly contested. The same is often true of Paramount chieftaincy.[5] In these competitions for high office, full brothers allegedly 'never rival each other'. The rivalries are invariably construed as occuring between 'houses' which originated several generations ago with a conflict and permanent rift between two half-brothers. This leads to the foundation of a junior and a senior 'house' which compete with each other for political office.[6] The competitiveness is interpreted in terms of *fadenye*.[7]

If a man is successful and fortunate in life, ill-feeling may prevail among his *fadennu* because natural or individual ability is only a partial explanation of success. The *jelibas* will praise the successful man, pointing out that his mother's conduct was exemplary and that his father and father's father made the sacrifices which secured his success and brought him the paternal ancestors' blessings. To the envious *fadennu* this may imply that they failed to respect their paternal ancestors or that their mother's conduct is being criticised. It is tantamount to casting aspersions upon their integrity, suggesting also that they neglected to strive for their father's prosperity and good name.

Therefore, a successful or fortunate man will exercise discretion and not vaunt his fortune lest his *fadennu* give vent to their envy in sorcery. It is often said that one's *fadennu* are one's severest critics, always ready to cry down one's success and disparage one's fortune. Although the tensions which characterise *fadenye* are most apparent in competition for political office, they are also evident in the rivalry between half-brothers for the paternal blessings and for the father's inheritance. The ideal principle of the unity of the sibling group is contravened by latent antagonisms and power struggles. 'Everyone strives for the father's place' (*bei fa ware l tirina*), say the Kuranko. If one dishonours the father's name, one's mother will be held accountable. It is said that if a woman is belligerent towards her husband, then her sons will lack eloquence. And eloquence, boldness and fearless in speech are highly-valued; a man's success and prestige is said to depend upon his ability to speak in public and to argue a case before an audience in the *luiye*. Some informants claimed that the sons of a junior wife are disadvantaged from birth: they are last in line of succession and their mother may be ignored by her husband and scorned by her elder co-wives.

Relations between uterine brothers are ideally characterised by cooperation, amity and mutual respect. Thus, if a man's uterine brother announces his intention to compete with him for political office or quarrels with him over the patrimony, he might say: 'Do you want to show *fadenye* to me?', meaning 'Do you want to compete with me and rival me as our *fadennu* do?' The difference between *fadenye* and full siblingship is also borne out by fostering patterns. Real brothers 'circulate' their sons amongst themselves. The suggestion that a man might foster his child with his *fa dan* is met with amusement; 'that would be unthinkable!' The theory is that if one dies then one's children (particularly one's sons) should be already familiar with one's brothers who will act as proxy fathers and raise them as if they were really their own children. A man simply does not expect this kind of care and regard from his 'father's sons' (his *fadennu*).[8]

The kinship ethic of sharing and of mutuality is contradicted and often nullified by the geographical and genealogical distance between *kebile* brothers, a distance which is expressed in terms of *fadenye*. The greatest threat of sorcery is 'from those who feel that they share a common inheritance'. These latent antagonisms reflect, in the Kuranko view, the differentiating nature of uterine affiliations. '*Fadenye* comes from the mothers', was the blunt assertion of one informant. By relating the conflicts among non-uterine brothers to the conflicts among co-wives (or between husband and wife), the Kuranko make male-female and female-female antagonisms appear to be the true sourse of male-male antagonisms. A profound ambivalence is created by virtue of the fact that uterine ties connote the unique and personal bond between mother and child (which is the metaphorical model of kinship), while agnatic descent denotes a 'centripetal' ideal of jural solidarity in relation to which uterine ties are construed as divisive and 'centrifugal' In later chapters I suggest that the polarisation of the complementary principles of uterine and agnatic descent is effected through the ritual segregation of the sexes in initiation and cult activity. It is only by organising members of the entire community in terms of identifications which eclipse and transcend descent, kinship, and marriage that the Kuranko ideology—founded upon a strict distinction and separation of the sexes—is affirmed.

Notes

1. This structural symmetry recalls Lévi-Strauss's comments on the 'atom of kinship'. The relationship between maternal uncle and nephew is to the relation between brother and sister as the relation between father and son is to that between husband and wife. Thus if we know one pair of relations, it is always possible to infer the other (1963:42).

2. Griaule 1973:12.

3. Refer Jackson (1975) for a discussion of actual cases.

4. This is clearly indicated by the customary form in which a husband curses his wife: 'If it is not my labour that I paid/gave for you, or if I did not do my best to maintain you, well, if you leave me you will find a good husband; but if it was my labour that I gave for you and I did my best to maintain you, then if you leave me you will never be happy or prosperous in this life.'

    If the wife acknowledges that she is at fault then she falls at her husband's feet and begs his forgiveness, praising his virtues and confessing her wrongs.

5. Warren records that in June 1925 the Paramountcy in Kalian was contested by Amoro (the son of the late chief) and Fina Mara Karifa ('member of another branch of the family'). The elders were divided and when the votes were counted (one vote for each house) the results were as follows:
    Amoro: 13 villages and a portion of 3 villages containing 210 houses.
    Fina Mara Karifa: 7 villages and a portion of 3 villages containing 198 houses.
    'I accordingly informed the meeting that Amoro had been elected Chief at the same time pointing out that this was as it should be, since by Kuranko customary law, a chief's son of full age, if there is nothing against him, has prior claim over everyone else to the chieftaincy' (Koinadugu District Intelligence Diary 1900-1925:221). Warren also recorded that Amoro was 'second surviving son of the late chief Ba Farra, his elder brother having resigned his right to be made chief, in favour of his brother' (ibid). Fina Mara was town chief of Baudaukoro.
    A more recent example of the resolution of conflicts over chiefly succession is as follows. Manse Pore Kargbo, presently town chief of Kamadugu Sukurela, spent 3 years and 9 months in the army during World War II. Not long after he returned home, his father died. The contest for the vacant town chieftaincy continued for a year The candidates were: two of the late chief's half-brothers, Pore, and one of Pore's half-brothers. One of Pore's father's half-brothers renounced his

claim and gave support to Pore. Chief Balansama Marah of Sengbe came and asked the men of the village to stand behind the man they favoured. Most were for Pore. In the first place, he was the youngest. In the second place, his father and father's father had been respected and successful town chiefs. But considerable importance was given to the necessity of electing a chief without alienating one section of the competing Kargbo lineage. Here, the appointment of a son as successor helps circumvent the rivalries between *fadennu* in the previous generation.

6.   Noah (my field assistant) is a member of a senior ruling house, but for several generations the Barawa chieftaincy has been held in the junior line. The suspicion and antagonism between members of each 'house' is considerable. Not long after I had begun my fieldwork I interviewed a young Firawa man on the subject of chieftaincy. He became irritated by my inquiries and broke off the interview. Noah later told me that I had been undiplomatic in asking a member of the junior 'house' about the Barawa chieftaincy. He said 'These people would not want me to know details of the succession in Barawa; they feel that this would give me an advantage over them.' People are extremely secretive about chieftaincy and ruling clan genealogies and I was obliged to vow that I would not publish genealogical material lest it be exploited by political opponents in contests for chieftaincy.

7.   Among the Mandinka of western Mali a distinction is made between *baden* ('children of the mother') and *faden* ('children of the father'). *Badenya* means 'kinship', while *faden* are 'traditionally hostile to one another—rivalry between half brothers appears as a major theme in the Soundiata story (Niane 1960)—and the word has come to be extended from the rivalry between actual half brothers or their descendants to mean any rivalry, even one not based on kinship (Hopkins 1971:100).

8.   It should also be remembered that debts can be contracted between non-uterine brothers and *kebile* brothers; mutual assistance is not characterised by the altruism that obtains among uterine brothers (refer chapter 4).

PART III

9. The Dynamics of Age Status

Ninki min kosa, Altala le wol'sisenu gbina a ye (If a cow has no tail, God will drive the flies away)
—Kuranko Proverb[1]

In chapter 2 I anticipated an analysis of Kuranko social structure which related the system of age status distinctions to Kuranko concepts of time. This analysis, which is presented in this chapter and the next, is intended to show how the Kuranko employ the principle of age differentiation as a means for arranging and ordering categories of persons into a system; the significance of each category derives from its relative position in the total system.

My first step will be to present the Kuranko theory of age status differentiation; I will then move on to a consideration of certain factors and particular relationships which reflect of confound this theory.

Fisa Mantiye

The concept of *fisa mantiye* ('*fisa*-than-ship') is central to understanding relative superordination-subordination in a variety of contexts. The concept connotes relative seniority in birth-order position, superiority of male over female, superiority of wife-givers over wife-receivers, superiority of the agnatic over the uterine line of descent, and, in the context of clanship, superordination of ruling clans and precedence in terms of the historical migrations of various clan groups into the present territory of the Kuranko (the *ferensola*). *Fisa mantiye* can also connote the superior status of persons *vis-à-vis* animals and things. In any relationship, the subordinate partner may say to his superior: *i fisa n'ko le* ('you are *fisa* than me'). *Fisa mante* denotes 'someone you are *fisa* than'; *fisa n'ko* denotes 'someone *fisa* than I am'; *fisa i ko* denotes 'someone *fisa* than you are'. Informants stress, however; that *fisa n'ko* implies the notion of superior position but does not mean that the other person is necessarily 'a better person'.

Before discussing the concept of *fisa mantiye* in greater detail it is worthwhile pointing out that Kuranko concepts which refer particularly to relative ability and personal power constitute a secondary system, discontinuous with the more formal concept of *fisa mantiye* which refers to relative status. *Fisa mantiye* refers to system and necessity. At any point in social time or space a person's social status is fixed according to the principles of sex and age distinction. Indeed, the principle of sex differentiation is subsumed by the principle of age status differentiation: men are *fisa* than women. For example, it is said that 'a

149

boy is *fisa* than a girl in the family because the girl goes away into marriage and the boy stays to build up the father's house', and 'you are *fisa* than your sister; even your younger brother is *fisa* than the elder sister because he is a man and she is a woman.'

The Kuranko recognise non-systematic or contingent aspects of social reality which constitute a kind of counterpoint to the formal order of things.[2] *Miran* refers to a person's charisma; it is an innate power which gives one ability in oratory, splendour in appearance, natural dignity and presence. Persons with great *miran* possess an almost mystical quality, a force which lends weight to their words, which can overwelm or amaze others. Of *miran*, the Kuranko say 'Some are born with it, others aquire it.' The phrase *ke miran a la* ('this person possesses *miran*') is used to describe a person with a commanding personality. The phrase *miraiye ke bolo* ('this person possesses *miran*') implies that the person referred to has acquired *miran* through manipulating external objects; his *miran* is not innate.

The second kind of innate, though non-hereditable, power that the Kuranko often alude to is *yugi*. While *miran* can be roughly translated as 'personality', *yugi* denotes 'temperament'. *yugi* is said to be a force which inclines a person towards either exemplary or evil conduct. It is abstract, intangible and invisible, and only manifests itself in a person's behaviour. *Yugi* exerts its influence despite a person's willpower. If a person is unfortunate enough to 'have a bad *yugi*' (*ke yugi ma kin*, 'this *yugi* is not good', by contrast with *ke yugi kin*, 'this *yugi* good') then he or she will be the unwitting and perhaps unwilling creature of malicious impulses, prone to lie, steal and cheat.

The third innate quality which should be mentioned here is *hankili* ('cleverness or commonsense'). A general phrase, *morgo kolo ma* (literally 'person not empty'), is used to refer to persons with superior inborn gifts. Of a dullard, the Kuranko say *kun to kolon* (literally 'head inside empty'); a person with a 'good head' will merit the statement *a kunye faan dun* ('his head is full') or *hankili me le kela* 'clever is this one'). But the phrase *ke ro kolo ma* (literally 'this one in empty not') means that the person referred to may possess extraordinary or even supernatural powers which could be either good or evil. They may have a bush spirit working for them or they may be possessed of a strong inner *miran*. *Hankili* is invariably regarded as a positive attribute.

It is useful at this point to recall that *baraka* (blessedness, fortune, luck) is regarded as a condition which is largly contingent upon one's mother's behaviour towards one's father and upon one's respect (*gbiliye*) for elders and ancestors. When the Kuranko speak of 'natural' gifts they in fact mean that certain innate powers or advantages are somehow 'God-given', by contrast with social identity (role and status) which is not subject to the vagaries of chance. Thus, *baraka* entails the idea of variable fortunes which depend upon individual dispositions; the concept of *fisa mantiye* defines a social system based upon invariable positions. One of the central problems in Kuranko social life (and one of which they are themselves acutely concious) is the discrepancy between status position, which is based upon the man-made social order, and individual abilities and dispositions which are based upon God-given or contingent factors.[3] In Kuranko dogma, senior status position implies superior powers of insight, fortitude, intelligence and capability. But the Kuranko also recognise that such factors as intelligence, appearance, disposition and temperament are often randomly or fortuitously distributed. That senior status positions do not always imply superior personal powers is indicated by the following comments of Keti Ferenke Koroma:

'We say kina wo and kina wo [respectively "beehive" and "elder"]. They are not one [i.e. the pronunciation of each word differs slightly]. If you hear kina [elder], he knows almost everything. But if you hear kina [beehive], it does not know anything. The elder could be found in the younger and the younger could be found in the elder.

'Even if a person is a child, but behaves like an elder, then he is an elder. If he thinks like an elder, then he is an elder. Even if a person is old and senior, if he behaves like a child then he is a child. Therefore this matter of seniority comes not only from the fact that one is born first, or from the fact that one is big and strong; it also concerns the manner in which a person behaves and does things. For example, you will see some old men who have nothing; they are not called 'big men' [morgo ba, i.e. 'elders']. But some young men have wealth; because of that they are called morgo ba. Therefore, whatever God has put in your head, that will make you what you are. Even I who am speaking now, my father Mansa Bala bore me; but some of these words of wisdom [bimba kumenu or kuma kore, 'ancestral words' or 'old words'] which I am explaining to you are not known by everyone. You may ask a man and he may know of them. But I have explained them. Therefore, am I not the elder? There are some elders who know of these things, but I have explained them. Therefore, if you hear the word kina you should know that it is cleverness/wisdom [hankili] that really defines it.'

The Kuranko say that the elder 'owns' the younger. Rulers 'own' (tigi) the chiefdom, its laws and its inhabitants in the same way as a household head (dembaiyetigi) 'owns' the household or a husband 'owns' his wife and children. 'Ownership' implies a hierarchy of command and control (over both persons and property) descending from 'first-born' to 'last-born'. In myths about the origins of the world, man was born before women. Thus, male is to female as elder is to younger.[4] It is not surprising, therefore, that younger sons, uninitiated boys and socially-marginal persons are 'psychologically feminised'.[5] This general theory of the difference between 'first-born' and 'last-born' is also consistent with the Kuranko model of time in which certainty, knowlege and social values are associated with the ancestral past (prior events) while uncertainty and ignorance are associated with the junior generation (prospective events) and women.

Fisa Mantiye and the Field of Clanship
In chapter 1 we saw that the original Kuranko clans entered and settled

Koinadugu in a series of migrations which probably date back to the early 17th century. The first conquering clans assumed control over large tracts of country and when other clans later migrated into the area they became subject to the rule and political authority of the ruling clan which 'owned' that area.

It is generally acknowledged that the first Kuranko clan to enter Koinadugu was the Mara clan. The Kuranko say 'a clan might be older than the Mara, but it was under a cotton tree planted by the Mara that you were raised.' Although some later migrants became rulers when the *ferensola* underwent partition, certain clans have always been subordinate in status. Thus, the *jeliba* and *finaba* clans are often thought of as 'the last born', by contrast with the ruling clans who are said to be 'first-born'. Status position is expressed in terms of birth-order position.

The clans in each chiefdom are differentiated according to traditional professional status and according to priorities in settlement order. The general divisions of clans into estates thus involves a hierarchical ordering. In Kamadugu the following order is recognised:

Kargbo are *fisa* than Mara
Kargbo and Mara are *fisa* than all other clans:
Sise, Norwe, Yaran, Fofona, Kande, Koroma . . .
These clans are all *fisa* than Kuyate and Gibate (the *jeliba* clans)
Kuyate and Gibate are *fisa* than the *finaba* clans
Finaba are *fisa* than no-one.

Because the Sise and Kargbo are *sanaku*-linked they are sometimes considered to be *fisa* than all commoner clans. It is also noteworthy that although the present chiefdom of Kamadugu is a part of the amalgamated Sengbe chiefdom (ruled by the Mara), the pre-amalgamation hierarchy is still recognised (the Kargbo are senior). But since both Kargbo and Mara have a heritage as rulers in this area they are sometimes classed together as *fisa* than all other clans. The *finas* and *jelis,* at the other extreme, together constitute a subordinate class: the *nyemakale.*

A member of a ruling lineage in one chiefdom has no comparable status in another. The Kuranko explain that 'every clan is *fisa* than another, so there is no supreme clan in the *ferensola*.' Accordingly, 'no one can say that any one clan is *fisa* than all the others because in one country you might be a ruler but in another country you will be a subordinate.' This principle indicates the extent to which each chiefdom is conceived of as politically autonomous. But changes in contemporary social and political life tend to contradict the traditional principle. A man from a ruling lineage in one chiefdom may achieve political position in the Sierra Leone government and so be accorded a position of authority over the entire Kuranko area, an authority which may extend (since tribal boundaries seldom coincide with the boundaries of political constituencies) into the territories of other tribes. Similarly, a man might achieve status through economic enterprise which will give him effective influence in chiefdom affairs, even though he does not belong to the ruling lineage in that chiefdom and may be from another chiefdom. Many literate Kuranko who have responsible positions in Chiefdom Councils or in local administration exert a similar kind of non-traditional but effective influence in local government. Perhaps the most influential of these opportunists are the court clerks. Many of the latent antagonisms between chiefs and political administrators centre around conflicts between customary law and the bureaucratic powers of the court clerks.

The Sanakuiye Tolon

The hierarchical structure of clanship is most dramatically challenged by the system of clan joking partnerships (the *sanakuiye*[6]) which entail a privileged, egalitarian, and symmetrical relationship where the politico-jural domain demands hierarchy and asymmetry. *Sanaku* bonds tend to blur status distinctions between clans.[7] *Sanaku*-linked clans are said to be 'one'; they are regarded as 'kinsmen' (*nakelinyorgonu*) or as 'one person' (*morgo keli*). Informants also compare the *sanakuiye* with the relationship between successive siblings of the same sex; in both cases the 'distance' between the clans or siblings is so slight that it is difficult to preserve unambiguous distinctions between elder and younger or superordinate and subordinate. I have already published an account of the *sanakuiye* and discussed the myths which the Kuranko adduce in explaining the origins and significance of these joking alliances[8]; my concern here is with the relationship between the *sanakuiye* and the Kuranko theory of age-status distinctions.

Clan myths pertaining to the origins of *sanaku* bonds fall into four categories: (1) one clan once assisted another clan and saved it from extinction, (2) two clans 'became one' as a result of continuous intermarriage, (3) two clans became rivals for a position of leadership, (4) the once distinct descent lines of two clans became crossed or confused. The mythical events establish an identity of interests between one or more clans; they explain why the ethic of kinship should now prevail between them. Among the Malinke, *sanaku* 'share obligations of reciprocal assistance' and the term can be translated as a 'duplicate' or 'double' ("You were two, henceforth you act as one").[9] Among the Kuranko, *sanaku*-linked clans are certainly one from the point of view of the fictive kinship and ideal reciprocity which unites them, but they remain disjoined by their different clan names, totemic symbols and marriage regulations. The *sanakuiye* is simultaneously a relationship of identity and difference. It is characterised by a mixture of affection and rivalry, formality and informality, respect and licensed abuse, equality and inequality. In theory the elder (senior clan or elder sibling) 'owns' the younger; in return for respecting the authority of the elder the younger is protected and cared for. In practice this principle is weakened in the equivocal relations between successive siblings and in relations between *sanaku*-linked clans.

The privilege or license to abuse one's *sanaku* partner signifies equality; it is often compared with the relationship between age mates. Contempories call each other *m'bo* and a joking relationship obtains between them, known as *boiya tolon* ('age mate joking relationship'). Yet the abuse exchanged between *sanaku* partners also signifies status inequality; it usually makes reference to master-slave or chief-commoner relationships. In fact, one could not call anyone but one's *sanaku* 'slave' (*yon*). The liberties which *sanaku* partners take with each other contrast with the lack of liberty which is implied by treating a person as if he were a slave to be bought and sold. This dramatic juxtaposing of altruistic gestures and derogatory images can be better illustrated if we examine the role of the *sanakuiye* in Kuranko rites of passage.

When a marriage is arranged it sometimes happens that a member of the *sanaku* clan finds some stones and a pariah dog which he then brings to the man whose son is getting married. He presents the dog and the stones to his joking partner, saying 'Since you are making a marriage here is our contribution; take this money/kola and this cow as our gift to you'. At the birth and naming ceremony of a child, *sanaku* clansmen may joke about the child's heritage in a similarly derisive manner, saying 'Ah he has got one more slave' or 'He will grow up to be a notorious thief', and so on. Just after initiation (on the final day of the ritual), a *sanaku* clansman may approach the neophyte's father with a bundle of ragged, discarded clothing, saying 'I have brought you these clothes of manhood for your son to put on', and at times the *sanaku* clansmen mob the young man and dress him in rags which they will make him wear until his father has given an appeasing gift. Finally, at mortuary rites the *sanaku* clan plays an important role which the Kuranko interpret as 'making light of a serious situation and taking people's attention away from the calamity of death'. A member of the *sanaku* clan enters the house of the deceased and binds the hands, feet and body of the corpse with rope. The joker may call out, 'Bring rope, I want to tie him up, he is a thief', and once the corpse is bound he may hold the free end of the rope and declare: 'He is not going to be buried, he is my slave.' Only when a token gift is given does he release his hold and allow the funeral to continue. Or, when the relatives of the deceased are weeping a *sanaku* clansman may come to them and say 'Now keep quiet, keep quiet, we are going to bring him back to life.' The same joking and teasing may be repeated during the funerary sacrifices; the *sanaku* might approach the man offering the sacrifice, saying 'Let us cut his throat first.'

These sketches of the *sanakuiye tolon* indicate the manner in which privileged identifications are expressed in terms of disrespectful actions: seizure, false promises, theft, slave-trading, debasement, etc. The ludicrous character of the exchanges springs from the fact that incompatible principles of identification are brought into conjunction.

Yet the raillery and abuse serve to polarise these principles since the liberties taken signify equality and unity while the images of exploitation and hierarchy signify inequalityand difference. That this form of joking play (*tolon*) should assume significance in the context of rites of passage is readily apparent. The rite of passage involves a transition from a disturbed, chaotic or incomplete state to a re-ordered, re-constituted or complete state. While the rite itself effects this transition serially, the *sanakuiye tolon* portrays the opposed states simultaneously.

From a structural point of view the *sanakuiye* may be compared with relationships of affinity since both mediate between the contrasting categories of kinship and friendship. Like friendship, *sanaku* ties are actualised as a matter of choice; they may be disregarded in the same way. But like kinship, *sanaku* ties are expressed in terms of mutual assistance and common origins. The clan myths which explain the origins of *sanaku* alliances usually relate or compare them with the relationship between a clan and its totem (*tane*). Both symbolise the moral axioms of kinship. Many of these myths indicate that the *sanakuiye* is related to either (1) potential affinity (*sanaku*-linked clans such as Kargbo-Sise prefer intermarriage) or (2) retrospective kinship (many *sanaku*-linked clans proscribe intermarriage because they are 'kin'). When clan myths refer to mutual assistance in the past between *sanaku*-linked clans, we are presented with an image of interdependence which the Kuranko themselves compare with affinity.[10] The *sanakuiye* thus connotes an ongoing dialectic between interdependence and independence, identity and difference, kinship and non-kinship, marriage and separation, friendship and enmity. Between *sanaku*-linked clans each extreme is simultaneously possible. In the same way age-mates are both friends and potential affines; a man might call his age-mate either *m'bo* or *m'biranke* ('male affine') regardless of whether or not they are in fact affines. And a man's *numorgo* are his potential 'wives', actually or categorically.[11] In Kuranko thought, affinity is a metaphor for the *sanakuiye*. Structurally, both mediate between contrasting categories; functionally, they create alliances between discrete groups.

But what is the relationship between the concept of *fisa-mantiye* and the *sanakuiye*? When one *sanaku* clan is a ruling clan and its joking partner is a non-ruling clan, the *sanakuiye tolon* grants a privileged status to the latter. In the past the *sanaku* clan would ritually officiate in certain ruling clan ceremonies: leading clan sacrifices, assisting with the purification of warriors before battle, purifying clan siblings who had commited incest. This ritual dependence of a ruling clan on a non-ruling clan tends to counterbalance the latter's politically-subordinate position. The asymmetry implied by *fisa mantiye* is challenged by the symmetrical relationship between *sanaku*-linked clans. At the same time, ancient alliances or associations between certain ruling clans and non-ruling *sanaku* partners betoken a relationship of indebtedness. A ruling clan must always protect the country and people which it 'owns'. But often, in the case of the *sanakuiye* between ruler and commoner, a founding ancestor of the commoner clan once sacrificed his own well-being to save the life of an ancestor of the ruling clan.[12] The commoner clan thereby has claims upon the ruling clan, and the Kuranko compare this relationship of indebtedness to the relationship between bride-givers and bride-receivers. The claims of the bride-givers upon bride-receivers are said to follow from the fact that the former group 'gave life' to the other *kebile*. As a general rule the Kuranko say that bride-givers are *fisa* than bride-receivers. But when they say that the sister's son has the right to claim assistance from his mother's brother 'because the mother's brother is *fisa* than the nephew', they refer to the principle that a person has the right to claim help and protection from anyone who is *fisa* than he or she.

It must be emphasised that in Kuranko thought, authority or control over someone else implies responsibility for that person's welfare. As one informant put it, 'The ones under you can beg you to give them something through *fisa mantiye*.' An example will clarify this matter. It is said that the daughter of a chief cannot be *fisa* than her *furunyorgoye* ('commoner') husband because she is a woman and because she relinquishes her *sunike* status when she marries. Nevertheless, her high birth is remembered and if her husband wants something from his wife he may say jokingly to her, 'Your father is *fisa* than my father, so give to me.' Here again one could say that the joking exchange refers to a structural contradiction: as wife-giver the father-in-law is *fisa* than the son-in-law (in this case the son-in-law has no claims upon his wife's group), but as a ruler, the father-in-law is also *fisa* than the son-in-law (in this case the son-in-law has the right to claim assistance).

Finally, I want to consider the manner in which *nyemakale* clans make formal claims upon members of the ruling clan by emphasising their subordinate position in terms of the concept of *fisa mantiye*.

The Status of Jelis and Finas

Although clans which are classed as *nyemakale* (the *jeli* and *fina* clans) have a politically-subordinate status, their role in the ritual life of the community gives them considerable influence over members of the ruling estate. It is often said that chiefs regard *jelibas* and *finabas* with apprehension 'because of their big mouths; if they scandalise your name they could spoil your character and reputation'. Some people go as far as maintaining that 'all the treacherous deeds in the past were caused by *jelibas*'. By this, the rulers mean that *jelibas* could arouse or incite people to do rash deeds by praising and flattering the chiefs, challenging them to wage war or commit themselves to actions which would make them worthy of their chiefly heritage.

Chiefs depend upon the *jelibas* who are the keepers of traditions, the praise-singers, 'remembrancers', and orators. At any major ruling clan sacrifice (*kofe*), a *jelibas* must be present to recite the names of the ancestors, to recollect their legendary exploits, and to praise the chieftaincy (*mansaiye*). Their mastery and control of chiefly traditions and genealogies give power and influence to *jelis* and *finas*. Although subordinate in status, they are entitled to 'beg' and makes claims upon their chiefs. Thus, a *jeliba* or *finaba* might approach a ruler with these words: 'Your grandfather was *fisa* than my grandfather, and your father was *fisa* than my father, so give me something'. A *fina* might even derogate himself by saying to a ruler, 'Even your wives are *fisa* than we are.' Whenever the services of a *jeliba* or *finaba* are required, payment must be made to them. But while many high-born Kuranko complain that the *jelis* are exploitative, the *jelis* do not necessarily become wealthy or powerful by claiming wealth from rulers; a *jeliba* can never rise above his station. At most he could become the head or chief of the *jelis*: a *jeli mansa*.

Like the relationship between *sanaku*-linked clans, the relationship of ruler to *jeli* or *fina* is ideally based upon reciprocity. There should be a balance between the services rendered to chiefs by orators and praise-singers and the gifts given by chiefs to the *nyemakale*. A Kuranko legend explains the origin of this mutual indebtedness between *finaba* and chief.[13]

Saramba was a *sunike* (ruler) and also a warrior of great renown. His *fadennu* (half-brothers) became jealous of his fame and decided to kill him. They plotted to ambush him along the road. The conspiracy was discovered but by that time Saramba was unable to delay his journey. Musa Kule, a *finaba,* decided to disguise Saramba in his clothes. He donned Saramba's clothes so that he would die and so save Saramba's life.

When the day of the journey came, they left together. A little way along the road Musa Kule took off his hat, gown, and trousers, and gave them to Saramba, his lord (*mansa*). Musa Kule then dressed in Saramba's clothes. They went on, riding on horses.

As usual Saramba was riding ahead. When they reached the place where the ambush had been laid, Saramba, in disguise, passed by. The men in hiding said 'Oh no, not that one, it is only his poor *finaba*.' When Musa Kule came, dressed in Saramba's clothes, they shot him.

Therefore, since the time of Saramba and Musa Kule they have always been together. Therefore they say 'Musa Kule and Saramba', meaning that they 'go together'.

This narrative may be compared with mythical accounts of the origins of *sanaku* links which also involve a momentary inversion of a traditional status difference. The subordinate clan saves the life of the superordinate clan, thus becoming its protector. The myths nullify the status distinction between the clans and emphasise their interdependency in terms of complementary functions. *Fisa mantiye* comes to imply, not simply relative social status, but relative personal ability. A complementarity is established between power and authority. In a narrative which deals with the origins of praise-singing, the ancestor of the *finas* is given the name Fisana by Mohammed becuase Fisana was 'wiser than other men' and, like Musa Kule, sacrificed his own well-being in order to support his superior. This contrast between the powers of *finas* and *jelis* and the authority of rulers is characterised by the same ambivalence that we have referred to in the context of marriage and affinity.

Although the prevailing agnatic ideaology allows women no central politico-jural status in Kuranko social life, women occupy important mediatory positions. We have noted the dialectic between structural necessity on the one hand (in this case the perpetuation of the patriline through marriage and the establishment of community networks through affinal and cognatic linkages) and the influence of interpersonal relationship on the other hand (between husband and wife, brother and sister, etc.)[14] If the interpersonal relationships are unstable then this leads to a disruption of affinal (inter-group) ties. Women are seen to be the source of such potential disruption because agnatic and affinal links are all mediated by them. In this way male dominance and authority are equated with the agnatic structure while female influence and power are associated with the interstices of the structure. Female roles are comparable to the roles of *jelis* and *finas*; in both cases the roles are structurally-marginal, yet they imply variable powers and influences which are, paradoxically, necessary to maintain the formal system by mediating between its discrete units.

Notes

1. The proverb means that the disadvantages of birth and the misfortunes of life will all be compensated for by the benevolence of God; no misfortune is absolute.

2. Fortes has elucidated this contrast in terms of Oedipal fate—an amoral force in social and personal development that cannot be changed or regulated by society—and Job's salvation—moral necessity based on and regularised by the social order (see Fortes 1959).

3. See Kuper (1961:chapter9) for comparable data on notions of individual variability among the Swazi.

4. This point has also been made by E. Goody (1973:211) on the Gonja, by M. Strathern (1972:162) on the Mt. Hagen tribes of New Guinea, and by Bateson (1958:243) on the Iatmul.

5. This is discussed in greater detail in my paper entitled *Dogmas and Fictions of Birth-Order Position* (Jackson 1977b).

6. Cf. the Malinke *sanaku ya* (Paulme 1973) and the Bambara *sanakuyé* (Paques 1954). Among the Maninka of western Mali the 'joking and aiding relationship' between clans is called *senankuya* (Hopkins 1971:101).

7. Labouret speaks of the *sanaku ya* among the Malinke as 'a kind of alliance uniting and at the same time opposing representatives of certain groups who have different names' (Labouret 1934:100).

8. Jackson 1974:408-11.

9. Paulme 1973:86.

10. Among the Malinke, marriages between *kalame* (cross-cousins) are 'sometimes permitted, sometimes proscribed: they are nowhere considered obligatory' (Paulme 1973:87). This is also the case among the Kuranko. Paulme describes *kalame* as 'foremost among the *sanaku*' (cf. Paques on the Bambara *kalame*, 1954:51-2). Of inter-clan joking relationships (*wutani*) among the Gogo, Rigby writes: 'By far the most common, and most important, explanation for *wutani* relations between clans concerns the existance of affinal links in the past, and the potentiality of affinal links in the present' (1968:140).

11. See chapter 6 for discussion of the *numorgo tolon*.

12. Refer Jackson 1974:408.

13. A comparable myth explains the origin of the mutual indebtedness between *jelıbas* and rulers. Sira Kaarta, the ancestor of the *jelis,* saved the life of Mohammed by sucking the venom from his leg after he had been bitten by a snake; the snake was one of Mohammed's enemies in disguise. According to this myth, Mohammed gave Sira Kaarta the name *jeli ba*; the etymology of the word is said to be *yeli* ('blood') and *ba* ('big' or 'great') because Sira Kaarta sucked the blood from Mohammed's leg and saved his life.

14. Evans-Pritchard makes a similar point in his analysis of Nuer kinship: 'In a sense all kinship is through the mother, even kinship with the father and hence with the paternal kin' (1969:156).

10. Birth-Order Position

In the previous chapter I presented an account of the Kuranko concept of *fisa mantiye,* relating it to the field of clanship. I showed how the Kuranko conceptualise and structure social relations in terms of birth-order position and noted that the contradistinction between elder and younger must be understood in relation to the Kuranko model of time; the primacy of elderhood is an expression of the priority of antecedent events. I also discussed the manner in which systems of alliance (such as the *sanakuiye*) cut across the hierarchical structure, and I indicated how there is some ambiguity in the concept of *fisa mantiye* since it can refer to both relative age-status postion and to individual differences in intelligence, personality and disposition. In this chapter I will examine the importance of the elder-younger distinction in the field of kinship.

In the first place it should be noted that the eldest brother is *fisa* than all his younger brothers irrespective of whom their mothers might be. The Kuranko say that the elder brother 'owns' the younger brother. One consequence of this principle of age-ranking (which is fundamental to succession and inheritance procedures) is that generational distinctions tend to be obscured since father's youngest brother and father's eldest son may be the same age. Generational lines are skewed because of the age-ranking within each generation. Moreover, even when father's younger brother and father's eldest son cannot be distinguished in terms of age differences, the former occupies a marginal position in the agnatic group while the latter occupies a central position in it. From the Kuranko point of view a man is 'closer' to his eldest son than to his youngest brother, especially when his youngest brother is a non-uterine brother. A diagram will illustrate the manner in which relative age takes precedence over generation.[1]

Both succession and inheritance procedures are based upon the principle of birth-order position. Succession to the position of family head (*dembaiyetigi*) follows the rule of primogeniture. The inheritance of wealth, widows and children is leviratic. But when the eldest son is of the same age as his father's younger brother, or more likely, is 'closer' to his father than is his father's younger brother, then he may be both successor and inheritor. Sometimes, when the inheritance is to be distributed, there is considerable equivocation and argument between the eldest son and his late father's younger brother. This is particularly common when the leviratic heir is the dead man's half-brother (*fa dan*). In such cases the eldest son may appeal to the chief's court and argue that since his father never 'pulled well' with his younger half-brother,

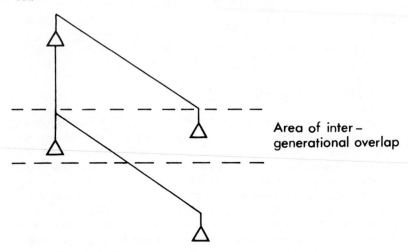

Area of inter –
generational overlap

the legacy (*che*) should not go to him. It may be argued too that the younger half-brother was, in any case, not directly involved in the production of that wealth. *Fadenye,* and the rivalries associated with this relationship, may thus be 'inherited' by successive generations. Dissentions among *fadennu* may in fact become, in the next generation, open breaches. For this reason leviratic inheritance often does not conform to the ideal pattern. Token parts of the legacy will be given to *kebile* brothers or non-uterine brothers, simply to maintain the illusion of amicability and respect. But even in reference to full brothers, a youngest surviving brother may never inherit the family wealth; an elder son of an elder brother may intervene and succesfully compete with him for the inheritance. In many instances this involves the father's widow going to live with her son rather than becoming a 'legacy wife' (*che musu*) of her husband's younger brother. However, this will only happen if the widow is elderly and past child-bearing age.

This contradistinction between lateral and vertical devolution indicates the primacy of *dembaiye* ties over *kebile* ties. Inheritance follows the leviratic principle only in theory (or in token form) where *kebile* relationships are involved. A man may often find himself in competition with his classificatory elder brother's eldest son. In any generation, younger brothers are on the margins of the agnatic group, often disinherited, dispossessed and disadvantaged. For them, uterine and matrilateral connections are often exploited as alternatives in their quest for wealth, particularly bride-wealth.

The rivalries for property and position that characterise relationships between *fadennu* tend to come into the open when a dead man's eldest son and his younger *fadan* brother 'compete' for the inheritance. This is often the point when the son moves away from his father's *luiye,* when the authority that he assumes on his father's death comes into direct conflict with the theoretical authority that his late father's *fadan* brother assumes within the *kebile* as a whole. Although all children are theoretically the property (*fan*) of their *kebile* 'father', in this case they have greater effective control over the distribution of their real father's inheritance than their father's *fadennu* have.

In an article in Sierra Leone Studies[2] Karifa Kamara argued that the eldest son inherits all his father's property, except for the widows. Kewule of Sokoro, in a rejoinder, challenged this assumption. 'Has not the leading principle of our jurisprudence in matters of succession always been that when the head of the family dies, the next eldest succeeds both to the rights and obligations of the deceased, not indeed selfishly to consume the property left, but as trustee to conserve the inheritance, and to preserve it from the greediness of eager youth in the interests of still weak infants and of generations yet unborn? And is it not to the brother of the deceased that as trustee the inheritance devolves? Does not he become the little father of the children? Is it not he who will pay both deceased's debts and receive those due to him?[3] This difference in opinion seems to reflect a discrepancy between the ideal (which Kewule describes) and the actuality (which Karifa Kamara emphasises).

An eldest son is marginal in the senior generation in the same way as a youngest brother is marginal in his own generation. This is comparable to the situation among the Konso of Ethiopia where 'the youngest son can be seen as having as much affinity with the junior generation as with his own senior generation—in short, as being a sort of very senior eB in relation to the generation below his own.'[4]

Agnatic descent accords superordinate status to the senior surviving member of the *kebile*. In theory this senior man is responsible for the welfare of all persons in the *kebile*. but since the agnatic group is only fully corporate at the *dembaiye* level of organisation, it is the family or household head (*dembaiyetigi*) who holds effective authority in the operative kin group. When a man dies, his eldest son becomes *dembaiyetigi* in his stead. The dead man's younger brothers retain only nominal authority over the eldest son, if the latter is adult. Consequently the application of the concept of *fisa mantiye* to *dembaiye* relations is more important than its application to *kebile* relations.

Elder Brother—Younger Brother

Elder brothers are *fisa* than their younger brothers. This means that the elder brothers are responsible for the welfare of their younger brothers as much as superordinate to them. One man explained to me that 'the ones under you can beg[5] you to give them something; the older brother is *fisa* than the younger brother because he 'owns' that one, he is responsible for that one. Even when the younger brother is wealthier than the older brother, the elder is still *fisa* than the younger'. Because the elder brother's children will tend to be older than the younger brother's children, it is sometimes asserted that the 'elder brother's sons are *fisa* than the younger brother's sons'. Within a ruling lineage, this distinction may give rise to senior and junior 'houses'. The relevant terminology is set out in the following figure.

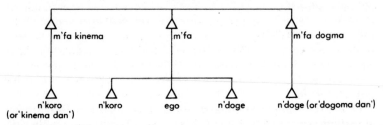

Figure 8. Elder-Younger Distinctions in Kinship Terminology

When the Kuranko refer to generations, the crucial criterion is relative age. A man might speak of *m'fannu tile* ('my fathers' day/time') or of *ma koron' tile* ('our elders' day/time'), the first category referring to generation, the second to age. In the second instance, elder brothers and classificatory fathers are classified together and an eldest son might think of himself as an age-equal of his father's youngest brother. Since this reflects a conflict between father's eldest son and father's youngest brother and suggests a structural similarity between the father-eldest son relationship and the elder brother-younger brother relationship, it is important that we examine the father-eldest son relationship in greater detail.

Father-Eldest Son

According to Kuranko rules of succession, the eldest son of the father's senior wife is destined to succeed to his father's position as *dembaiyetigi* ('family head'). Yet the relationship between father and eldest son is often characterised by emotional ambivalence on both sides, largely because of the tremendous significance which the Kuranko attach to the role of family head. While the father is alive, the eldest son is subject to his authority. A man must, however, raise his eldest son so that he will be capable of assuming that position of authority and responsibility. Paradoxically perhaps, a man must maintain a strict status distance between himself and his eldest son while at the same time preparing his son to be his successor. This anticipation that the eldest son will inevitably 'become' or replace his father is sometimes viewed as a threat to the father's role. Many informants express this idea by way of an analogy: it is often said that when father and eldest son resemble each other physically the tension and conflict between them will be greatest; ideally, the identity of the successor should be camouflaged.[6]

This emphasis on 'denying' the inevitable succession is further demonstrated by the Kuranko view that a father must feign or exaggerate antagonism towards his eldest son in order to deflect public attention from the privileged status of the eldest son. The restraint and formality that an eldest son should show in his dealings with his father's wives is another way in which this overlapping of roles is disguised. For instance, a son must not wear his father's underclothes or even inherit them; such an act would imply usurpation of the father's sexual role. Other customs, such as the prohibition on a son wearing his father's trousers or sleeping on his father's bed, have similar oedipal connotations. The father's authority is symbolically protected by the prohibition on the eldest son wearing his father's cap or gown during his father's lifetime.

One of the commonest rationalisations of the quasi-ritualised display of hostility between father and eldest son rests on the assumption that should a man show any real affection for his first-born son (*den ke sare*, literally 'child male first-born'), then the boy's *fadennu* might find cause to be envious of their brother's imminent position of authority in the family and seek to harm him and their father by sorcery. Therefore, many Kuranko say, the father is obliged to display hostility towards his son in public so that the identity of the true successor will be disguised and the potential *fadan* rivalries mitigated. In private, this hostility may be suspended. One informant reflected that 'a man's eldest son should avoid coming into contact with his father. But this is only in public. In secret they meet and it is during these meetings that the father shares the secrets of his protective medicines with his eldest son or tells his son the history of the clan. He also advises him on how to behave, because the eldest son will succeed his father. But the avoidance in public is only for show.'

Although there is sometimes reserve and even avoidance between a man and his eldest daughter (*dimusu sire*, literally 'child female first-born'), a mother and her eldest daughter are said to be especially close. A women instructs her eldest daughter in domestic science, mothercraft and various women's skills such as cotton-spinning and cloth-dying. But her eldest daughter is not a potential threat to her; her destiny lies outside the family as a wife in another *dembaiye* altogether. While she remains in her mother's home, an eldest daughter is a friend and helpmate, not a status rival.

To summarise and illustrate the characteristic pattern of the father-eldest son relationship I will recount (in loose translation) what one man told me about his own notoriously difficult relationship with his father. Discretion forbids the use of real names, but it is important to note that this relationship was doubly problematic. Tamba was aged about 25. His father was a petty trader and therefore, unlike most Kuranko, he possessed a considerable amount of personal property. From Tamba's father's point of view it was imperative that his eldest son acquire business acumen and responsibility and ultimately take over the trade store in the village. Tamba's ambitions lay elsewhere.

The following is Tamba's account:

'The father wants his eldest son to shoulder the family responsibility; he raises him to assume his position at the head of the family, and so delegates much authority in family affairs to him: he gets him to look after the household and family wealth, the granaries and valuables, whenever he is away from the village. And he allows his eldest son to punish the younger sons when they do wrong. So the father's affection is hidden and the eldest son often looks for this paternal affection from his father's brothers or his mother's brothers. In my case, however, my father's brothers and my mother's brothers are all dead and I feel deeply the lack of a real father. My mother tends to side with my father when I argue with him and she cries bitterly whenever I ask her to intervene on my behalf. Her hands are tied. After all, she must take my father's side in public even though in private she may feel differently. Once, when my father was away, I was left to look after the store. When he returned he told me that I had been negligent and irresponsible during his absence. He said, "When I am in my grave, who will continue the family? You are useless." Whatever I do I cannot please my father. He is constantly finding fault with me and criticising me.

'You see, a father prays to get a son who is better than he is. So the son feels that he can never please his father, no matter what he does. This is why a father will sometimes drive his eldest son away from home, though he will be careful to make sure his son remained in the same village, always near him, so he can watch him and marry him a wife from the village to ensure that he stays.

'A father treats his eldest son harshly as a training for the hardships of the future when he will have to shoulder the responsibility for the entire family. So he delegates authority to his eldest son, over wives, children, property.Yet he is always critical of his son's ability to assume this authority and responsibility.'

Geographical mobility and new alternatives nowadays enable sons to evade the onerous situations that sometimes develop. The army, the Kono diamond districts, the cities and large towns—these are often escapes for young men who feel themselves overburdened by customary kinship responsibilities. Within the villages it is unusual for adult eldest sons to actually reside in their father's *luiye* (refer Table 2). In many cases, the eldest son 'cuts his mouth off from his father's *luiye*' as soon as he is able to assert his independence (after his initiation). When his father dies he may return to his father's place and assume his responsibilities. In other cases, however, the eldest son alienates himself permanently from his father's *luiye*. When this occurs, nominal authority in the *dembaiye* usually falls to the second eldest son. One example will illustrate this.

When Fode's father died, Fode's elder brother—Pore— should have succeeded him. But Pore, a notorious wastrel, repudiated the responsibility for the care and welfare of the family; he left the village and district altogether. As second eldest son, Fode came to 'play' the role of the family head, but reluctantly. Although he has never refused help to his younger brothers and their families, he has always made it clear that the absent Pore is the proper and titular head of the family and should therefore honour the commitments of that position.

In conflicts between father and eldest son the son's mother is often placed in a difficult postion. She prays that her eldest son live up to the father's expectations, partly because her husband's attitude towards her is largely conditional upon the behaviour of their son. As we have already seen, mothers conventionally bear the blame for the misdemeanours of their children, just as they are praised for their childrens' good fortunes. If conjugal discord does exist, it is argued that the blessings of the patrilineal ancestors will not flow to the son since they are conditional upon the mother's behaviour towards her husband. For these reasons a woman strives to reconcile the differences between her husband and eldest son, tempering the father's criticisms and reproofs, reminding her son that he will understand, when he comes of age, the resons for the father's outward harshness.

Perhaps the most effective resolution of the conflict between father and eldest son is achieved by the father delegating authority to his eldest son over the younger sons. While remaining subject to the authority of his father, the eldest son becomes the 'owner' (*tigi*) of the younger brothers—in effect a kind of father to them. The term *koro* denotes both elder sibling and elder or senior person. My informants were quite explicit in comparing the father-eldest son relationship with the relationship between elder and younger brother. One man explained, 'Just as the father is *fisa* than the eldest son, so the elder brother is *fisa* than the younger brother'. Another elder commented, 'As with your father so with your elder brother after him; you do not just sit down and talk with your elder brother as with other men'. The general principal implied here can be represented in a simple figure:

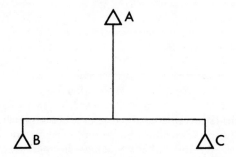

A is to B as B is to C. With regard to the foregoing discussion this means that, structurally-speaking, the inter-generational relationship is like the intra-generational one. From a psychological point of view there is a displacement of the resentments and tensions of the filial relationship onto the sibling relationship.[7]

The father's delegation of authority to his eldest son reflects in part his expectation that his eldest son will set an example to his younger sons. It is said that the younger brothers emulate the elder and if the eldest brother misbehaves then his younger brothers will tend to follow his bad example. One informant told me that in the case of his own family his father would rebuke the eldest son whenever a younger son misbehaved. Other people noted that a father delegates authority to his eldest son as a kind of trial, to see if he can cope with the responsibilities of family and household management. From a father's point of view, exemplary conduct from his eldest son is crucial to the integrity and continuity of the *dembaiye*. For the eldest son, his destiny is inextricably bound up with his *fa ware* ('father's place'), not just because he is his father's immediate successor but because he depends upon his father to secure the bridewealth necessary for his marriage. A younger son, by contrast, depends more upon his elder brother since, when he reaches marriageable age, his father may be very old or deceased.

We have noted how the Kuranko sometimes explain the formality and distance between father and eldest son in terms of the need to minimise *fadenye* rivalries, particularly among the elder sons of a man's wives. Thus, a father must never appear to favour or prefer his true successor. The structural proximity of father and eldest son may be compared to that of first-born and second-born brothers. The eldest son acts as a shadow father, in authority over and responsible for the welfare of his younger brothers. Theoretically, the role of father's younger brother is defined similarly. In the following figure A is to C as B is to C.

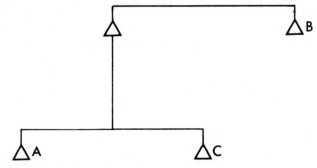

This structural equivalence (which again transects generational lines and emphasises the overriding importance of age) sometimes means that eldest son (A) and father's youngest brother (B) compete for authority. This is particularly common when decisions must be made concerning marriage arrangements. If a man dies then his younger (inheriting) brother assumes responsibility for the deceased man's daughters; he must arrange their marriages and decide how incoming bridewealth from these marriages will be used. In many cases, however, the deceased man's sons arrange their sisters' marriages in order to gain direct control over the bridewealth (which they require for their own marriages). But, say the Kuranko, this happens only when an heir neglects his obligations to his deceased brother's sons.

Successive Siblings

The Kuranko frequently allude to tensions between successive siblings; squabbling and fighting are allegedly common between successive brothers, and relations between them in public tend to be distant and reserved. The usual explanation is that 'the second son feels that the first son is only a little older than he is; he therefore does not feel inclined to accord that one the kind of respect he would accord an elder' (Seku Kargbo). At the base of these problems, therefore, is a conflict over authority and control rather than envy of the sibling who has displaced the subject in his mother's affections. This conflict over authority reflects a kind of status blurring at the point where elder-younger distinctions are most finely drawn.

The successive sibling is called the *gbarase* (literally 'comes after'), as in the phrase *ke ta gbarase le kela* (this comes after this one'). Obviously, the last-born child (*de na ban; denke ban*—last-born son; *dimusu l ban*—last born daughter) is *gbarase* to the second-to-last-born child, but he or she has no *gbarase*.

In the case of women, successive sisters cannot be married to the same man (nor can sisters with the same father and same mother) because it is considered impure for them both to have sexual contact 'through the husband'. This prohibition may serve to prevent rivalries between successive sisters extending into the already problematic domain of co-wifeship. With successive brothers, the problem of the younger bucking the elder's authority is resolved sometimes by rather ingenious means. Yandi was *gbarase* to Bala. They were always quarreling. To resolve their differences once and for all their mother organised a wrestling bout between them. She knew that Bala, the eldest and strongest, would probably win and so she ensured that the bout was witnessed by many villagers. As she predicted Bala defeated Yandi and thenceforth Yandi accepted and respected the authority of his elder brother. In the eyes of the village the status distinction between them was quite clear.

In Kuranko thought, the status distinctions among brothers tend to be nullified in the presence of the father or elder brother. One man remarked that 'every brother is one in the presence of an elder brother. If the brothers are sitting together and an elder brother comes, then they are all one under him. But if the father comes, then all the brothers are one under him.' This ideal unity and mutuality of the sibling group is, however, contradicted in some ways by evidence adduced from Kuranko oral narratives.

Sibling Rivalry

During my fieldwork I recorded and translated over 200 Kuranko narratives. The extent to which these stories indicate areas of tension and crises in actual social relations is remarkable. Stories concerning male-female and elder-younger oppositions afforded me insights into some of the problematic aspects of Kuranko social organisation and they also served as means for discussing with informants the interplay between latent and manifest social patterns.

About 20% of the stories which I collected concern the familiar fictional protagonists: hare and hyena. These stories elaborate a formal contrast between status position and personal capability. A contrast between those who are directly concerned with maintaining the status quo (elders) and those who are liberated from the normal constraints of the given order (the clever youngsters) is often expressed as a contrast between the inflexibility or inadequacy of status superiors and the flexibility and cleverness of status inferiors. Thus, elders are caricatured as being inflexible, stupid and backward-looking; they are hyenas. Youngsters are characterised as flexible, clever, insightful; they are hares. Typically in the stories a stupid, unjust or irresponsible elder is outwitted, manipulated and displaced by a clever youngster. The narratives often end with the death or displacement of a chief or elder brother; the youngster 'becomes' the elder and the elder is then someone whose personal ability is commensurate with the high status he has won.[8] This fictional pattern in undoubtedly reflective of real latent tension, particularly between elder and younger brothers.

Ideally, elderhood (*koroya*) signifies both authority over and responsibility for younger or junior persons; this dual and reciprocal character of relationships between superordinates and subordinates is implied in the concept of *fisa mantiye*. But in reality the authority of the elder is often regarded as bullying dominance. People say that an elder brother or father may impose certain idiosyncratic rules upon the family which disadvantage the younger members. Youngsters often deride their elders by referring to their conservatism, their strictness, their gravity. Some claim that the elders put their own selfish interests before those of the family; others speak of the indignity of always receiving clothes that older siblings have grown out of, being constantly told what to do, subject at all times to the authority (and whims) of others. Such resentments are not without foundation in some cases. Nonkowa Kargbo, an elder of Benekoro, explained:

'The elder brother is at times inclined to abuse his authority and neglect the welfare of his younger brothers. The younger brother is often made to run errands, fetch water, and summon friends for his elder brothers. The younger brother may seek the support, protection and friendship of an elder brother if another one fails him. So younger brothers may sometimes outsmart the elders by playing them off against one another. The elders fear the possibility that a younger brother may cause dissensions among them by telling one that another insulted him or rufused to help him. By enlisting the support of a sympathetic brother he can cause rifts among his elder brothers. This is why the elder should not underestimate the younger and why the elders look after the younger ones.'

An elder brother is thus admonished to care for his younger brothers lest they disrespect him. And a younger brother is reminded that he should show forebearance and patience simply because he is last in line of succession within the family. One stoic injunction takes the form of an adage: *sare ya ro, sare koma* ('first-born son first, first-born son last'). This implies that should fortunes change than the last-born son could indeed find himself in the position of the first-born; the last-born son should never give up hope of ultimately succeeding to headship of the family. 'Positions are like garments', one elder commented. 'your father has the gown of authority over you all; perhaps his son or a responsible brother will put on that gown when the father dies, to show his change of position.' And a Kuranko song goes: 'Whatever the elder brother or the younger brother find, the one that lives longest will inherit it.' I have heard it suggested that fortune is not always determined by one's social position; it is often determined by whether or not one outlives other claimants and rivals.

The marginality of the youngest son (deprived of any real authority and having no effective control of the family property) does however, have its compensations. The relationship between a man and his youngest son is especially intimate, partly because there is no status rivalry between them. The last-born child is always at his father's side fussed over, petted, given favours, supported in his quarrels with domineering older brothers. Reciprocally, the attachment of a youngest son to his father is especially strong. The structural explanation for this close *rapport* between father and youngest son is as follows: the typically great age difference between them means that they are, so to speak, separated by an entire generation; their relationship is thus directly comparable to the relationship between grandfather and grandchild. This is clarified by a remark which Noah's father once made to him, emphasising Noah's position as youngest son: 'I have five sons; you have no one to favour you and you will never challenge my authority. Because you have no grandfather alive and nowhere else to go (i.e. Noah had no uncles alive), I will be more sympathetic towards you.' In this case, Noah's father deliberately assumed a grandpaternal attitude towards his youngest son.

Grandparents and Grandchildren

The affectionate and caring attitude of Kuranko grandparents towards their grandchildren is so noticeable in everyday life that it is easy to appreciate the Kuranko adage: 'The grandchild is sweeter than the child' (*mamane di den ko*). Kumba Doron elaborated: 'Just as when you plant a tree and the tree starts producing fruit, so if you have your own child and he or she starts producing, the fruit of that one will assure you that your name will not be lost; therefore the grandchild is dearer to you than your own child.' Small boys particularly spend a great deal of time in the company of a favourite grandparent; and they are often favoured and indulged. One old man from Fasewoia (whose grandson was always at his side) averred that in the event of war he would save his grandson before anything or anyone else; recollecting this remark on a later occasion he stressed that he would do the same for his son. When dispensing medicines I often found that grandparents showed as much concern as parents for sick children. And in domestic disputes a grandparent frequently intervenes to prevent the punishment of a grandchild. When a child is thrashed by a parent for some misdemeanour it is often a grandparent who is sought for comfort and sympathy.

Even more unrestrained by conventional formalities is the relationship between great-grandparents and great-grandchildren (*tolobire*, literally 'ear-hole'). On one visit to Chief Fakuli Kargbo of Dankawali I commented upon the affectionate manner in which he treated his *tolobire*. Chief Fakuli said that one's grandchild (*mamane*, literally 'small grandmother'[10]), particularly one's son's son, would not take the same liberties; he could tug at one's beard, pull one's nose or poke at one's eyes, and be indulged in all this, but he should never pull the grandfather's ear—this could make the grandfather deaf. This prohibition does not obtain in the case of the great-grandchild. Since the ear is associated with respect for the words of the elders (*kuma kore*, literally 'words old/venerable') it is implied that the grandchild should recognise, despite certain joking conventions and privileges, the authority of the grandfather. Indeed, the term *m'bimba* ('my grandfather') denotes both grandfather (paternal or maternal) and ancestor.

It is also noteworthy that the symmetrical joking play between grandparents and grandchildren (the *mamania tolon*) is suspended during the distribution of a legacy in the *kebile*. On such occasions the grandfather plays a nominal role as head of the *kebile*. The Kuranko also point out that a man and his son's son will both be claimants to a portion of the inheritance (*che*). If the conventional levity is sustained then, it is said, the grandfather may jeopardise his chances of getting a share of the property. Therefore, 'joking play between grandfather and grandson is not proper on the day of the legacy division' (*mamania tolon ma ben che fare lon*).

The informality which usually characterises the *maman'ye* (or *mamania*, i.e. 'grandparent-grandchild relationship') is probably a consequence of the fact that grandparents and grandchildren are not ordinarily concerned with matters of property management or authority in the *kebile*. In particular, grandparents are not directly involved with the resposibilities of raising and disciplining children; they can enjoy the pleasures of 'parenthood' unburdened by its various obligations. This may be why it is often said that 'a grandparent could love his or her grandchildren more than his or her own child.'

I have suggested that a degree of ambivalence characterises the relationship between grandparent and grandchild; the *mamania* involves elements of intimacy and distance, respect and privileged disrespect, distinction and identification. Like certain other joking relationships (the *numorgo tolon* especially), images of anticipated marriage and sexual intimacy figure in the conventional expressions of the joking play (*tolon*). A man calls his grandfather's wife 'my wife', a woman calls her grandson 'my husband'. I often observed Ali's son, Bokari, who was no more than 7 years old, lovingly addressing his father's mother (with whom he was living) as 'my wife'. Ali's mother would reciprocate, addressing her grandson as 'my husband'. This was partly because of the joking convention, partly because Bokari was her late husband's actual name.[11] With older grandchildren of the opposite sex the typical banter consists of lewd references to the genitalia. Ordinarily it is considered indecent to even mention the words for sex organs in the company of the other sex.

One joking exchange which I overheard went as follows:

Grandson to grandmother: 'Grandmother Samanomo, your goitrous neck is so wrinkled'.[12]

Grandmother (in reply): 'Ah my father, your scrotum (*kili*) is just as wrinkled'

Then, several other small children gathered and turned the lines into a song, chanting them over and over and clapping their hands.

Even a granddaughter could 'insult' her grandmother in a similar way, with such comments as 'Ah my mother, your vagina is so wrinkled.' These and other sexual allusions are not thought to be obscene; this is because, as the Kuranko point out, very young children are sexually innocent and very old people are incapable of sexual activity. But the identification of non-adjacent generations is based upon several factors, some of which are largely metaphorical: absence of procreative sex life, no dependent children, no real control over the property or wealth of the family, no effective authority. A grandfather is, by virtue of his age and status as an elder, superordinate to his grandchildren. But he is marginal or anterior to the effective kinship grouping (his son's *dembaiye*) and therefore occupies a position which is structurally similar to that of his grandson. This similarity is sometimes expressed in terms of temperament and sensibility. In old age there is an observeable regression to child-like behaviour, a regression which the Kuranko note with the same mixture of bemusement and melancholy as we do. As one informant put it, 'A man's age increases and his wisdom (*hankili*) increases up to a certain point; then he becomes less wise and he returns to the stage of a child.' It is not uncommon for the young to taunt, cry down and laugh at the very old. The dependency of the aged is quite explicitly compared with the dependency and 'uselessness' of the very young. It may be that the juxtaposition of disparate factors— the 'elderhood' status of the old on the one hand, their physical and temperamental decrepitude on the other—underlies and explains the *mamania tolon*.

This particular discrepancy between personal disposition and social position is resolved to some extent during mortuary rites (*sa ya koe*, literally 'death happening') and it is the *mamania tolon* which assists this

resolution. In the context of mortuary ritual the category *mamanianenu*
(pl.) includes 'all those who call the deceased *m'bimba'*, i.e. sons'
daughters, younger sons' wives, grandsons' wives. It should be noted
that although these women do not belong to the same generation they
will tend to be of an age and, moreover, all share the same privileges of
the *mamania tolon*.

During a mortuary ritual, two categories of persons are permitted to
'insult' the deceased: members of the deceased man's *sanaku*-linked
clan, and the *mamanianenu*. The *mamanianenu* wash and dress the corpse
and also mimic various idiosyncrasies of their late grandfather—his
manner of walking, dancing and speaking. Kamara has described these
performances as follows:

'One of the deceased's sons' wives dresses in the Chief's clothes and tries to
imitate his walk and speech, for doing which he receives presents. Another puts
on big trousers, goes to the bathing place and falls into the water. She comes out
with the trousers full of water and then walks from Chief to Chief with a pestle
which she uses to throw water on people. Anybody disliking dirty water buys
her off with a present as soon as she tries to come near him.'[13]

Sayers describes the '*mamani*' at a funeral, running about with a pestle
and mortar looking for rice to pound (presumably to prepare *dege* for a
sacrifice); this behaviour is interpreted as 'feigning madness'.[14] I have
not observed this behaviour, but it is not uncommon for the *mamane* to
don the gown and cap of the deceased. This, like the other mimetic
performances by the *mamanianenu*, is explained by informants as a way of
showing that everyone is confused and emotionally upset. In my view,
these performances assist the polarisation and separation of two aspects
of the identity of the deceased: his idiosyncratic and his social
personality. The comic and inept imitations of his idiosyncrasies are
necessary preliminaries to his assumption of the abstract and idealised
ancestor role. It is only when memories of the dead person's personal
deficiencies and mannerisms are repressed or masked that the dead can
exemplify, as an abstract category, the values and customs of the
society. This theatrical 'setting apart' of the dead person's idiosyncratic
personality is paralleled by various usages which excommunicate, as it
were, the dead person's spirit (*nie*): continued mourning is prohibited
lest the spirit remain among the villagers as a malevolent shade (*yiyee*),
the immediate bereaved (especially the widows) are isolated for a
period of 40 days, the grave is sealed by heavy stones and logs to prevent
the spirit returning to the body, and sacrifices are offered in order to
speed the spirit to *lakira* (where ancestral spirits dwell).[15]

It is my view that the emotional ambivalence towards the dead
person which is conveyed by the mimetic performances of the
mamanianenu and *sanaku* partners is an extension of the emotional
ambivalence towards elders. There is a mixture of respect and
disrespect in the performances: mourning for a loved one and ludicrous
imitation of his mannerisms (in the case of the *mamanianenu*), references

to status differences coupled with status derogation (in the case of the *sanaku* jokers). As we have seen, elders are simultaneously the exemplars of customary values and, in some cases, unjust in the exercise of their authority, selfish, unable to curb their appetites—in brief, like children. The Kuranko way of expressing this is to refer to old peoples' insatiable appetite (*meeye*) for 'sweet' (*mindi*) things. It may be that this contradiction between official and unofficial conceptualisations is resolved through those aspects of mortuary ritual which we have discussed above. By isolating and derogating the idiosyncratic personality of the deceased, the person as ancestor—a collective category—emerges as transcendent. In more mundane terms, this transformation involves the separation of the body (*bonke* or *fere bonke*, literally 'dust/dirt') from the spirit (*nie*), the body being closely associated with the idiosyncratic personality, the *nie* with ancesterhood. I have already referred to the malevolent shade of a dead person, the *yiyee*, which will haunt the living until this transformation has been effected. The *yiyee* is said to be a kind of shadow (*ninne*), anomalous because it shares attributes of the body (audible—usually as ghostly footsteps—and visible) and of the spirit (insubstantiality). The *yiyee* thus ceases to exist when the complete separation of body and spirit has been ritually accomplished.

Having advanced a general explanation for the mimetic performances we can now consider why it should be appropriate for the *mamanianenu* to be the performers. For the bereaved wives and children, profound emotions determine their attitudes to the deceased. By contrast, the association or identification of the *mamane* with her grandfather is founded upon an artifice of logic. But, as we have seen, a girl often develops a strong emotional attachment to her father's father or husband's grandfather simply because a formal principle of the social system—the identification of non-adjacent generations—makes such attachments possible and appropriate. Structurally speaking, the *mamane* is placed in an ambiguous position: closely identified with the grandfather yet also a 'stranger' because of obvious age and status differences. As a real or fictive affine (a man jokingly refers to his granddaughter as 'my wife') she is, so to speak, halfway between strangerhood (*sundanye*) and kinship (*nakelinyorgoye*). She is therefore well situated to act out (on behalf of bereaved wives and sons), during mortuary rites, the emotional confusions and anxieties of the bereavement reaction.[16] At the same time she can remain sufficiently aloof to perform a more general service in mediating the passage of the dead person's spirit from the world of the living (governed by close attachments) to the world of the dead (where personal attachments cease to exist).[17]

Twins and Triplets

Kuranko beliefs about twins can be understood in structural terms by considering twinship in the context of ideas pertaining to birth-order position. Among the Kuranko twins are not age-differentiated. They are structurally anomalous because near-simultaneous birth and near-identical appearance (in some cases) preclude the possibility of differentiating them in terms of birth-order position or physical appearance. In short, twin births nullify the principle of *fisa mantiye*. Yet, the Kuranko do not take the view that twins should be killed because they are monstrous or like the offspring of animals. Rather, a more positive attitude prevails.

Twins are known as *feranu* or *filanenu* (literally 'little twos', from *fila*— two). It is often said that twins are like two persons in one or one person in two. Twins receive special names: Ferenke or Lansana for a male twin, Feremusu, Mense or Bamba for a female twin. However, because personal names are inherited within a family, not all persons bearing these names are themselves twins. It is commonly believed that twins are doubly-gifted, possessing the power to protect kinsmen from witchcraft and evil influence. Yet such powers are ambivalent since twins can bring misfortune upon their family by withholding their protection. The usual way of referring to the special powers or gifts which twins possess is to say that they have 'four eyes' (*ye nani*), a sort of double vision which enables them to see bush spirits, to read peoples' minds, and to see the conspiracies of witches. It is pointed out, however, that twins must be treated with great respect because, if they take offence over some minor slight, they could turn their powers against their own parents. A twin can make a person deaf, for example, by tapping him or her on the head in some mysterious way. But if one twin wishes to harm its mother or father, it can only do so with the assent of the other twin. There is thus some check against the whimsical use of these powers. Nonetheless, I have heard of cases where twins have been held responsible for the death or disablement of one of their parents. If a parent becomes deaf and he or she has twin children, the twins may be blamed. One woman, I was told, had four sets of twins. Her husband's death was attributed, in local gossip, to the twins. Consequently, Kuranko parents tend to regard twins as a mixed blessing. They are sometimes regarded as 'good fortune', because as one man commented 'the parents get more than one child at once', but they are just as often regarded with suspicion. Similar attitudes obtain in the case of triplets (*sawanenu*, literally 'little three' from *sawa*—three).

The child born after twins is known as the *sayon* and its personal name is always Sayon. The *sayon* has all the gifts and special powers of twins but in greater measure, a notion which probably derived from the idea that the successive sibling (*gbarase*) shares some of the status attributes of its immediate elder.

Twinship also serves as a more general symbol of the strength and complementary of paired elements. Although the concept of twinship among the Kuranko is not as conspicuously or consciously elaborated as it is among other West Sudanic peoples (notably the Dogon and Bambara), it is used as an image of the ideal unanimity between husband and wife. Mother and father share the status of parents vis-a-vis their children. Accord between the parents is to some extent encouraged by the threat of mystical sanction associated with twins. The twins protect the family from external mystical attack and they may punish their parents if the mother or father causes discord within the family. The punishment is usually blindness or deafness. Further evidence of the significance attached to complementarity is adduced when we consider certain beliefs about a witch's ghost (*pulan*). It is said that when a witch's ghost enters its victim's house, it proceeds to count the sleeping occupants in pairs. It is the person who is 'unpaired' who is most vulnerable. Because twins are naturally paired they are not vulnerable to witchcraft attack; indeed, their special powers are sometimes compared with those of witches except that twins do not kill or 'eat' people.

Status Distinctions among Women

Generally speaking, status distinctions based upon birth-order position are less significant and less problematic among women. The reasons is quite simple: in secular life[19], women—like younger sons in the family and *finas* in the community—theoretically command no real authority and own no real property.[19] Thus, although an elder sister devotes much of her time to looking after her younger sisters and is delegated authority over her younger sisters (by her mother), she is never a rival for her mother's position. Her destiny is to marry out of her father's lineage. A women does not regard her eldest daughter as rival or potential usurper (as a man regards his eldest son); rather, she is considered to be helpmate and companion. Young children often address an elder sister as *n'na* ('my mother') as if in recognition of this identification. One man commented that 'since the elder sister (*koromuse*) is a kind of mother to you, her blessings also influence your destiny; therefore the mother's blessings may come to you through the elder sister.'

The influence of the mother and, to a lesser extent, the elder sister does not imply, however, that the mother is *fisa* than her sons or that the elder sister is *fisa* than her younger brothers. The Kuranko are adamant that 'all men are *fisa* than all women'; in other words, sex is given priority over age in determining *fisa mantiye*. When a woman is older than a man this connotes not authority over (i.e. superior status) but influence upon, for examples the mediation of the paternal ancestors' blessings by the mother, and the influence of the sister upon her younger 'bridewealth-linked' brother.

Women can also achieve positions of authority within the female community which enable them to exert influence upon the male community. The position of *dimusukuntigi* ('head of the women') is a notable example, and there is one male cult—the *Doe* cult—which admits older women to its membership. The rationalisation of this is that wisdom is not invariably determined by age and sex.

There is one set of relationships where age-status distinctions among women are significant and problematic, namely relationships among co-wives. The term of reference for co-wife is *sinemuse;* thus *n'sine*—my co-wife'. In practice a woman addresses a co-wife according to relative age status. A junior wife (*gberinya*) calls her elder co-wife *n'koro* ('my elder sister'). The senior wife (*bare* or *baremusu*) calls a younger co-wife *n'doge* ('my younger sister'). These usages may reflect the frequency of sororal polygyny among the Kuranko but it is also the case that a man compares the relationships among his wives with the relationships among his children. Just as a father delegates authority to his eldest son over his younger sons, so, the Kuranko point out, a husband delegates authority to his senior wife over his junior wives. 'The first wife is second to you', one man observed, 'the next wife is younger and she will accept the authority of the elder co-wife; the first wife should lead the way in bringing the second wife into the household.' In fact, when the senior wife is much older than a junior wife, the latter may address her as 'my mother'. This is particularly common when the senior wife plays a significant role in choosing a new wife for her husband. It is also noteworthy that this mode of address indicates once more how relative age overrides and even ignores actual generational boundaries.

The parallelism between relations among siblings and relations among co-wives is demonstrated further by the Kuranko notion that when the age difference between co-wives is minimal the interpersonal tensions will be greatest. Tensions between a wife and her immediate successor are thus compared with tensions between the child and his successive sibling (*gbarase*). Finally, it is important to allude to earlier discussion of the manner in which *fadenye* rivalries and antagonisms are related to or seen as projections of tensions among co-wives. In this case the rivalries of half-brothers and ortho-cousins for power and property in the family are related explicitily to the struggle among co-wives for preferential positions in the household.

Notes

1. The application of this principle often leads to interesting variations in kinship nomenclature. For instance, a woman sometimes addresses her husband's father as 'grandfather' and her husband's mother as 'grandmother. Morowa's wife explained that 'the husband is thought of as a kind of father because he should care for his wife just as a father cares for his child; that is why when they give a girl to her husband they will say that the man should be her father, her mother, her everybody, just as if she were a child'. In some cases, a woman will address her husband's elder brother as 'grandfather' for the same reason: the latter is, jurally speaking, a kind of father.

2. Kamara 1932:94-100

3. Kewule 1932:100-1

4. Hallpike 1972:110-12. Among the Pare (W. District, Kiunga sub-district, Papua) age takes precedence over generation; here, however, this principle is recognised in the formal relationship terminology itself: FyB = eB; FeB = FF, MF; BS = yB (Voorhoeve, personal communication).

5. The noun *tarle* signifies a demand, but to beg is signified by the phrase *fe na bor* (literally 'thing take out', i.e. 'give me something'). A plea is usually expressed as *n'ko* (literally 'me give', i.e. 'give me'), and one can beg for forgiveness in a similar way, e.g. *m'a ko to* ('forgive me').

6. Ingenious literary devices for masking the identity of the true successor often figure in Kuranko narratives concerned with inter-generational conflicts.

7. It could be argued that there is a further displacement of fraternal tensions which expresses itself in the concept of *fadenye*. *Fadenye* rivalries are, in turn, thought to originate in tensions among co-wives.

8. This narrative scheme is discussed in detail in my paper: *Dogmas and Fictions of Birth-Order Position* (Jackson 1977b).

9. It should be remembered that children are often fostered with their grandparents; occasionally the fosterage becomes permanent (particularly if the child's parents die while it is in the care of its grandparents) and for this reason one sometimes finds men residing in the *luiye* of their maternal or paternal grandfather (see Table 1).

10. The usual explanation for the term *mamane* is that person is 'a little one of them (the grandmothers); you came from them'.

11. Ali had, according to convention, named his first son after his father, Bokari. He would often call his son *'m'fa togoma'* ('my father's namesake') and his mother would often call her grandson *'m'buin togoma'* ('my husband's namesake'). Because a man's eldest son takes the name of that man's father it is arguable that the tension between father and eldest son is a reactivation of unresolved conflicts between a man and his own late father.

12. A woman's neck is said to be one of the most attractive parts of her body; the allusion to the neck in this joking exchange has sexual connotations.

13. Kamara 1933:156

14. Sayers 1925:24

15. A complete account of Kuranko mortuary rituals is in preparation.

16. For instance, the *mamanianenu* customarily sing the mourning songs and dirges while the widows remain indoors.

17. *Sanaku* and *Mamane* may ritually debase themselves by dressing in rags, covering their bodies with ash, carrying bundles of faggots on their heads. When not involved in mimetic activities, the *mamane* must assume a completely deadpan face; this is, conceivably, a symbol of her emotional disengagement.

18. It will become clear in Part IV that in the context of cult activity women do command authority through the control over 'sacred' properties (*sumafan*—'secret thing'). It is noteworthy that the term *fan* is used to refer to property, goods, material objects and often means simply 'thing'.

19. This is not to deny the 'influence' of women, nor the fact that women accumulate and even inherit some personal property (usually domestic articles, trinkets, some gold); we are here speaking in terms of the male view, i.e. jural notions.

PART IV

11. Crossing the Water

'For where most things are concerned, the main pre-condition of happiness is not, of course, that contradictions be cleared up, but that they should be caused to disappear, as the gaps between the trees disappear when one looks down a long avenue.'

—Robert Musil, *The Man Without Qualities*

This chapter, which takes its title from a Kuranko metaphor[1], bridges the gap between Part 1 (in which we explored the ideological landscape of Kuranko culture) and Part II (in which we investigated particular aspects of the cultural terrain). The following account of Kuranko initiation rituals is thus transitional and mediatory, in both a literary and a sociological sense. It refers us back to the abstract principles which underlie Kuranko thought and social structure, but at the same time it carries us forward once more to an examination of the problematic aspects of that structure. By placing this account towards the end of this book I am echoing Kuranko thought, for initiation is considered to be at once the midpoint and apogee of personal and social existence. But the structural position of this chapter in our argument is intermediary. In a work whose artificial form imposes linearity and sequence upon events which are in reality always repetitive and simultaneous in character, this intermediary position reflects a sociological truth: the Kuranko situate initiation ritual at a transitional point in a system of transformations which cannot be understood either in terms of its discrete elements alone or in terms of serial description.

For this reason I propose to analyse Kuranko initiation ritual as if it were a myth, a myth staged rather than spoken, acted out rather than voiced. In the course of this analysis I shall endeavour to show how the Kuranko think through and act upon some of the contradictions and problems which confront them in their social life. It will be already clear that I am borrowing my method of exposition from Lévi-Strauss. It will be also clear that a problem arises here which is far less intransigent in the study of myth, namely the problem of translating ritual and symbolic actions into words. The complex and fascinating round of events which one observes during initiations articulates a world of meanings, but these meanings are not often verbalised and perhaps cannot be because they surpass and confound language. This is why the anthropologist, held back by his conviction that a literate sensibility can bring him closer to conveying and expressing truth than

181

any other medium of communication, is often estranged. As he is observing ritual action he is also (as an outsider) involved in a 'private' and simultaneous ritual whereby he seeks to reduce acts to words and give objects a specific vocabulary. Inasmuch as ritual often makes language redundant, the anthropologist himself becomes redundant and his questions tend to be superflous. Perhaps all that is open to us is a strategy of literature, rather than a method of sociology. As Borges puts it, 'To eliminate a word completely, to refer to it by means of inept phrases and obvious paraphrases, is perhaps the best way of drawing attention to it.'[2]

In Kuranko initiation ritual a variety of themes and thematic variations are ubiquitous and simultaneous. The initiations are like bas-reliefs in art—the meanings which are communicated or apprehended depend upon three variables: the point of perceptual or conceptual focus, the sensibilities of the participant, and the role of the participant. Any account of ritual must therefore pay attention to these three perspectives. Some of the themes of Kuranko initiation ritual were immediately elucidated for me in the extempore comments of informants; others were brought into focus in the course of searching discussions with participants during or just after the events; others were suggested as I came to appreciate the total social context in which certain symbolic actions occured. As we shall see, my own interpretations are never at variance with Kuranko interpretations although some of the anthropological glosses which I place upon them would undoubtedly mystify many Kuranko. Yet, in Victor Turner's terms, we should not be necessarily limited by the paucity of 'exegetical' data, for meanings must also be elaborated by careful study of the 'operational' and 'positional' aspects of symbolism.[3]

The system of transformations in which these various themes are embedded is, in one sense, described by the most commonly-used model for analysing ritual events—that of Van Gennep. But I have been cautious in my use of this model since it is, in my view, relevant at a low level of abstraction but not illuminating at a higher level. In other words, by describing the most obvious form of ritual events— the serial form—it fails to focus the deeper infrastructure which I have called here the 'simultaneous' and 'ubiquitous' form. As Lévi-Strauss expresses it, speaking of the structural analysis of myth, such a model would enable us to re-tell the events, but not help us to understand them.[4]

In these ways the problem of translating ritual actions into words is compounded by other problems. How can we describe in a single narrative, events which are meaningful in several diverse ways simultaneously (depending upon individual sensibilities, roles, and levels of focus)? And how can we clarify the multi-faceted and polysemic structure of ritual without elementary disortions or reductions? In the following account of Kuranko initiation ritual (based upon direct observations in Firawa during January and February 1970)

13. A group of visiting kin from another Barawa village arrive in Firawa the day before initiation festivities begin.
14. The *serewayili* ('praise-singer of the hunters') has journeyed to Firawa for the initiations: Karifa Mansaray of Momoria Badela (Barawa Section).

15. A group of neophytes, led by drummers, moves on to another *luiye* to dance. 16. A girl performs the vigorous and graceful *yatuiye* or 'happiness dance'.

17. The 'plaiting day' (*kundan lunye*), the girls just returned to the village after purification rites by the stream. They are dressed in long white country-cloth gowns, made especially for this occasion. The *dimusukuntigi*, switch in hand, keeps men and children away from the neophytes.

18. The 'operation day' (*simbire*). The young men's cult—*gbansogoron*—performs. They are accompanied by a young *jeliba* playing his *balanje* (xylophone). The men's cheeks are pierced by porcupine quills and they carry medicines to bolster their courage and fortitude.

20

19. The 'Little *Sewulan*' or *tatati mama*. Note the *tatati* performer at the left of the picture; she is dressed in a man's gown and hat and she carries a warsword. A wad of cloth is held tightly against her closed mouth.

20. *Sewulan*, also called *Komantere*. Note the male attire and the *gbuse* fruit on her forehead.

19

21. *Forubandi binye*: the 'chimpanzee boy' with his age-mates. 22. *Kamban dunse* and *Kamban soiye*: note woman wearing a hunter's 'buffalo' cap and men's trousers, and carrying a rifle; her companion holds a war sword and remains expressionless. 23. *Kamban dunse* and *Kamban serewayili*: woman on right wears a hunter's attire; her companion imitates the harp-playing of the *serewayili*. 24. *Tefera kundi* dancers.

25

2

25. A group of senior village women belligerently 'beg' the *keminetigi* for the money which he holds aloft. 26. *Yefera kundi* dancers bring out the women's cult object—*Kawulikile*—to parade around the village. One woman precedes the group holding a dish to collect gifts. 27. Doron Fina after initiation, her hair plaited in customary post-initiation style: cowrie-shell headband and side plaits decorated with bright red berries. 28. Four boys from Kamadugu Sukurela, just returned from undergoing circumcision in the hospital at Kabala. They wear *gbangbale* gowns and carry elephant-grass staves. The school caps suggest an identification with graduating school boys.

27

28

I do not pretend to have overcome all these difficulties, but by bringing them into perspective I hope that it will prove possible to move a little closer to their solution.

Girl's Initiation (dimusu biriye)

By December most of the rice harvest is done. For the first time in many months families return to their village from the farmsteads. With the arduous and desolate months of the rainy season behind them, villagers can relax and enjoy the happier and more casual routines of dry season community life: repairing houses, spinning and weaving cotton, making mats, dyeing cloth, marketing rice and purchasing imported commodities, visiting kin and entertaining friends. Even the interminable round of court hearings, which occupies much of the men's time, is regarded as an opportunity for re-establishing social ties and an occasion for rehearsing the customs of community life.

The granaries are full, the houses are full. It is a time of collective endeavour. During the cooler morning hours village women work in cooperative groups (*kere*), pounding rice in readiness for the forthcoming initiations. The women's work-songs, sounds of laughter, chatter and the incessant thud of mortars commingle to create an atmosphere of excitement and affability. Women discuss impending marriages, what arrangements are to be made for the ceremonies, who will be visiting the village for the occasion, and so on. Whether it is a group of men involved in a court case or the ebullient conversation of women in a cooking compound, the mood is one of collective effort, community spirit and good humour.

Every day small groups of neophytes leave the village with kola which they give to relatives in other villages to notify them of the date of the initiations. The girls usually spend several days moving around the countryside, from village to village, contacting distant and dispersed kin. Although each village (even hamlets) organises its own initiations, they are seldom arranged so that they take place at exactly the same time. This allows people to attend initiations in other villages within their chiefdom where they have kin; it also means that people are involved in rituals outside their own village, united in a common purpose which has social consequences that extend far beyond the boundaries of the nuclear family and individual groups.

Each evening the dancing begins. The rapid syllabic sound of drumming fills the village night as the girls gather for the pre-initiation dances. The *sunkuronnu* (neophytes) assemble in a *luiye* area, chorussing and clapping as one after another they perform the graceful and bird-like 'happiness dance' (*yatuiye*). As each girl comes forward from the circle and dances, with increasing energy and tempo towards the male drummer (*yimbe forle*, literally '*yimbe* drum beater') her companions chant her name. During the days immediately preceding initiation the girls perform another dance, the final dance of girlhood: the *yamayili* or *biriyedon*. Now they sing of the waning of girlhood days, repeating over and over 'Girlhood days are done, girlhood days are done' until, late at night the conclusion of the dancing is signalled by the refrain 'Girlhood days are done and the dancing ends.' From time to time another dance is performed (*sogo*), during which the girls sing the praises of their prospective husbands with words such as these: 'Mara is working hard, Mara is working hard, therefore I like him. . .' The *sogo* and *yatuiye* dances can be, however, performed by girls of any age, even at times by initiated women (*musubannu*). The *yamayili* dance which concludes the preliminary entertainments and marks the imminence of initiation is, by contrast, performed only by the *sunkuronnu* (neophytes).

The neophytes are already dressed for the first phase of the ritual. Their long hair is brushed and oiled, then with a mother's help is braided so that four plaits form a crest across the top of the head, each plait passing through a white snail-shell toggle (*inwora*) or an elephant-tusk ring (*kolkore*). This plaiting style is called *lol-lore*, or, if there are only two plaits, *kankansare*. A beaded headband is worn high across the forehead and a small 'country cloth' apron together with several red and black beaded strings (*baiye*) is worn at the waist. Nowadays, however, many girls prefer to wear a lapa and headkerchief made from imported material; they are often embarrassed to go about dressed in the traditional way.

Towards the end of January, diviners are consulted by parents who will be 'putting a daughter into womanhood'. The diviners direct appropriate sacrifices (*sarake*) to God and to the ancestors to ensure the success of the venture. Some girls wear red ochre (or lipstick) on their lips and adorn their faces and bodies with white ochres and talcum; some wear metal charms around their necks or metal amults; others carry small double-bladed knives. All such variations in apparel or adornment are the results of diviners' instructions. The assiduous and conscientious manner in which parents follow out their instructions is an indication of the seriousness with which they regard their child's initiation; any deviation from the prescribed ritual would, it is said, jeopardise the safety of the child. Although a spirit of celebration and carefreeness invests the public entertainments and dances there is, at the same time, an undercurrent of uncertainty and nervousness. Once one's child is taken from the village for the operation and following period of seclusion there is little one can do to comfort her. The dangers attending the actual clitoridectomy are well-known. Within a few days we would hear rumours of a girl bleeding to death and find ourselves powerless to intervene.

The Day of the Riceflour Sacrifice (dege bo lunye)
The town chief (*sutigi*) has consulted a Muslim diviner and set the date for the initiations. The operation always takes place on a Saturday (*simbire*), the first day of the week in the Islamic calendar. There are

about fifty neophytes from Firawa, though, for reasons of prestige, the Paramount Chief had hoped for more. Many of the girls are pre-pubescent, others are adolescent.

I am staying in Abdul's house at Firawa. Already I am involved in events because Abdul's wife's sister's daughter—Doron Fina—is among the girls to be initiated. From daybreak the village has been invaded by scores of visitors, mostly women, all dressed in their finest clothes. As various groups arrive thay are welcomed by their hosts with singing and dancing. Gifts are immediately given to the host (chickens, rice, money, salt, mats, cloth), and these will help defray the expenses of the festivities.

The responsibility for planning and supervising the entire *biriye* is in the hands of the senior village woman—the *dimusukuntigi*. Only two weeks ago a new *dimusukuntigi* had been elected by the women of Firawa and she is obviously eager to show that her capabilities are equal to those of her predecessor—a formidable and powerfully-built woman of whom many men spoke with awe. Some men recollected how, as audacious youngsters at former initiations, she had tackled them, beaten them and driven them away from the girls. It is already clear to me that the men of Firawa have been made aware that this is not their affair; they are reduced to being mere onlookers, marginal participants. In fact, Chief Sewa and some of his 'big men' announce that they are leaving the village and going to Yifin on 'chiefdom business'.

Throughout the day visitors continue to arrive. At the same time the neophytes are moving about the village, from house to house, in the company of drummers, dancing, singing, clapping. I follow them for several hours, recording the words of the *yamayili* dance songs, observing, questioning, taking photographs. The *dimusukuntigi* is with the girls all the while, striving to keep to an itinerary which includes practically every house in the village, ensuring that the dance circle remains large enough to allow the girls room to dance, chasing away over-excited children with a hearth-broom, supervising the distribution of gifts. At each house the girls are given small gifts of money or kola which are used to pay for the services of the indefatigable drummers who accompany them. As the neophytes continue to circulate around the village, other groups of initiated women begin to assemble. One group is chanting the refrain, 'Dont be afraid of the operation.' The woman who is leading the group holds a cane with two feathers attached to it. It signifies a flute, an instrument normally played by men only. She mimics the flautist's finger movements as she sings, 'Don't be afraid of the operation, don't be afraid of womanhood, you must always be obedient and cheerful when you are among women.' I am told that such reassuring phrases are appropriate at this time; they are meant to allay any rumours that might make the girls afraid of the operation. These women also receive gifts from the households for whom they sing and dance.

During the late afternoon, preparations for the *dege* sacrifices are made. In each *luiye* kinsmen gather in front of the *lutigi's* house and then, in the warm twilight silence, you hear the murmured *aminas* (amens) as the *lutigi* recites the names of the ancestors in a rapid, whispered incantation. Doron Fina was both Abdul's sororal neice and his *kebile* sister. It was in his role as 'elder brother' that he assumed partial responsibility for her initiation and marriage expenses. So I joined Abdul who was going to participate in the *dege* sacrifice at Doron Fina's father's house.

As soon as we are all installed inside the house, Abdul addresses Doron Fina's immediate family. He presents gifts of salt, money, thread and cloth (Abdul is a tailor), and then says, 'The respect that you accord us is the reason why we are sharing in this *biriye*; we are responsible for everything that concerns our sister's *biriye*.' Doron Fina's father accepts the gifts, saying '*ko baraka baraka*' and then we all leave the house and assemble in the *luiye* for the sacrifice. Doron Fina's father leads it and explains that the *dege* is being offered to the patrilineal ancestors. When this is done and the riceflour is shared among the assembled relatives,[5] we repair back to Abdul's house where the second sacrifice is to be offered. This time the sacrifice is offered to the matrilineal ancestors; it is offered in Abdul's house for two reasons, first because he is a senior member of Doron Fina's *kebile* and second because Abdul is married to Doron Fina's mother's sister.

With the conclusion of the sacrifices the events of the day come to a close. But during the night the men's witch-finding cult (*Gbangbe*) moves about the village to ensure that the neophytes will not be endangered by witchcraft. I am told that the girls are particularly vulnerable to witchcraft attack at this time and therefore every precaution is taken to ensure their protection. It is a disquieting comment; it is as if the goodwill and conviviality which pervade the community by day is a kind of mask beneath whose surface one can detect the shadows of equally forceful fears.

The Plaiting Day (kundan lunye)

It is the second day of the ritual cycle. More visitors arrive in the village, including the woman who will perform the operations tomorrow. She is Mantene, from the neighbouring chiefdom of Kamadugu (Sukurela village). People say that she is renowned throughout Kuranko country for her skill. Later in the day another woman will arrive from an even more distant town (Yifin in Nieni chiefdom)—she will be present at the operations as an assistant. In many cases the initiator (*biriyele*) inherits her skills from her mother. These women often wear ceremonial dress, usually made of red or russet cloth and decorated with cowries (*sebe*), pieces of mirror and mica. During the day I see the initiators from time to time, always in the company of a group of Firawa women, moving about the village from house to house. The name of the *biriyele* is sung and she is praised with these words: 'She knows how to do it, there is no one who knows as well as she does.' At each house the group receives gifts which will go towards paying the initiators for their services.

Late in the morning various groups of male performers arrive from neighbouring villages. The Firawa men's hunting 'society' assembles at the hunters' shrine (*Mande Fabori bon*) and the hunters fire their guns as a salute to the festivities and to show their enthusiasm for the occasion. A singer with attendant rattle-players passes about the village, and like the pied piper, the praise-singer of the hunters (the *Serewayili*) threads his way among the houses at the head of a column of excited children, playing his harp and recounting in song the legendary feats of the ancestral hunter— Mande Fabori.

It is late afternoon when the main event of the day begins. All the women gather in a *luiye* at the western end of the village for the final dancing. For about half an hour the neophytes perform the *yamayili* dance then several older women lead them from the village along the narrow path which ends at the part of the village stream where women customarily wash, launder and bathe. Men are forbidden to go here at any time; today the women are particularly anxious that children and men should keep their distance. The *dimusukuntigi*, with mock ferocity, lashes out at us with her hearth-broom. The only men who remain in the *luiye* now are those who have become interested in my camera work. We sit on the porch of a house and, as dusk gathers, we wait for the return of the women and neophytes from the streamside. I ask the men what is happening. Since the pattern of events is, to them, a simulacrum of male initiation, they are able to give me some answers. At the streamside the girl's plaits are undone and their hair is washed, brushed and cut. They are undressed and the genital areas are carefully washed. Then they are dressed in long white 'country-cloth' gowns which have been specially made for the occasion. I recall how Abdul spent several hours yesterday sewing together the long strips of new cloth to make Doron Fina's gown.

Quarter of an hour passes. Now the women and the neophytes are returning to the village. The girls are all dressed in long white gowns, grouped demurely and slightly bewildered among a throng of older women. There is a little more dancing, but night is falling and the neophytes are soon ushered away towards the house where they will spend the night. It is an ordinary house but it has been specially consecrated for this occasion; it is called the *marbon*. The girls will sleep here under the watchful eyes of older women until daybreak; then they will taken from the village for the operations. However, some of the girls are operated upon during the night. The irregularity of this procedure is said to be a way of outwitting any witches who may be scheming to harm the girls during the time of tomorrow's operations.

The Day of the Operations (simbire)

At first light I am roused from sleep by the sound of gunshots. Outside, groups of women are running about the village shaking leaves and branches, chanting the names of the neophytes, extolling their bravery and saying how well prepared they are for the ordeals of the operation. There is a sense of impending climax. I notice one group of women moving around, shaking small bells. The *biriyele* is with these women, who are singing her name and praising her skills. Apparently the operations have been performed at first light. By mid-morning the village is almost deserted of women. I am told that they have gone to the *biriyedon* (the initiation site) to help dress the girls' wounds and to take the girls to the *fafei* house where they will remain secluded for the next few weeks. I am eager to know exactly what is going on, but all men and uninitiated persons are forbidden to go anywhere near the *biriyedon* and *fafei*. With the women absent from the village, the men are obliged to cook for themselves. It is the first time that I have ever known men to cook meals. But the women's absence does not mean a cessation of the festivities. Throughout the day, various entertainments are given by children's and men's groups; in the following pages I describe them.

Gbansogoron (*The Cheek-Piercers*)

This is a male cult association which practices the art of self-inflicted ordeal as a way of displaying their bravery and fortitude. Their command of special medicines which they brandish proudly in public, allows them to pierce their cheeks painlessly with porcupine quills. Since the *Gbansogorontigi* (Master of the Cheek-Piercers) is said to possess mystical powers, people who are not members of the cult (especially children) keep at a safe distance. If one eats, smokes or drinks in their presence one will contract a disease 'which causes holes in the face' (perhaps smallpox). I asked people to explain the role of this cult association and was told that it 'was just to provide entertainment' and 'to show that not everyone is equally gifted with mystical powers'. Apparently any man who wants to demonstrate his superior bravery can join the cult; after the payment of a membership fee (comprising a red cock, red kola and red cloth) a man is initiated in the use of the secret medicines.

Tatatiye

There are both male and female *Tatatiye* groups. Young girls perform during female initiations, young boys during male initiations. But the pattern of the performance is the same in both cases. The *Tatatiye* affords an opportunity for non-initiates to participate in the initiation rituals. Many of the children dress up as neophytes, especially if they are nearing the age of initiation. At Firawa the small girls circulated around the village from house to house; as they sang and danced they received token gifts. In each group there is one girl who is dressed in a man's hat and gown. She holds a cutlass in one hand and covers her mouth with a cloth wad. The name of the group derives from the nonsense word which they chant constantly: '*Tatatiye, tatati, tatatiye, tatati.*' I am told once again, that the role of the *Tatatiye* is 'just for amusement, just to entertain' and that these performances only occur during initiations. One should not see the mouth of the group leader, which is why she keeps it covered by a cloth wad.

Sewulanne (*The Little* Sewulan)
Sewulan (*wulan* means 'red') is a women's cult association which performs in public on the day following the day of the operations. The *Sewulanne* is a children's version (or imitation) which, like the *Sewulan* proper, is characterised by a certain style of body painting. The body is plastered with white clay and then spotted with red ochre and charcoal; sometimes two symmetrical lines are painted under the eyes with dampened charcoal. The performers wear a deadpan or mask-like expression and frequently carry a red flower clenched in the lips. The *Sewulanne* group approaches a house and waits outside, hands outstretched, until someone gives them a small gift.

Komantere (*The Scapegoat*)
The *Komantere* (literally 'everything that is put on a person') is sometimes referred to as *Sewulan*. It is a women's association and the leading performer is said to be like a scapegoat because 'people can put everything on her'. She is usually dressed in men's clothes and strung around her forehead and neck are various wild fruits, notably the *gbuse*—a kind of wild apple. As she dances she imitates the dance steps and gestures of men and her attendants sing, 'It is the *gbuse* fruit that is hanging around her neck, *Komantere*'. Her expression is deadpan throughout the performance and one is struck by the contrast between the amused and exuberant expressions of the audience and the seriousness of the performers. As with many other of the initiation entertainments one is immediately intrigued by evidence of role-reversal and the mimicry of masculine apparel and gesture.

Forubandi Binye (*The Chimpanzee Dancers*)
In the early afternoon a group of small boys enters the village, one of them completely covered in a mossy grass (*forumadinti*) which gives him the appearance of a chimpanzee. I had often heard people refer to the ugliness of the chimpanzee with such adages as *n'de ya wuron sunnye lon a sasa fe ti-na-la, koni ma lon a kinya ti-na-la* ('I know that the chimpanzee's nostrils are for blowing snot through, but I do not know the chimpanzee's nose for its beauty'). But in the particular context another aspect of this 'ugliness' was brought to light. It is said that chimpanzees thrash their children mercilessly and irrationally; they can therefore be expected to show no sympathy whatever for the children of other

chimpanzees. As the boys lightly beat the 'chimpanzee boy' with elephant grass switches, they chant the following words: '*Fa wuru ma a dentu morgo de morgo gbere de*' ('the chimpanzee father/elder persecutes its own child, therefore it will have no sympathy for another person's child'). As this chanting continues the 'chimpanzee boy' falls to the ground from time to time, only to be revived by the increasingly fervent singing of his companions. I was interested to learn whether this idea of the overbearing and unsympathetic elder or parent was in any way associated with the trials and ordeals of initiation. In particular, was the transition from childhood to adulthood understood as a violent shift from the relative security of the child in the natal family to the more onerous and responsible roles of adulthood within the wider community? Yes, I was told; there is a Kuranko proverb which expresses the inexorable and irreversible passage from childhood to adulthood: '*Mor' mera i bon na forumadinti binye la nyawonya an si i te bi*' ('No matter how long a person wears the chimpanzee grass, one day someone else will wear it').

Other Entertainers

Everyone contributes something to the day's entertainments. Groups of local or visiting flautists, *jelibas* playing their xylophones, girls dressed up like the neophytes, and children with makeshift toy drums all play their part. One group of small boys gave their version of a Krio cult performance, their heads hidden under masks made from roughly-stitched sack cloth. But few people paid them any attention and the boys received no gifts for their performance; they were, it was said, imitating a foreign dance which had no place in the Kuranko ritual.

This collective participation, characterised by the constant giving and taking of token gifts and the involvement of entertainers from elsewhere in the chiefdom nonetheless belied a forceful division within the community—between male and female. And within thse categories other divisions became apparent, notably the division between initiated and uninitiated. These divisions became even more obvious in the events which ended the day's activities.

Towards sunset, kinsmen of the neophytes are seen carrying calabashes or basins of cooked rice and meat to an assembly point on the eastern side of the village. There, the *dimusukuntigi* is supervising the distribution of food for the neophytes' evening meal. It is significant that this first meal after the operations is supplied by the women of the community; the girls thus share a communal meal rather than eat food prepared especially for them by their own mothers. As soon as the women have left the village to take this food out to the *fafei*, word passes around the village that the women's main cult association is about to 'come out'. In a frantic flurry, men, boys and uninitiated girls flee indoors locking themselves in, closing shutters and waiting for the music of the cult. In Abdul's house I am surrounded by a group of excited children. One of Abdul's sons— Sewa—is tugging at my sleeve, cautioning me to be quiet and to stay away from the door. Then we hear the singing of the women. The cult association is *Segere* and I am told that if a man should see *Segere* he will be afflicted by some dreadful disease of the sexual organs and probably die. It is a rather awesome moment and we are all obliged to remain in the house for about half an hour while the women parade their secret cult object around the village. When I finally leave the house I am met by a curious sight. To celebrate the plentiful supply of rice and the sociability of the occasion, women from each household place basins or calabashes of rice in the *luiye*. Then, like flocks of hungry birds, the children scramble for the food and, in a wild melee, eat as much as they can of it. As this rice is being given away to the children, girls and women rush about the village throwing handfuls of rice in the lanes and over the house tops. This is known as *kordiye* ('rice dance' or 'rice song') and it signifies the abundance of rice and celebrates the fact that everyone has eaten well and enjoyed the day's festivities. These events mark the close of the first phase of the initiation.

In the late evening I sit down with a group of elders and discuss with them several points that my sketchy fieldnotes have left vague and inconclusive. But it proves difficult to add much to my observations. The purpose of the ritual performances and various entertainments is said to be 'just for amusement', 'to show how happy everyone feels at this time'. The constant giving of token gifts and the generous distribution of rice are explained as ways of affirming participation, 'so that people will not feel that you are standing aloof', means of 'involving everyone in the events'. I am told that the gift-giving 'makes people feel that they are all moving together'. But these comments seem superficial, for I am searching for remarks which might help me understand the symbolism of the body painting, the significance of role-reversal, and the events which occur during the secret episodes of the ritual. It is only later that I realise that by taking these comments at their face value, I am able to appreciate what the events mean to the participants. I realise that my role as anthropologist has led me to take seriously events which are, for the Kuranko, commonplace and entertaining. It is the spirit or mood of the ritual, not the intellectual commentary, which the Kuranko themselves place greatest value upon.

The Sleepless Night (Kinyale)

Exactly three weeks have passed since the Saturday in January when the girls were initiated. During this time the neophytes have been living in the *fafei* house some distance away from Firawa; there, under the surveillance of older women, their wounds have been dressed and they have received continual instruction in sexual knowledge, marital duties, the values of womanhood, and in the secret lore of the women's cult associations.

Throughout Friday, groups of women move around the village announcing the events which will take place the following day. One group chants, 'Tomorrow will be a big day, the Firawa *Kamban* does not play/joke.' *Kamban* is one of the women's cult groups; the unrelenting chanting of its name evokes a mood of awe and expectancy. At about 10 o'clock at night rumours begin to circulate that the neophytes are entering the village. Accompanied by a group of senior women and the *dimusukuntigi*, they proceed directly to two adjoining houses which have been specially consecrated for the night's events. The houses have been surrounded by high fences of elephant grass to ensure privacy. The girls, dressed now in long white robes (*gbangbale*), are ushered into the houses and before long the silence of the night is broken by the sounds of women keening and wailing within the houses. This keening continues all night. It is impossible to sleep, but I derive some comfort from the fact that the neophytes inside the *Kinyale* houses are not permitted to sleep either. The houses are filled with smoke, the fires being fed with green leaves and sappy wood. If any girl shows signs of drowsiness then pepper may be rubbed into her eyes. This ordeal presages the hardships of womanhood to which the neophytes must become inured. Informants explain that 'it is not easy to be a man or a woman' and that the purpose of *Kinyale* ('sleepless night') is to prepare the *bire ke* (male initiates) or the *bire muse* (female initiates) for the hardships of adulthood. During the night the initiates are often thrashed by the older women, and as the *Kinyale* songs indicate, the express purpose of the ordeals is to show the initiates that they must now prepare themselves for a life in which sympathy and kindness cannot always be expected from others. 'Eh, *Sewulan,* if you put on the gown then you should not expect any sympathy'— these are the words of one song. But for the initiates there is some solace and pride in knowing that they are now truly initiated. In one of their songs they cry '*Sulima kun gbe, ya la ko ko fule ma, i mar wo lon*' (Sulima, white/pure-headed non-initiate, you know nothing of the events which take place at the *fule*). The *fule* is the site where the operations are performed.

Late on Friday night the initiates' prospective husbands bring mats to the *Kinyale* house, and early on Saturday morning the girls are released from the ordeal of the smoke-filled house and they catch a little sleep on these mats. Since they have now passed the final endurance test, they are considered worthy of their husbands and ready for marriage.

Kamban faga le sina ('Kamban *killing tomorrow*')

At first light the village is awoken by the sound of gunshots. The initiates gather in the company of their prospective husbands to dance and sing and praise their names. As each girl sings to her intended (or to a proxy delegated by him to officiate in the ceremony) he fires his gun into the air. The song goes as follows: '*A dinge, a dinge Mara, a dinge, koni n'tamasoro; eh, nimbi Mara bolo konko timbira'* ('I love, I love Mara, I love him but I cannot possess him; eh, if I am in Mara's hands hunger will never afflict me'). If a man's gun fails to fire, then something is amiss with the intended marriage. As I am observing the ceremony one man's gun fails to go off. He tries again, and again, and then on the fourth attempt it fires. People are amused, for each time he tries to fire the gun he declares (as is customary), 'If there is something amiss in this matter and I do not know about it, then may this gun misfire.' The implication is that if the gun does not fire then the girl is probably contemplating an affair with another man. The general amusement belies the concern with which the girl's father regards this event. I am told that a great deal of 'palaver', involving consultations with diviners, will occur before this particular marriage is allowed to take place.

The gun-firing ceremony lasts about an hour. When it is over the girls leave the village once more for the *fafei;* they are not directly concerned with the events which will occupy the rest of the day within the village. Already the appearance of *Kamban* has been announced. From daybreak the initiates from last year's *biriye*—the *biril'gbagbe*—around whom the events of the day now centre, have been moving around the village singing 'We cannot sit, we cannot stand, we cannot wait until we have seen the seed (secret) of *Kamban*'. Today these young women will be initiated into the secrets of the women's Kamban cult association. Several groups of older women circulate around the village, calling upon these young women to come out. '*Biril'gbagbe* should come out, *Kamban* is always on the alert.' Other women are chanting 'Eh skull, eh skull' to evoke dread and excitement. The girls are instilled with a dread of *Kamban* right from early childhood. They are told that *Kamban* will one day swallow them up, regurgitate them, swallow them again and then regurgitate them once more. It is obvious that the *biril'gbagbe* are in a state of nervous anticipation, uncertain of what will really happen when they finally encounter *Kamban*. One old woman blocks my path as I make my way towards the other end of the village. Bellowing at us and rolling her eyes, she frightens the children with me and they scatter with panic and delight on their faces.

All the performances on this day are given by groups of women. All relate to the *Kamban* cult association. In the following pages these performances are recounted in the order of their appearance.

Sewulan *and* Kamban Yuwe ('*Mad* Kamban')

At about 9 a.m. a group of women pass around the village; one woman is known as 'mad Kamban' and with deadpan expression, clumsy dancing, distracted gestures, a switch in hand (which she uses to chase away men and children) and wearing a man's clothes, she occupies the area within a closed circle of women (*bolofafolenu*, literally 'hand-clappers'). The *Sewulan* are also in this group. They too wear deadpan expressions and they are not allowed to move a muscle of their faces.

One is painted with white ochre on one side of her body, with black charcoal on the other. Her lips are caked with red ochre and she holds the stem of a bright red flower in her mouth. The *biril'gbagbe* kneel on the ground on one side of the circle, clapping their hands to the music as the *Sewulan* sprinkles water over them in preparation for their initiation. As the group moves from house to house they receive gifts.

Kamban Soiya ('Kamban *soldiers*')

A circle of women forms around two women who have dressed up as soldiers. With old rifles over their shoulders they march up and down in mock military style, each one shouting commands to the other. Their masquerade is so effective that it takes me some time to realise that they are really women. I am curious to know why women should mimic soldiers and men on this occasion, but my questions are rebuffed. 'It just adds to the spirit of the occasion,' one man tells me. But later I learn that the mock military parade shows that 'women are demonstrating their ability to withstand the same kind of ordeals that men can withstand as soldiers and warriors'. As the *Kamban* soldiers finish their performance in front of Abdul's house we give them gifts to show our appreciation. Soon, another group of women appears. One is masquerading as a hunter (*Kamban dunse,* the *Kamban* hunter), another as the hunter's praise-singer (*Kamban serewayili*). A woman with the masqueraders sings, 'If you are extending a kindness then extend it to someone who will appreciate it'. It is only when we have given further gifts (5 cent pieces) that this group also continues on its way to other houses.

Yefera Kundi

By noon the pace of events has quickened. Women, singly or in small groups, are rushing about the village announcing the arrival of the *yefera kundi* performers. The female performers are painted with white or red ochres, over which daubs or spots of red, black and white ochre are laid. Each performer carries a makeshift percussion instrument—a cloth-covered dish with pebbles inside, or several brass bells—and some brandish a hearth broom or cutlass which they use to attack the men and children. These histrionic 'assaults' are inevitably amusing and the children take a great deal of delight in escaping them. But the mask-like expressions of the performers betray no amusement, no emotion. Rattling their 'instruments' they approach elders for gifts. The raucous tones and demanding actions with which they address the town chief and the *keminetigi* were the reverse of normal female behaviour towards men. A group of women mill round the *Keminetigi*, who holds a leone note high above his head. Then, in the midst of the melee one woman snatches the note from his hand and the women retreat, laughing and clapping. These performances continue for most of the afternoon. It is about 4 o'clock when the arrival of *Kamban* is heralded. Women rush about the village with leaves and branches, flailing the air with them as they chant, '*Kawulikile* is coming out', over and over again. The *yefera kundi* performers now retire from the scene; they are the same women who in a short while will carry the *Kamban koli* (*Kamban* seed, i.e. the cult object) from the house where it is now being prepared for display.

Kamban *or* Kawulikile (*literally 'A Million Bows and Arrows'*)

We wait for about half an hour outside the house from which the *Kamban koli* will emerge. Several women are sitting on the porches of houses in the *luiye,* others are dancing, and one elderly woman is grimacing and bellowing at a group of small children. When *Kamban* finally appears both men and children retreat from it. The cult object is a large sagging bundle wrapped in an embroidered red cloth and hung from a long pole which is borne on the shoulders of two women. The bearers are *yefera kundi* performers, their body painting now flaking off, but their expressions as mask-like as before. It is easy to imagine that the bundle contains bows and arrows but it is not possible to discover whether this is so. In the midst of a throng of women the *Kamban* bearers now begin to move away from the *luiye.* Some of the women lash out at male bystanders with leaves or hearth brooms. The group then passes around the village, from house to house, receiving gifts as they go.

By nightfall the performance is over and with it the public aspects of the *biriye* also come to an end. There now remains only the secret initiation of the *biril'gbagbe* who, during the night and after ceremonial bathing and purification in the village stream, will be shown the seed (or secret) of *Kamban* for the first time.

Postscript

Two days after the initiations had ended, I left Firawa to rejoin my wife in Kabala. During the following two weeks I made several visits to other Kuranko villages and observed episodes in other *biriye.* Even in a small hamlet like Fasewoia (population about 100) initiations were in progress, the events identical to those which I had witnessed at Firawa. At this time I concentrated my research on initiation ritual and as a result of many conversations with informants in many villages, I gradually began to amplify the account which had been based on my observations at Firawa.

Then, one day in late February, Doron Fina visited us in Kabala. I hardly recognised the girl who, only a month before, had sat outside Abdul's house combing her hair in preparation for plaiting. Her hair was now braided in a different style, a string of cowries was drawn across her forehead, and dozens of red berries were threaded onto the long plaits which hung down the side of her head. This was the customary plaiting style for newly-initiated girls, and Doron Fina would wear her hair like this until her marriage which was planned for two months hence. During this period she would travel around the country, visiting and staying with relatives. Doron Fina's shyness and sense of propriety made it difficult for me to discover very much about her attitudes towards and experiences during initiation. Although I felt immensely fortunate to have observed the Firawa initiations, I was disappointed that male initiations rarely take place nowadays. Young boys (*bilakorenu*) are usually circumcised either at the hospital in Kabala or by the hospital dispenser who, in his spare time and for a small fee, makes visits to various outlying villages during the dry season to perform the operations on several boys at the same time. It was imperative for me to record details of male initiation, even at second hand, and so I interviewed a number of men and slowly built up a picture of these rituals and the meanings·which informants ascribed to them. In the following account it will be evident that the form of the male initiations is almost identical to the form of female initiations. Yet this parallelism at the level of event masks certain differences at the level of function and meaning. These parallels and differences are elucidated in terms of Kuranko commentary and exegesis.

Boy's Initiation (denke biriye)

Traditionally, boys had their hair plaited in the same way as girls. Although the customary identification of boys and girls is rarely evidenced today, it is still considered significant. It is immediately apparent in the way boys are prepared for *biriye*. Both boys and girls wear the *kankansare* or *lol-lore* coiffure during the weeks preceding *biriye*. One man explained that this 'shows that someone who is not initiated is just like a woman; he knows nothing of manhood.' The boys also perform special pre-initiation dances (the *kontadon* and the *gbonbodon*) and, just before initiation, the *kalgbese* dance signifies the imminent end of boyhood.

Pre-Initiation Activities

During the weeks before *biriye,* the *bilakorenu* travel to neighbouring villages to inform kinsmen of the date of the *biriye*. Four kola nuts are wrapped in leaves and tied in a unique way to signify this message. As the boys enter a village they beat small drums (*tamba*) which they carry under their arms; some boys play flutes to announce their arrival. Village girls (*sunkuronu*) greet the visitors and arrange trysts for the evening before conducting the boys to their respective kinsmen's houses (usually the house of a maternal uncle). In the afternoon, wrestling bouts are organised between the local boys and the visitors. The local boys issue challenges by presenting the visitor with seven red peppers wrapped in a leaf. If the challenge is accepted, the boys (accompanied now by their girl friends) make their way to the wrestling ground (*tunilketene*) in separate groups. Here the boys challenge each other with taunts and insulting gestures, such as spitting on the earth and inviting the opponent to 'come and clean up your younger brother's excreta' or grabbing the opponent's testicles and then tapping him on the head. In these play-fights and verbal gibes the social distance between the two communities is expressed and the latent hostility between them is 'played out'. The conflicts between village boys and visitors also involve a jealous vying for the affections of local girls. In the wrestling bouts the boys are mindful of the attention of the girls who applaud and encourage their favourites. The wrestling follows strict rules and village elders referee the contests.

When the afternoon's sport is over the visitors return to their lodgings for the evening meal. During the evening dancing begins and further trysts are made for the night ahead. At about 9 o'clock each boy retires to the main room of his host's house with his girl friend and there the young couple amuse each other, the boy counting the beads on his sweetheart's waist, recounting stories or parables or telling of his own village childhood. Sexual intercourse is forbidden. Until the time of initiation boys and girls are supposed to be both ignorant and innocent of sex. It is believed that if a boy or girl does have sexual intercourse before initiation then they will bleed profusely during the operation and the wound will not heal quickly afterwards. I have been told of cases when a boy is bleeding to death after circumcision and is asked to name the woman with whom he has had intercourse so that the bleeding will stop.

The boys remain in the village for two or three days before moving on. Sometimes they will rest and sleep a night in a village where they have no kinsmen, but the energetic round of wrestling bouts, playful courtship and generous hospitality continues. When the boys leave a village, in the morning their girl friends accompany them half way on their journey to the next village and they may give their paramours an armulet, a beaded headband (*fatakone*) a ring, necklace or trinket as a remembrance gift.

After this period of visiting, during which dispersed kinsmen are notified of the forthcoming *biriye*, the boys return to their own village. Dancing continues, women in cooperative groups prepare rice for the occasion, diviners are consulted, sacrifices are made, and events move towards the initiation according to the pattern already described for girls.

The Plaiting Day (Kundan Lunye)

The riceflour sacrifices have already been made. On the day preceding the actual circumcisions (the plaiting day) the boys have their hair unplaited, cut and washed. The last pre-initiation dance (*kalgbese*) is performed, then the neophytes are taken to the men's bathing place at the streamside where the washing of the hair and genitals is carried out. They then put on special caps and long 'country-cloth' gowns called *gbangbale* which are worn throughout the period of initiation. The neophytes also carry small bows (*kale* or *kile*) to signify their forthcoming entry into manhood. Each *bilakore* sits on the shoulders of a man who is a trusted friend of his father, 'playing' the bow like a harp. This day marks the first phase of ritual separation from boyhood; the boys' mothers and kinswomen weep and wail to show the grief of separation. Village sweethearts help wash the feet of the neophytes before they too are separated from them. The boy's parents customarily give gifts to their son's girl friend (sheep, goats, big pots, rice, etc.) before the neophytes are led away in a group to the *marboneke* ('the men's *marbon*) where they will spend the night watched over by village elders. From the time that they enter this house until the time that they leave the *fafei* as men, no women, girls or uninitiated boys are allowed to see them.

The Operation Day (Simbire)

Early in the morning, the boys are led out of the village to the bush. There a specially cleared site known as the *fule* marks the place where the circumcisions will be carried out. If a woman's first-born son is among the neophytes she lines up with other mothers along the path leading from the village and as her son passes he stops and binds his mother's wrists with a rope of woven cotten (*gbalgbalan*). The mothers remain bound in this way until guns are fired from the *fule* later in the morning to signal that the operations have been performed.

The initiator (*biriyele*) performs the operations with skill and speed. Certain men are famed for their skill and it is said that some do not even touch the penis when they operate; they collect some limes (as many as there are neophytes) and then incise them with the operating knife (the *biriyemuri* or *lilan*), calling the name of each boy as they take the limes from an assistant. Immediately blood appears on the penis and the prepuce is miraculously severed.

The Kuranko regard circumcision as an act of purification, a way of removing the 'taint' or 'dirt' of childhood. Through enduring pain, the child becomes a man. The prepuce itself symbolises this childhood 'taint' and it is usual for some clay to be packed around it prior to the operation to accentuate this symbolism. Informants do not regard the prepuce as a 'feminine' part, though they readily admit that the various purification rites (washing and bleeding) are ways of effecting a social differentiation of male and female. The 'impure' state of the male child implies that he or she has not undergone complete socialisation and therefore is, from a social point of view, sexually undifferentiated.

As the operations continue, flautists play to distract the neophytes' attention and assist them to endure the ordeal. Any cry of pain or sign of weakness or complaint shames a boy and will mark him as a coward for life among his initiation mates. Some boys, determined to show their bravery and fortitude in the face of the initiator, will boldly snatch the cap from the initiator's head as he operates on them.

As soon as circumcision has been performed a male nurse or dresser (*seme*) immediately wipes the penis free of blood and applies a herbal dressing to it. When all the operations are completed a hunter fires his gun to notify kinsmen and friends in the village. The neophytes are then taken to the *fafei*, situated near the *fule*, where their nurses again dress the wounds. The *seme* are assigned to take care of the neophytes by the boys' fathers. They are responsible both for the medical aftercare of the neophytes and for attending and advising them during their period of seclusion in the *fafei*. For seven days after circumcision a small disc is worn over the penis to prevent chafing. On the seventh day the boys are taken to a stream where the wounds are treated with a bark concoction, made from the *yisan* tree. As the wounds heal the neophytes begin their education under the tutelage of village elders. Instruction is given in warrior arts, the virtues of manhood (forebearance, stoicism, honesty, loyalty, bravery) and in the use of special medicines. The neophytes receive instruction in sexual knowledge, and in the final weeks in the *fafei* they learn the principles of conduct associated with membership of various male cult groups, notably *Gbangbe* (witch-finding), *Konke* (hammock-bridge making), and *Kome*.

While the neophytes are in the *fafei* the boys who will be initiated the following year (they are known as *yibankore*) are appointed to act as messengers to mediate between the neophytes and their kinsmen in the village. If the neophytes want water they must sing for it. The *yibankore* (literally 'water finished elder brothers') hear these requests and return to the village to pass on the message. Food and water is usually brought from the village to the precincts of the *fafei* by the neophyte's father, elder brother or younger brother, and, occasionally, mother. As they approach the *fafei*, the neophyte cries '*hera hera*' ('good ho!') but no face to face contact is permitted during the 14 day period of seclusion. The Kuranko emphasise the importance of the neophytes' separation from the mundane and village world. This is why the *seme* are never kinsmen of the neophytes, why the initiator is usually brought in from another village, why non-initiates are not permitted to enter the *fafei*, and why the various indoctrinations and tests administered in the *fafei* are supervised by the most senior men of the village.

The Sleepless Night (Kinyale)

The *fafei* is a tent-like structure, thatched with palm leaves and built around a long pole (*lumbon*) which extends several feet above the peak of the roof. The word '*fafei*' derives from *fafa*, meaning 'hot', though the usual term for hot objects is *wian* and the usual term for hot liquids is *kalme* or *kale*. Informants explained that the *fafei* is thought of as a hot place because 'it is where you are thrashed and subjected to various ordeals; even if your father or maternal uncle are present they are not permitted to interfere or sympathise; what happens in the *fafei* is not their business'. One informant translated *fafa* as 'troubled' since, on their final night in the *fafei* the neophytes must undergo the ordeal of the sleepless night. The *fafei* is filled with smoke. Green leaves, sappy wood and peppers are thrown onto the fire until the smoke not only fills the house but billows upwards through the thatched roof and completely covers the top of the *lumbon*. The smoking of the neophytes is regarded as a way of 'drying' them or 'cooling them'; the term *gbala* means both 'smoked' and 'dried'. One informant drew an analogy between the troubled period in the *'fafei'* and a household 'palaver'; 'a person might say that that place is hot, but when trouble is over he will say that the place has become cool'.

When the neophytes return to the village they wear the long red-dyed *gbangbale* gowns. The red colour is said to be a means of disguising bloodstains and of symbolising the neophytes' vulnerability. New initiates are said to be especially vulnerable to witchcraft attack throughout the period of initiation. For the first time, initiates also wear their 'caps of manhood'. For an initiated boy (*bire ke*) of the Mara clan, leaving the *fafei* as a young man (*kemine*), his new status is signified by wearing the special 'crocodile cap' of the Mara (the *bambedon* or 'crocodile mouth'). The initiates also wear long silk scarves around their necks and carry elephant grass canes with which they strike out at uninitiated boys to show publicly that they are now superior in status to them. But in the presence of elders, the initiates must kneel and remain silent and respectful, for although they have passed from childhood into adulthood they are still merely junior adults (*kemine*). Their anomalous status position is manifest in their behaviour during the four weeks following their return to the village. They are permitted to indulge in petty theft and exempted from many domestic chores. This indicates, as one elder put it, that 'they are above the law'. In this sense they are still regarded as child-like and irresponsible. But the neophytes' attitudes to unitiated boys indicate that they already regard themselves as adults. At Sukurela I observed four young initiated boys taunting a group of youngsters with the refrain, *'Oh bilakore, i ma ta, i sume n n'toro la'* ('Oh *bilakore*, go away from me, your smell disturbs me'). Upon asking them what they meant by these words they explained that uninitiated boys smell quite different from initiates and they asked me, rather surprised by my ignorance, whether I could not smell the difference.

In fact, it is only when the initiates take off the *gbangbale* gown that they are considered to be fully responsible adult members of the community. The gowns are given to the boys' nurses, their childhood clothes are given to younger brothers. The Kuranko say that just as a young man will never put on the clothes of childhood or initiation again, so he will never behave as a child or as a neophyte again. After initiation, the boys are expected to lead a new life as men. It is said that if an initiate leaves the *fafei* with any bad habit, uncorrected trait of boyhood personality or remnant of childhood behaviour then it will remain with him for the rest of his life. The most serious impediment to this transition to full adulthood is disrespect towards elders, particularly one's *seme*. I have often heard elders jokingly refer to someone's bad habits with the words, 'He came out of the *fafei* like that, there is nothing that can be done about it.'

On the day that the initiates return to the village, the *fafei* is burnt down by the *seme*. Initiates must avoid seeing the smoke from the burning house and hide indoors until it is completely destroyed. If an initiate even glimpses the smoke it is said that he will die; he is leaving not only boyhood behind but initiation too. He must turn his head away from the *fafei* and from the life which preceded his entry to it.

Discussion and Analysis

Ritual events transcend mundane reality; they are 'bracketed'. In ritual, people are disengaged from everday roles and the theatrical self-consciousness of ritual behaviour allows people to bring into focus an abstract image of their social ideology and to tolerate a dramatic rehearsal of the contradictions within it. In the Kuranko *biriye* we glimpse the fundamental principles of their social ideology (such as the different but complementary domains of male and female, elder and younger, initiate and noninitiate, kinship and community, village and bush). But this insight is reached through the focussing of antithetical images and dramatic contrasts (such as the contrast between the 'social bisexuality' of the child and subsequent polarisation of the sexes, the women's mimicry of male roles and the men's arrogation of maternal functions). It is as if the social world were being shattered only to be rebuilt, as if chaos had to be entertained before order could be achieved. In my view it is possible to make sense of these ritual transformations only when one recognises that the ritual process enables the Kuranko to actually become self-conscious arbiters of events which ordinarily reduce them to passivity. The apparent absurdity of an endeavour which works to destroy the world only to reconstruct it as it was before can only be understood, it seems to me, by recognising that in the process man becomes momentarily the master of his own destiny. Events which are ordinarily adventitious and arbitrary are anticipated and subjected to symbolic transformations which are the result of human volition. Merleau-Ponty writes:

What defines man is not the capacity to create a second nature— economic, social or cultural—beyond biological nature; it is rather the capacity of going beyond created structures in order to create others. And this movement is already visable in each of the particular products of human work.

This power of choosing and varying points of view permits man to create instruments, not under the pressure of a *de facto* situation, but for a virtual use and especially in order to fabricate others. . . These acts of the human dialectic all reveal the same essence: the capacity of orienting oneself in relation to the possible, to the mediate, and not in relation to a limited milieu; they all reveal what we called above, with Goldstein, the categorical attitude. Thus, the human dialectic is ambiguous: it is first manifested by the social or cultural structures, the appearance of which it brings about and in which it imprisons itself. But its use-objects and its cultural objects would not be what they are if the activity, which brings about their appearance did not also have as its meaning to reject them and to surpass them.[6]

Death, destructive propensities, and the extraordinary powers of bush spirits, God and the ancestors, are factors over which the Kuranko have, in the normal course of events, only partial control. Innate factors pertaining to individual temperament and personality such as *yugi, miran, hankili* and *baraka* (discussed in chapter 9) are randomly and arbitrarily distributed despite the fact that official ideology presents them as systematically attributed. Whenever I discussed with informants the causes of affliction, sickness and death, I would be told of the distinction between *altala kiraiye* (afflictions caused by God) and *morgofi' kiraiye* (afflictions caused by 'black'/evil persons). In the latter category the Kuranko place witches and sorcerers. All these special powers or character traits, whether positive or negative, are regarded as lying outside the bounds of certain human control and understanding. They are factors which are not absolutely governable by human will or social action.

Yet, in the initiation rituals, life and death are transformed or reconstrued as factors which are subject to human control and manipulation. They are 'disengaged' from subjectivity. This point is well made by L. V. Thomas:

Pour mieux siteur la notion de personne, il importe d'insister plus spécialement sur l'opposition *mort réelle* (physique, sociale)/*mort symbolique* (rituel d'initiation). La premiére est subie, individuelle et individualisante. La seconde, au contraire, est voulue, collective et communautarisante. Avec celle-là on reste malgré tout du côté de la nature; mais celle-ci nous introduit en plein coeur de la culture. En outre, la naissance biologique qui n'aura de sens social vrai qu'avec l'initiation, aboutit nécessairement a la mort biologique tandis que la mort culturelle permet au groupe rituellement donc symboliquement (imaginalement) de se régénérer par la naissance (ou re-naissance) initiatique.

C'est donc par la vertu du symbole ou de la démarche utopique (l'idéel, l'imaginal) et la conduite communielle (union communautaire) que le Noir echappe à la naturalité de sa condition.[7]

The symbolic death and rebirth of the neophytes is only one aspect of a complex of activities whose common theme is regeneration. It might seem that this 'control' over the forces of life and death (biogenetic factors) is illusory and even pathetic if we failed to take into account certain axioms of Kuranko thought. In previous chapters I have shown how the Kuranko conceptualise their social universe as an enclosed space, characterised by life-giving reciprocal interactions. Outside this space are darkness, death and uncertainty. Life is social life, death the absence of it or the consequence of anti-social behaviour. To ensure that life continues the Kuranko must ensure that the ideals of social behaviour within the community are maintained. Ideologically, individual life is viewed as a condition of social life, identified with it rather than apart from it. What unsettles or makes imperfect this identification are the uncertainties of nature, the capriciousness of personal affections, the unpredictability of death and affliction, the idiosyncratic variability of man.

What we may discern in Kuranko initiations is a brave invocation of these forces and a concerted effort to transcend them, to make them subject to human control. Mortality, facial expressions, idiosyncratic gestures, individual attitudes, personal affections and emotions . . . these are all eclipsed by the 'masks' which people wear and the collective symbols which they employ. In the rituals, behaviour becomes standardised, stereotyped, model. And there is a conscious and deliberate assumption of the ritual roles. While ordinary life is characterised by taken-for-granted routines, ritual activity is the very reverse. It is this dramatic splitting of the individual and the role which may explain the comic effects of the public performances. Although performers are transformed into stage figures by virtue of their masks and disguises, they remain perceptibly themselves. At Firawa it was impossible for me to discern anything of this for I knew very few of the performers. But local people would recognise a familiar face behind the staid and fixed expression of the 'mask' and laugh, for they were being confronted by that most improbable and ludicrous of spectacles—a familiar person behaving like an automaton. One sees a familiar face and an individual person vanish into the mimetic role and become consumed by it; suddenly one fears for their safety, one is desperate to know whether the idiosyncratic personality will disengage itself again from the ritual *persona*.

But these transformations which occur during the public performances differ significantly from the transformations which the neophytes undergo. While the public performers will return to their familiar form, the neophytes will not. With regard to the transformation of personality, we may say that the former movement is reversible and the latter movement is irreversible. This may be why the public performances have a comic effect (indicating the ambiguities and uncertainties of a momentary transformation) while the secret initiation procedures have a serious effect (for the neophytes there is no return to their former selves). Nonetheless, both the public and secret performances are complementary. The symbolic de-personalisation of the neophytes is part of the process of enculturation. At the same time, the de-personalisation one observes in the public performers (it takes the form of impersonating ideal others) is also a kind of enculturation process. By transcending their ordinary selves and through playing extraordinary roles, the performers project an image of social principals and categories. Just as the neophytes transcend their childhood identifications, so too the community transcends the divisions and conflicts which threaten its solidarity and integrity. In other words, processes of ritual separation (male from female, initiated from uninitiated, married from unmarried, ignorant from knowing, etc.)

must be viewed as running in parallel to processes of ritual unification (the unity of the dispersed community, the solidarity of men *vis-à-vis* women, the solidarity of initiates *vis-à-vis* non-initiates, etc.).

Kuranko initiation rituals thus create and project an idealised image of social reality, the distinctions and unities of which are never as well focussed in ordinary life. The dialectic of the ritual is not unlike that involved in mythological argument. Like myth, these rituals seem to turn the world upside down as a preliminary to reconstituting it. They seem to create, by symbolic means, an abnormal state of affairs before recreating the ideal condition. The rituals, in short, bring people together in a common enterprise which is nothing less than the reshaping of the social universe. It is, of course, not the case that each individual participant or performer is identically motivated. The real point to be stressed is that *both organised and spontaneous social movements and processes are possible not because all individuals participating in them are identically (and sociologistically) motivated, but because a variety of authentically subjective motives may seek and find an ego syntonic outlet in the same type of collective activity.*[8]

In the following pages I shall analyse the symbolism of *biriye* and discuss various sociological and psychological aspects of the ritual. My aim is to explore the meaning and functions of *biriye* in terms of both Kuranko exegesis and anthropological theories of initiation.

From Childhood to Adulthood

The Kuranko emphasise that the purpose of *biriye* is initiation into adulthood, a process which involves separating the child from its exclusive attachments to and identifications with the kinship group. This crucial and irreversible transition necessitates a transformation of both the social status and the personality of the child. Since the Kuranko consider children to be 'dirty' or impure, they often speak of *biriye* as a ritual of purification or cleansing. Informants substantiate their notion that children are impure by pointing out that children are innocent or ignorant of sexual matters, that they play in and with dirt, that they go naked (i.e. the sex organs are not covered). I have often heard elders objecting to the way in which Kuranko schoolboys pay so much attention to personal cleanliness and clothing. For them, this is inconsistent with the idea that childhood is a state of impurity; it presumes initiation before it has actually occured. But most important, the idea of impurity is, in this context, associated with the child's psychological attachment to its mother and its dependence upon its parents.[9] The child's dependent status and jural minority are implicitly related to the child's primary attachment to the immediate kinship group(*dembaiye*).[10] As jural minors, attached to and identified with the kinship group, children do not really have any status in the wider community. As such, they are only partially socialised; they are socially marginal.[11] The Kuranko terms for particular stages in the life cycle of the individual all relate to the event of initiation when complete socialisation is effected (refer chapter 2 for details).

The Kuranko conceptualise the progressive stages of the individual life cycle in terms of the all-important ritual 'divide' of initiation. But initiation transforms this naturally-determined sequence of events (biographical time) into a culturally-determined cycle (social time). The birth and life of the individual are symbolically recapitulated, and in the process the ideological foundations of the society are simultaneously rehearsed. In the context of initiation ritual the themes of death and birth are culturally elaborated so that the neophyte moves from kinship group to community, from descent group identification to cult group membership, from a status given at birth to a status arrived at through wholly cultural means.

This enacted transformation is comparable to that which Lévi-Stauss uncovers in his brief analysis of the Oedipus myth.[12] In Kuranko initiations we also discern a clear contrast between features which *overrate blood relations* and features which *underrate blood relations*. I have already alluded to the manner in which the Kuranko characterise childhood (*dininye*) as a period of dependency on the mother. The child usually sleeps in the same room as its mother; for boys this may continue until about the age of 10. The child shares the same sleeping mat with its siblings (of either sex), depends entirely upon its parents for protection and sustenance, and has no status outside the kinship group. Adult status is, by contrast, characterised by independence and separation from the family of origin and the assumption of responsibilities which involve and incorporate a person in the life of the entire community. At initiation the child passes from the possession of the *dembaiye* into the possession of the community. This transition is expressed in many features of *biriye*.

In the weeks preceding *biriye*, mothers of the neophytes circulate around the village singing songs such as: 'Oh my belly Ferema Sise[13], oh my belly, the day after tomorrow the children will be initiated into womanhood (*musubaye*)'. Informants commented upon this song by emphasising that initiation severs the child from the mother; the image of pregnancy and pain in childbirth expresses the finality of this severance. After initiation, the daughter will be given in marriage to her husband (and leave her natal home), the initiated man will be no longer permitted to sleep in the same room as his mother, sisters, and uninitiated brothers. Another song, sung during the day that female initiates are introduced to the secrets of *Kamban*, conveys a similar meaning. '*Hali i fa ya a ya wulan la bor ma si ke bo i ro, yenye, dannu yenye*'— 'Even if your father (the song is repeated and the word '*na*' [mother] is substituted for the word '*fa*' [father]) looks at you with red eyes we will take you from him children, we will take you from him.' In this context, red (*wulan*) signifies annoyance, lust or irritation, and, in a more mundane sense, weeping and mourning.

The sudden emotional separation from parents and kin which the neophytes must endure is illustrated in other ways: the binding of the mother's wrists as her eldest son leaves the village for the *fule*[14], the ban on parental intervention during the course of the ordeals in the *fafei*, the public displays of grief by kinsmen as their sons or daughters depart for the operations, and the restrictions imposed upon kinsmen who may not make direct contact with their children during the period of seclusion. In the next chapter we will see how the initiation of neophytes into various secret community cults carries this separation even further. But it is appropriate here to mention the role of surrogate parents during initiation.

The *seme* ('nurse' or 'dresser') who attends the neophyte in the *fafei* is accorded considerable respect; any failure to respect or obey the instructions of the *seme* would, it is said, impede the initiate's progress to full adulthood. The *seme* may be a clansman, but never a father, brother or mother's brother. The *seme* is usually a respected neighbour or contemporary of the neophyte's father. Thus the neophyte's care and life is in the hands of a member of the community who is not a kinsman. When the initiate has recovered from the operation, his gown(*gbangbale*) and other gifts (money, a fowl, a cooking pot[15]) are presented to the *seme* by the initiate's father. Throughout his life the initiate must respect his *seme* and heed his advice. This relationship is comparable to the relationship between a person and his or her *yigi* (literally 'hope'). Most people recognise at least one *yigi* who may be a man or a woman, but who is invariably an older person. One's *yigi* is rarely, if ever, a kinsman; he or she could be from another village or chiefdom. A child's father might approach a respected contemporary or friend with a small gift and ask them to remember his child, or a person could make a similar request of any elder, saying '*ne n'yigi sigi bi ma na sina*' ('let me place my hope/trust in you, not for today but for tomorrow'). In times of personal misfortune a person could ask his *yigi* for material help or to act as a spokesman in a legal dispute. Kinsmen are regarded as partisan, and the neutrality of the *yigi* is recognised in such cases. But one uses kinship terms of address, one's *yigi* being called *m'fa* ('my father') or *n'na* ('my mother'), so that a parallel with kinship bonds and responsibilities always remains obvious. Like the relationship with one's *seme*, the relationship with one's *yigi* creates affiliations and ties which extend beyond the closed circle of family and sub-clan. But unlike the parent-child relationship, which is ascribed and given, relationships with one's *seme* and *yigi* are achieved and chosen.

The officials who direct and plan *biriye* (the *keminetigi*—'leader of the young men'—and the *dimusukuntigi*—'head of the women') are also regarded as alter-parents, entrusted with the responsibility for transforming the neophytes into adult members of the community. The manner in which initiation eclipses kinship affiliations and bestows community status on the initiate is also evinced by the initiate's introduction to community cult associations.[16] In the cults, kinship terms of reference and address are often used among members irrespective of whether or not real kinship ties exist.

A further dimension of meaning in *biriye* is disclosed when we take this contrast between *natural birth into the kinship group* and *culturally contrived rebirth into the community group* one stage further. As in the Oedipus myth[17], we can isolate features which, on the one hand concern the *autochthonous origin of man,* and on the other hand concern *denial of the autochthonous origin of man.* Expressed more simply, this contrast implies the problem: born from one or born from two?

The Kuranko theory of procreation denies the woman any part in creating the child; she is regarded as a vessel in which the male seed grows. This dogma clearly underwrites the patrilineal ideology according to which procreation is seen as male-determined. However, the raising of the child is always regarded as being in the hands of the mother; the child's destiny (*latege*) depends upon the mother's behaviour and influence. The patrilineal dogma is challenged, as it were, by the facts that sexual intercourse is necessary in order to conceive a child, that cooperation between both mother and father is required in the raising of the child, and that the mother plays such an important role in shaping the destiny and character of the child. The passivity which is, in theory, ascribed to women is contradicted by the central and active role she plays in child-rearing.

The themes of procreation and birth are pervasive features of *biriye.* But unlike the circumstances of natural procreation, birth and child-rearing, the ritual separates men from women and women from men in an absolute sense. The symbolic rebirth of the girl as a woman is entirely in the hands of women; the symbolic rebirth of a boy as a man is entirely in the hands of men. And it is through the manipulation of external symbols that young women are 'borne' by older women and young boys are 'borne' by older men.

In the case of male initiation, the ritual separation of the sexes during the initiation process enables the Kuranko to make good a discrepancy in the patrilineal dogma: the symbolic rebirth of the neophytes serves to realise the ideal of male control over the procreation and raising of males.[18] Moreover, the substitution of cult masters or ritual experts such as the *biriyele* and *seme* (who are not related by kinship to the neophytes) for real fathers or elder brothers, helps to disengage this new birth from subjectivity. With reference to such factors as primary attachments, separation anxieties and oedipus conflicts, the ritual officials and the ritual events make possible a kind of defence against the spontaneous and random expression of individual emotions by re-presenting these factors in a form significantly remote from the original or idiosyncratic context to permit mutual identification around a common object, concept, cult figure or impersonal other.[19]

Bettelheim has stressed that 'One of the purposes of male initiation may be to assert that men, too, can bear children. It has been fully recognized that one of the purposes of the ceremony is to give the boy and often also the women the impression that the boy was reborne by the father, and therefore owes his life to the father.'[20] But, in the Kuranko case, we would need to add that if 'male envy' exists it is more envy of the women's influence in child-rearing than envy of women's child-bearing capacities. This psychogenic explanation (which stresses 'envy') must, moreover, be modified to accommodate the fact that quite disparate individual motives find outlet in the same collective activity.[21] The fact that men 'imitate' maternal functions or the fact that women 'parody' certain male roles does not mean that there is, in the unconcious of each individual, a kind of 'womb envy' or rebelliousness. It is the dissociation of affect and behaviour which characterises ritual action; no Kuranko would regard the *Kamban Yuwe* ('Mad *Kamban*') performer as really insane (*yuwe*) simply because she imitates or affects insane behaviour. Another important point is that the male neophyte is not so much 'reborne' by the father as by the initiated male community.[22] From the neophytes point of view, he is taught to suppress narcissistic inclinations (expressed in terms of his emotional attachment to the mother) in order to realise his responsibilities within the male community. The development of this 'abstract attitude' depends upon the initiate's ability to think in symbolic terms and to defer immediate gratifications. Images taken from the natural world express this transformation: the neophytes are 'gathered' or 'harvested', cut off from the kinship domain, then isolated in a 'bush' house. During *kinyale* ('the sleepless night') they are symbolically 'cooked' or 'dried' in a smoke-filled room. They are swallowed up and regurgitated, the girls by *Kamban*, the boys by a male equivalent called *Kigbofuri* (literally 'bachelor dead').[23] The socialisation of the neophytes is at the same time a symbolic recreation of social ideology, for their rebirth as men (a process involving men only) or as women (a process involving women only) is in perfect accord with an ideology which demands a strict separation of the sexes. 'Although experience contradicts theory, social life validates cosmology by its similarity of structure. Hence cosmology is true.'[24]

We have seen how notions of impurity, irresponsibility and confused sexual identity are ritually exaggerated in the preliminary stages of *biriye*. I have suggested that such features as the neophytes' licence to steal, play cohabitation, and general permissiveness are symbols of disorder in a much wider sense, first emphasised then expunged. The transformation of child into adult is simultaneously a transformation of chaos into order, and the Kuranko stress three aspects of this change: first, purification through a series of ritual cleansings or washing followed by the circumcision or clitoridectomy itself; second, changes in attire; third, changes in hairstyle. Male and female are initially confused, for both boys and girls commence *biriye* dressed in the same way, their hair plaited in identical styles, their manners undistinguished. The separation of male and female is shown outwardly by changes of dress and hairstyle.[25] Occasionally people say of an initiate (*bire*), 'he/she has put on clothes' (*a ra fanita*) and this implies mainly the covering-up of the genitalia. But an inward transformation also occurs as neophytes are instructed in the code of conduct governing relationships between the sexes. Prior to initiation, a child is not expected to be able to exercise much self-control. The Kuranko fully recognise the parallelism of intellectual and physical maturation, so that the puberty rites serve to instruct the neophytes in how to assert conscious control over both the body and the mind. Physical control is taught through the ordeals in which the inhibition of impulsive and egocentric actions is emphasised[26]; mental self-control is taught through the inculcation of the 'abstract attitude' in which long-term needs such as cooperation with others are emphasised over narcissistic and immediate gratification. After initiation, strict rules apply determining what a person may see and may not see, what he may hear and may not hear, etc. These restrictions and prohibitions refer to what the Kuranko call *sumafan* ('secret things') and the same term denotes what are commonly called 'secret societies' and 'society devils'. The cult associations, into which the new initiate is inducted, serve to bind together the men of the community because of the strict code governing the keeping of cult secrets. Emphasis is placed, by the Kuranko, on the social regulation of the senses (*ka sumafen kwe mara*, literally 'to secret things keep/command/control'). It is often said that a person's life (*nie*) will not be long unless he learns to control his eyes and ears; 'if you are told not to look at something but then you look at it, you will die because of your "curious eyes", and if you are told not to speak of certain things but then you speak of them, you will die because of your "big mouth".'[27]

Not only does this control or regulation of the senses specify the proper code of conduct between the sexes; it also signifies the correct form of relations between elders and juniors. Initiation introduces the neophyte to the first stage of an adult cult association; there are still secrets which he is not permitted to know, songs which he should not hear, objects which he should not see or touch. The neophyte's relative ignorance or innocence and his subordination to cult elders or masters continue to impose a strict separation between elders and juniors. The neophyte's passivity, malleability and dependency in relation to the ritual elders and officials is comparable to the child's relationship with its parents. However, whereas the world of kinship is subject to the influence of personal disposition, the world of the community cults is comparatively impersonal, relating to forces and elemental agencies that are always marginal to the domain of human existence: God, the *sacra* of the cults, the spirits of the wild. In a sense, community ideals are constant and infallible because individual persons cannot gain total access to them or influence and control them entirely. Kinship ideals are, by contrast, inconstant and fallible because they are comparatively accessible and attainable, far more subject to the influence of individual persons. This may be why the ritual expression of community ideals involves an underrating of and a symbolic disengagement from kinship affiliations.[28] This process of impersonalisation is most dramatically shown in the ordeals which neophytes must undergo in order to become adults, that is to say persons who can 'see the two kinds of bush spirits (*konke* and *gbangbe* or *kuruwe*) which non-initiates cannot see'. Utter subjugation to the dictates of the ritual elders and direct confrontation with the cult *sacra* (*sumafen*) instruct the neophyte in ways in which he can stand outside his familiar world and transcend his individual self.

During the period of mid-transition, the neophytes are 'at once no longer classified and not yet classified'.[29] This critical interval in a person's life is at the same time a period of hiatus in social life. The ambiguous character of the neophyte dramatises a contrast between nature and culture, the unsocialised and the socialised. During the liminal phrase of *biriye* the neophytes are already superior to uninitiated children, yet they are inferior to full adults. When greeting an elder, the young initiate must kneel and take off his cap of manhood. Yet he is permitted to disdain the company of uninitiated children by mocking their infantile manners and by brushing them aside with a blow of his elephant grass cane. The attitude of abasement is identical to that adopted by a woman when she greets her husband; it suggests that the young initiate is classified with women. But the gestures of avoidance and abuse with respect to non-initiates signify superior status; the initiate is thus separated from childhood. Whilst in the *fafei*, the initiates are subject to the control of elders, yet they are licenced to steal food (notably eggs) and domestic animals in the village (though not from inside houses). They are clothed, yet not clothed, for the *gbangbale* gown marks them apart from non-initiates as much as it distinguishes them from adults. They are married, yet not married, for until the girls are formally installed in their husbands' home they are virgins (physically) but knowledgeable about sex; the boys are permitted to embark upon adulterous affairs (*kemine koiye*) after initiation, but they are not allowed to marry until five years have elapsed. The neophytes are sworn to keep the secrets of manhood or womanhood, yet they are considered to be 'outside the law' and incapable of full self-control. In Kuranko folktales, the trickster hero is almost always a young man (*kemine*), initiated but not yet married, and the narratives which are centred around the exploits of this character are, like the rituals, concerned with confusions between sentiment and structure, personal affections and social obligations.[30]

Precisely the same kind of ambiguity characterises the secret objects and bush spirits on which the community cults are centred. They are capricious and dangerous, they can give life or take life, they may be predictable one moment and intractable the next, they are simultaneously wild and tame. Both neophytes and bush spirits signify a mediation between nature and culture. This is why the events of mid-transition take place on the margins of the community, in a 'bush house'. And it is also why the neophytes at this stage are considered to be in a state of danger themselves and at the same time capable of endangering others. The reintegration of the community as a whole depends upon their successful transition from childhood to adulthood. The rumours and fears of witchcraft which possess many villagers during this time, the ritual use of red (signifying danger and uncertainty), the scrupulous attention given to diviners's instructions, the adherence to strict routines, the isolation of the neophytes, and the various rites which bring irregularities to light (such as the gun-firing rite during the girls' *biriye*) are all indications of this suspense. The acceleration of movement which presages the completion of the transition from childhood to adulthood during the final phase of the ritual is, at the same time, a movement through which the interrupted cycle of community life is resumed.

The Separation of the Sexes

Many Kuranko remark that one of the main purposes of *biriye* is 'to maintain respect and distance between men and women'. Initiations involve a separation of male and female domains and a differentiation masculine and feminine attributes. It is said that men and women possess exclusive and secret powers which can be used if a person of the opposite sex infringes one's rights or trespasses on one's domain. Significantly, these powers are alleged to affect the sexual organs. During the Firawa initiations, several men commented that they feared women at this time 'because they are doing things which we do not understand'. They acknowledged that should a man intrude during the secret rites of the girls' initiation then, not only would he himself suffer (by being afflicted with elephantiasis of the testicles), but it would mean a breakdown of the social order. Nonetheless, fear alone does not maintain this segregation of the sexes; it is also the result of a voluntary collusion, a decision on the part of both men and women to feign total ignorance of the mysteries of the other sex.

The separation of the child from its natal group is paralled by another transformation in which male is separated or differentiated from female.[31] The child is socially 'sexless' or bisexual; his or her sexual ignorance or innocence, physical immaturity, nakedness and irresponsibility place him or her outside the exclusive male-female divisions of adult life. In the preliminary phases of the *biriye* sexual differences are symbolically 'played down'. Identical dress, hairstyle and body decoration serve to disguise sexual differences. Moreover, during the course of the initiation there is a pattern of sex role reversals in which women performers assume the status trappings of men. We are faced with the problem of explaining why women should act as men during the period of mid-transition, and we must also account for the fact that while women masquerade as men (during female initiations), men do not actually masquerade as women (during male initiations).

Gluckman has stressed the psychological and cathartic aspects of these role reversals, pointing out that in a society which is pervaded by the jural and political hegemony of the male it is imperative that women's frustrations be given some socially-prescribed outlet.[32] Kuranko women are bemused by this idea, though they acknowledge the venting of frustrations through rebelliousness and recalcitrance in other areas of social life. First, they emphasise the comic effects of their transvesticism. Second, they say that their mimicry of certain male roles is indicative of their aspirations to become like men. By this they mean that the neophytes should inculcate those virtues which men exemplify: superior fortitude, bravery, loyalty, the ability to keep secrets and control refractory emotions. It is not that women are expressing grievances against men, rather that they are striving to emulate certain virtues or principles of behaviour associated with the male domain. The comedy of these transvestite performances may be simply a consequence of an improbable juxtoposition between the mimetic and the actual, between male guise and female person. The unusual association of male and female in these abstracted performances may have the effect of not so much confusing the spectator but of making him more keenly aware of the differences between masculinity and feminity.[33] Thus, the awkwardness of the mimetic performances, the expressionless faces of the performers, and the buffoonery which is displayed among the spectators, all serve to sharpen one's awareness of male-female differences. If some women do use these performances as occasions for giving vent to private antagonisms, then this is incidental; an explanation of the role reversals which stressed this aspect alone would fail to account for the reasons that make such mimetic ritual socially appropriate during initiations.

Ordinarily, women are dependent upon men but during the secret rites of initiation they become independent of men. They, and they alone, 'conceive' and give symbolic birth to the female neophytes.[34] Yet this process, in which women play at being men, is founded upon impossible aspirations; it remains a masquerade and its artificiality is signified by the deliberately gauche and ludicrous character of the mimetic performances which take place in public.[35] Similar incongruities are betrayed during male initiations when the men 'give birth to' and 'raise' the male neophytes without the intervention of women. The patrilineal dogma of total male control is enacted theatrically in the rehearsing of procreative and child-rearing processes during the secret rites. But the absolute separation of male and female, like the separation of the idiosyncratic personality from the social personality, can only be affected, momentarily, synthetically, theatrically.

The male and female cult associations are also founded upon the principle of total sexual segregation. The actual complementarity and interdependence of the sexes in the domain of kinship and marriage are again 'played down' in the cult context. As Turner pointed out in his analysis of the Mukanda rite of circumcision among the Ndembu, 'categorical relationships which stress likeness rather than interdependence (are) the basis of classification'.[36] Categories such as men, women, elders, children, the unmarried, the married etc. are constituted in binary oppositions; they cut across and interlink kinship or descent groups, defining the community in terms of 'the universal constants and differentiae of human society, age, sex, and somatic features'.[37]

The Unification of the Community

The oscillations between wet and dry seasons impose a pattern of social contrasts upon Kuranko life, notably between the dispersed, kinship-group-centred farm life during the rains and the more fully integrated community life of the dry season. Although the cooperative labour system, village visiting and the proximity of other farming families offset the isolation of rainy season life, this isolation still contrasts with the sense of community which is expressed in dry season social and ritual activity within the village. Moreover, the hardships, hunger and misery of the rainy season stand in direct contrast to the atmosphere of well-being, security and goodwill which village life establishes. The initiation rituals are the high point in the dry season. They celebrate the abundance of rice, the success of harvest and the regeneration of society itself.[38] Generous hospitality, sharing and exchange all serve to reunite kinsmen and villagers who have been separated or estranged during the long months of the rainy season. In this sense, initiations are annual rites of passage in which the community crosses the threshold from one phase of social life (dispersed, kin-centred) to another (collected, community-centred). In part, initiation rituals and festivities help to re-establish the bases for economic cooperation which are essential to the success of the next farm season. During the dry deason, debts are cleared, court cases resolve issues which may have been long-postponed, marriages are made, and sacrifices are offered by the ruling lineage to secure the protection and prosperity of the entire chiefdom. In all these activities, the relationships among members of the community are reformed and revitalised.

This regenerative process incorporates a series of transformations which I have already discussed: wet season to dry season, unmarried to married, deprivation to abundance, kinship affiliations to community identifications, and so on. For the initiates, two significant transformations occur. They are prepared for marriage and taught the rules and regulations governing proper relationships between the sexes, and they are inducted into the community cult associations. The cult associations define a microcosm in which the principles of Kuranko social ideology achieve strict definition; categorical relationships such as sex and age eclipse kinship or descent-group identifications. Throughout this chapter I have sought to emphasise the manner in which initiation rituals express and focus the values of community. The various descent and kinship groupings in the local community are united in terms of a higher order of collective identity, a more abstract frame of reference, the focal point of which is the system of sexually-exclusive and hierarchically-structured cult associations. In the next chapter I will present an account of these cult associations and indicate where their force and significance lies.

Notes

1.   Initiation ritual (*biriye*) is sometimes referred to as *koiyige* (literally 'riverside down' or 'going down to the riverside'). My field assistant, Noah Marah, suggested that 'crossing the water' would be an acceptable translation of the term.

2.   Jorge Luis Borges 1965:91

3.   Turner 1970:50-1.

4.   Lévi-Strauss 1963:214.

5.   Uninitiated persons of either sex are not permitted to eat eggs. The neophytes are not permitted to eat any *dege* on the day of the riceflour sacrifice; it is said that the *dege* would appear at the clitoris during the operation and prevent the wound healing. Although both eggs and *dege* are regarded as white or pure (*gbe*), informants could not elaborate upon the significance of these prohibitions. It may be suggested, however, that it is because the neophytes are symbolically 'impure' that they are not permitted to eat the *dege*; such an act would 'spoil' the *dege* sacrifice which is offered to the ancestors.

6.   Merleau-Ponty 1965:175-6.

7.   L. V. Thomas 1973:407-8.

8.   Devereux 1961:236 (italics in text).

9.   In referring to 'attachment' I mean to denote 'attachment behaviour' as discussed by Bowlby (1971).

10. In fact, many informants take the view that the mother is *fisa* than the child 'because she is the mother, she bore you'; in this instance it is the child's dependency upon the mother as well as the fact that the child is younger than its mother which define its subordinate status position (see chapter 9 for further discussion of the concept of *fisa mantiye*).

11. Thus, a child who dies before it has been initiated is buried in the *sundu kunye ma* ('the rubbish heap area at the back of the house') which lies half-way between the domain of the kinship group (*dembaiye*) and the wider community. An initiated adult is buried on the margins of the village area, i.e. half-way between the community and the wilderness (an area associated with bush spirits and the ancestors). In these ways, spatial

CROSSING THE WATER   215

and the adult (see chapter 3 for further discussion).

12. Lévi-Strauss 1963:213-8.

13. Ferema Sise is the name of a particular girl.

14. That only the eldest son does this may indicate the stress which the
Kuranko place upon the eldest son as his father's successor; in the case of
younger sons the separation from and avoidance of the parents is less
emphatic.

15. The gift of a cooking pot may suggest that the *seme* is assigned a role which
is modelled on both paternal authority and maternal care.

16. In his discussion of Plato's *Republic,* Stanley Diamond advances the view
that this kind of obliteration of primary kinship bonds is a precondition
for the transition from primitive social organisation to the proto-state
(1969:174-5). A similar view is presented by Paula Brown in her essay on
patterns of authority in West Africa (1951:261-78).

17. Lévi-Strauss 1963:213-18.

18. Cf. Lévi-Strauss's observation that 'the Oedipus myth provides *a kind of
logical tool* which relates the original problem—born from one or born
from two?—to the derivative problem: born from different or born from
same? By a correlation of this type, the overrating of blood relations is to
the underrating of blood relations as the attempt to escape autochthony is
to the impossibility to succeed in it' (1963:216).

19. Cf. Róheim 1971:chapter 3. It is noteworthy that among the Temne the
man who performs the operations wears a mask, allegedly borrowed from
the Kuranko; it is an 'impersonalised' ancestor mask known as *ka bimba*
(*bimba* also being the Kuranko word for ancestor) (A. K. Turay, personal
communication).

20. Bettelheim 1954:109.

21. Devereaux (1961) has quite rightly insisted that 'one must sharply
differentiate between psychologistic conceptions of motivation and
sociologistic conceptions of motivation, both in the construction of
models of "modal personality" and in the interpretation of participation
in social movements'. He notes that in the psychologistic model the
motivation is and must be subjective. Hence, the motivational structure
of the 'modal' personality of a given group must be made up of motives
and needs which are systematically stimulated—either through constant
and expectable gratification or through systematic frustration—in that
society. In the sociologistic model, the motivation must be collective and
the motivational structure of the 'modal' personality of a given group
must be constructed out of the type of 'common sense' motives which the
social scientist must impute to all members of a given group in order to be
able to explain their participation in collective activities . . . (1961:238-
9).

My analysis of Kuranko initiations is primarily sociologistic, partly
because I do not have comprehensive data of the kind that would permit
psychologistic analysis, and partly because it is imperative that
sociological and psychological modes of discourse and explanation be
differentiated. Moreover, my analysis does not attempt to discover or
demonstrate universally invariant functions or meanings in initiation
rituals. In fact, it seems to me, from my own observations of Kuranko
initiations, that just as highly variable and idiosyncratic interpretations

are made (by informants and participants) of the standard and collective events, so the same ritual events (which we classify together as 'initiation ritual') in several different societies do not necessarily have identical significance or serve the same functions. The manifest similarities of initiation rituals among many different societies do not, in my view, justify *a priori* statements that their functions and meanings are identical for each society, or, within one society, for each individual. Nevertheless, it is clear that Kuranko initiation does permit general comparison in terms of both function and meaning with initiation rituals in other societies. This fact, while enabling comparative generalisation, should not blind us to the possibility that the 'universal invariants' we discern may not necessarily have a primary significance or function in each case; moreover, we should be cautious about regarding the idiosyncratic or cultural-specific variations in function or meaning as mere secondary elaborations or contingent factors, demanding far less theoretical attention than the universals.

22. Cf. Wiko initiations in which 'the boys are ritually separated from their mothers to be identified with their fathers' (Gluckman, cited in Turner 1970:153).

23. The appearance of *Kigbofuri* is heralded by the blowing of a horn and the chanting of the refrain: '*Ta i la konkola Kigbofuri, ta i la konkola*' ('Go into your room"bachelor dead", go into your room'); one informant supposed that the room was the *fafei*.

24. Lévi-Strauss 1963:216.

25. In psychoanalytic terms the head hair symbolises (through a process of displacement from below to above) the genital organs; hair-cutting is thus a symbolic 'castration'. For the Kuranko, the plaiting, unplaiting, cutting and washing of the head hair are means of symbolically identifying the neophytes in terms of the distinctions between noninitiate-neophyte-initiate, and male-female. The purification process thus implies a public ordering of social categories; the genital operations involve a less public process of differentiating male and female characteristics. But circumcision is not regarded as a kind of 'castration', nor is the prepuce considered to be a 'feminine part' (see Leach 1967).

26. The performances of the *Gbansogoron* masters are noteworthy here.

27. The deadpan expressions, the covered mouths and the averted gaze of the *Tatatie, Sewulan* and *Yefera Kundi* performers exemplify these principles.

28. In my analysis of Kuranko sacrifice I have suggested that God is invoked in sacrifices involving persons from several different descent groups because God (unlike the ancestors) is a symbol of community, transcending particular kinship and descent-group alignments and identifications (Jackson 1977a).

29. Turner 1970:96.

30. This idea is discussed in detail in my paper: *Dogmas and Fictions of Birth-Order Position* (Jackson 1977b).

31. The separation of the son from his mother is most important. Whiting's argument that male initiation rites are a consequence of sex identity conflicts engendered in infancy and early childhood (Whiting 1961, 1962) may have value in understanding Kuranko initiation (cf. Koch's application of Whiting's hypotheses to Jalé initiation, 1974). But

Whiting's explanation has less value when we consider girls' initiation among the Kuranko. A girl never sleeps with her father, her principle identification is with her mother, and initiation is concerned with managing her separation from her mother so that she can become a mother in her own right. Young's emphasis on male and female solidarity is of value in understanding the manner in which *biriye* serves to shift the initiate's identification from the context of the natal group to the context of the wider community (Young 1962).

32. Gluckman 1970: chapter 5.

33. Cf. Turner 1970:105-6.

34. Of female initiation among the Kissi, Denise Paulme writes:
'During the retreat no instruction is given and no mystery revealed: but the women taking part in it absorb, from talking among themselves, a much clearer idea of their importance as women, as opposed to the male element in society. Women are the 'guardians of life', for to them alone belong the secrets of birth: 'men'—so runs the conviction, more or less clearly formulated, which they bring away with them from their stay in the bush—"cannot do without us" ' (Paulme 1948:44).

35. Cf. Bateson's explanation of transvestism in the *naven* of the Iatmul:
'The ethos of women . . . has been built up around certain types of situation and that of men around very different situations. The result is that women, placed by culture in a situation which is unusual for them but which is usual for men, have contrived a transvestite costume, and this costume has been accepted by the community as appropriate to these abnormal situations' (1958:200).

36. Turner 1970:264-265.

37. Turner 1970:265.

38. Cf. Bettelheim who argues that 'Initiation rites, including circumcision, should be viewed within the context of fertility rites . . .' because they occur at puberty, the age when procreation becomes possible, and because fertility 'is the foundation of social survival' (1954:105).

12. Cult Associations

'. . . The cult groups are too fleeting and shifting in composition to develop internal stresses and divisions. It is, I suggest, because the organizational principles which govern the secular structure are contradictory and produce perennial conflicts between persons and groups, that rituals are constantly being performed by unitary though transitory associations, and that these rituals stress common values over and above the clash of sectional interests.'

—Victor Turner (1972: xxi)

In Sierra Leone, the term 'secret society' is widely used to refer to various indigenous cult associations whose structure and functions are often comparable from one tribal group to another.[1] Among the Kuranko, there are numerous recreational or festival groups (such as those described in the previous chapter) as well as cooperative associations (*kere*) which are not 'secret' societies; membership of these groups is restricted but the group activity and ceremonial is carried out in public. These work and entertainment groups may be compared with the Bambara and Malinke *ton* (or *to*)[2], though the Kuranko do not employ any general term to describe such groups. In Kuranko, *ton* is synonymous with *seria* and means 'rule' or 'law'; thus chiefs are often referred to as the *tontigi* or *seriatigi* ('law owners'). Secret societies are known as *sumafen* (sing. *sumafan*), a word which means literally 'secret things'. The cult association is thus defined by and named after the cult object and *sacra* which only adepts of the cult are permitted to see. Cult activity and ceremonial are *duworon* ('private/secret/hidden/covert') by contrast with the activities of the work and entertainment groups which are *kenema* ('public/open'). Some groups, such as the hunters' association (*dunse* or *donse*) or the *gbansogoron* ('the cheek-piercers'), practice 'secret' ceremonials and employ 'secret' medicines (*besekoli*) or incantations (*haye*), but, like the blacksmiths (*numunake* or *nume*), many of their activities take place in public. The cult objects or *sumafen* are usually embodiments of or give the 'master' (*tigi*) of the cult access to the powers of a particular bush spirit. The power of the cult association thus derives from a kind of alliance, mediated by the master of the cult, between man and the spirits of the wild. These powers are contrasted with the secular powers of chiefs.[3] But, like the various work, entertainment, recreational and professional associations (the *jelis* and *finas* excluded), membership of the cult groups is not based on birth or adoption into a kinship unit.[4] Moreover, the manipulation of external powers through the use of sacred objects, medicines and verbal formulae characterises all these groups. In every case, but especially

219

with the cult associations themselves, the members are bound together by a pact of secrecy; 'nothing which takes place in the context of an association meeting should be repeated outside it.'[5]

One of the objectives of my field research was to understand the role and significance of the cult associations in Kuranko society. But this endeavour was, predictability, frustrated. It became apparent to me that an avowed interest in the Kuranko cults would inevitably confirm Kuranko suspicions that I, like other Europeans, was determined to steal tribal secrets. Even when certain Kuranko friends and informants acknowledged my academic disinterestedness I felt that it would be wrong to urge them to divulge cult secrets or privileged information to me. And when approached by the occasional eccentric who promised to supply me details of cult ceremonial, I refused the offer lest it compromise the trust of friends. From a more mercenary point of view, it would have been unethical to publish accounts of cult secrets. The descriptive material in this chapter is consequently superficial and limited, partly because no esoteric data are presented and partly because many of the cult associations are today on the decline. My concern here is with discussing the structure and functions of the cult associations and elucidating the principles around which they are organised.

It will be already evident that the idea of secrecy is of immense importance in Kuranko social life. The ability to keep secrets (*ka sumafen kwe mara*) is perhaps the most profound expression of the virtues of loyalty, solidarity, and trust. With one's initiation mates and contemporaries (*bonu*) one is open, with others one is guarded.[6] Men should be open in their dealings with one another, guarded in their dealings with women.[7] In this way, the category distinction between elder and younger (of the same sex) is subsumed by a more general category distinction between men and women. In both cases the Kuranko speak of this distinction in terms of 'respect' (*gbiliye*), 'distance' or 'darkness'.

I once asked the Firawa *Komotigi* ('Master of the *Komo* cult association') what the 'work' of the cult was. In reply he said: 'That is a good question, I'm glad you asked me that. The work of the cults (*sumafen*) is to maintain the distance between men and women. If the women see the men's *korte* (an "arrow medicine") then the men may use it against them; therefore they will avoid seeing it. And women also have their ways of protecting themselves. They can give a man elephantiasis of the testicles (*kee*) through the power of their *sumafen*. Therefore, men and women live in fear of each other and respect each other.'

I then asked why the sexes should be kept apart. The *Komotigi* expressed amusement at the naivity of my question. 'Because God made them different; because, if a man goes near a house where a woman is giving birth to a child then he will die at once.' This kind of comment is typical. Another informant said that the 'work' of the cult associations was 'to keep men and women separate, to make them respect each other; the women cannot understand the men's cults and the men cannot understand the women's cults, therefore a darkness exists between them which maintains the mutual respect between womanhood and manhood.' Some informants confessed that within the cult 'there isn't really very much, though for the women it is awesome.' The secret objects themselves are far less significant than the principle of secrecy and the mystical powers which they symbolise. The betrayal of cult secrets leads not only to the punishment of the offender (by the cult adepts), it also threatens the social order. For, 'if women have no respect for men then the principles of manhood will be as nothing.'

The cult associations are primarily community groups, but a member of a particular cult may attend meetings of the same cult in other villages or chiefdoms if he is invited. Unlike Lodges, the cult associations do not have cells or chapters, but a common charter or constitution does unite groups of the same cult from different localities. Membership is always restricted and as we noted in the previous chapter, rights to membership are acquired by undergoing the initiatory ordeals. Induction into a cult also involves the payment of a fee, passing certain tests, and taking oaths of secrecy. Membership is limited to initiates only in some cases, to men only or women only in other cases, and the exclusiveness of the cults confirms the major social category distinctions in Kuranko society: elder/younger, male/female, initiated/uninitiated. Since the cults are hierarchically structured, a person is first initiated into the lowest or junior grade and is subsequently initiated into higher grades until, finally, he or she may become a leader or master (*tigi*) of the cult.[8] But the attainment of such positions depends upon a person's ability to command special powers. When the Kuranko refer to a person with the phrase '*ke ro kolo ma*' ('this person is not empty'), they mean that he possesses abilities and talents which are extraordinary. The person may be exceptionally clever (*hankili* or '*a kunye faan dun*', literally 'his head is full'), or he may possess some inner vitality (*miran*) which gives him commanding presence, dignity or bearing, or he may have a bush spirit (*nyenne*) working for him as an ally. The ability to have access to and employ the powers of a bush spirit are perhaps most important in the context of cult leadership.

The ability of a cult leader to mediate mystical powers which are external to the secular domain (and therefore regarded as dangerous and ambiguous), together with the fact that a cult leader achieves his position by virtue of exceptional personal ability, mean that the cult system and the secular system of chieftaincy are characterised in quite different ways. The authority and power of a chief are sanctioned by genealogy. By contrast, the authority and power of cult leaders are based upon their ability to attain command over forces which are marginal to the secular domain, namely the spirits of the wild. We can express this diagrammatically as follows:

```
                                                              T
                    Ruling lineage
                                                              I

                                                              M
                       Chief
                                                              E
Bush spirits           Cult leaders

            S    P    A    C    E
```

The social significance of these complementary sectors of authority is considerable. It has been attested that the frailty of chiefly authority originates in a discrepancy or conflict between the ideals of leadership (the social role) and the weakness of the leader (temperament or personality).[9] In the rituals associated with divine kingship we see abundant evidence of devices which mankind has employed in order to make the office of kingship uncorruptible, infallible, transcendent. Among the Kuranko the institution of divine kingship is absent, but some of its principles are present. The discrepancy between personal ambition and public duty, responsibility to protect subjects and inability to do so, the conflict between partisan interests and community commitments . . . these are instances of the problem. First Kuranko chiefs are dependent upon ritual experts for the medicines which both protect them personally and protect the country as a whole. Second, Kuranko chiefs must act in concert with the elders of the community when settling legal disputes. Third, Kuranko chiefs are dependent upon the *jelis* and *finas* whose knowledge of chiefly traditions and genealogies is indispensable. But the resolution of the problem also assumes a more abstract character. Inasmuch as the cult leaders transcend secular authority and derive their powers from outside the secular domain, they embody and exemplify the abstract principles which underlie authority *per se*. In the past, new laws or decrees had to be debated publically in the council of elders (i.e. before the people— *nyama*, literally 'a gathering/crowd/audience') and the *Kome* cult also had to be consulted before such new laws were approved. It is, however, difficult to ascertain to what extent the cults acted to check abuses of chiefly power.

The validation of secular authority would seem to depend upon beliefs which made that authority appear to be a manifestation of extra-social agencies. In some societies the king is divine, in others he is associated and identified with forces which both give him power and prevent him from abusing it. Among other societies the secular authority of chiefs is complemented by the mystical authority of ritual experts or religious officials. Unlike the Temne and Mende, where chiefs were often closely and directly associated with *Poro*, the Kuranko *Kome* cult seems to have always defined itself apart from secular authority.[10] In this sense, the Kuranko *Kome* is comparable to the Bambara *Komo*. Tauxier notes that 'le Komo est principalement un organisme destiné à faire meilleur, plus prompte et plus efficace justice que ne pourrait le faire le chef du village, le dougoutigui, agissant en plein jour avec ses pouvoirs publics.'[11] One of the *Komo* cult songs expresses this opposition between what Tauxier calls 'Sacerdoce et de l'Empire': 'Le chef du village commande le village, mais qu'il ne laisse pas cependant sous fils se disputer avec le Komo!' Tauxier comments, 'Ceci c'est l'affirmation de l'indépendance et même de la superiorité du pouvoir spirituel sur le pouvoir temporel.'[12] In a small-scale community justice must be meted out disinterestedly lest through partiality or nepotism, it seem unfair, and so precipitate further conflict. By settling many issues (mendacity, theft, adultery, illegitimate use of sorcery) out of court with the judges masked and the trial secret, the *Komo* cult among the Bambara arrogates some of the legal powers of chiefs. When judgements are made and punishments carried out, the cult announces that it is *Komo* who has killed, not a person[13]. Among the Kuranko the legal powers of the *Kome* cult are more limited and they apply only when a member of the cult breaks one of the rules or oaths of the association. But the powers of *Kome* are formidable, greater than the powers of ordinary bush spirits (*nyenne*) and greater than the powers which chiefs command. The incomparable powers of *Kome* are vaunted in one of the cult songs: '*Sembe, sembe, sembe li, Kome la eh Kome wo, n'de min i li nyonto ken yen*' ('Extraordinary power/strength has *Kome*, eh *Kome*, I have not and you have not seen the like/equal of him').

Children's Associations

From a very early age, Kuranko children are told about the bush spirits. Various *nyenne* figure prominently in folktales told to children and I have often overheard parents admonishing a grizzling or ill-tempered child with the words, 'Stop, a *tutu* is coming'. The *tutu*, *tutuwe* ('the big *tutu*'), or *tutufingbe* ('the black white *tutu*') as this *nyenne* is variously called, is a cannabalistic 'bogey-man' which adults admit is imaginary, but which young children often fear as real.[14] It is no exaggeration to say that the *nyenne* dominate the imaginative life of children, holding the same fascination as fairies, ogres, hobgoblins, ghosts and witches hold for European children.[15] I have, on many occasions, observed groups of small children drawing with sticks in the dust of a village path, sketching the bizarre outlines of some bush spirit and gleefully pretending that they have seen it or heard it. And I have watched children dancing long into the dry season nights, ceaselessly chanting the names of certain bush spirits and, in their play, imitating what they believe to be the ritual actions of the cult masters.

Nowadays, children delight in making toy trucks or aeroplanes; such mystifying and powerful artefacts of the European world may have, for them, the same symbolic value as the *nyenne*. These are symbols of the world beyond the parental, domestic or village worlds. Through manipulating or making contact with these 'foreign' objects or powers, a person can transcend the circumstances of his birth and of his ordinary social world. The Europeans are both compared with the *nyenne* and are said to derive their inventive powers from alliances with the *nyenne*. Association with the European world is regarded as being just as risky as alliance with a *nyenne*. Both domains are outside complete Kuranko control and understanding, yet the forces associated with these domains allow a person to contemplate, at least, rising above the ordinary and inflexible conditions of his lot.[16]

There are two main childhood associations: *Gbongbokode* and *Tulbare*. Both are basically semi-formal play-groups for uninitiated boys. As soon as small boys are 'capable of keeping secrets' (age 8-10) they may join the *Gbongbokode* association. New recruits are led blindfold from the village to a place in the bush where they must run the gauntlet between lines of older boys. The boys learn secret signs and code words and they meet in secret from time to time to initiate new members. Sometimes the boys parade through the village singing a warning song: 'Whoever betrays the secrets of *Gbongbokode* will suffer the penalty'. Because these parades are generally held at night, when women and children are indoors anyway, the dread which the association should inspire is more theatrical than real. But such parades and clandestine activities anticipate the more dramatic activities of the cult associations which the boys are destined to join in early adulthood. The cabalistic atmosphere, the code of secrecy, the mastery of a secret object (*Gbongbokode*), the solidarity of the age-group, the submission to ordeals and to the authority of the group leaders serve to prepare the boys for the more demanding disciplines of the cult associations which they will join later in life.

At about 10 years of age, boys join a second childhood association called *Tulbare*. The boys meet from time to time and go out together to raid farms or gardens, stealing groundnuts, bananas and cassava. This theft is tolerated by adults who often pretend to be overawed by the audacity and guile of the boys. Occasionally the *Tulbare* boys 'invade' the village at night. They take the women's mortars from house compounds and then pile them on top of each other to make a tall column. This is regarded as an innocent way of frightening the women, a sign of the growing powers of the boys. In another activity, the boys tie thread to the thatched cones that surmount house roofs and then interlink several houses in the village with long strands of thread. It is said that this 'shows how powerful the group is, by putting things up high'. But for the boys it is also an occasion for shared daring and devilry. One could suggest that when the boys bind the houses together or stack the mortars ('stolen' from several households) on top of each other, they are symbolically confirming their common identity as an age-group, an identity which cuts across household or descent-group lines. What is quite evident, however, is that these escapades bolster the solidarity of the age-group and throw into relief the exclusiveness of male and female domains. In this way, the *Tulbare* association gives form to the less disciplined play-groups of children, forcing recreational groups (randomly recruited and comprising both sexes and children of all ages) into the mould of social structure (recruitment formalised, the sexes separated, and age becoming a criterion of membership). Adult men do not participate in the activities of these associations, but they encourage boys to join them. As one informant observed, 'Once you are a member of *Tulbare* or *Gbongbokode* you remain a member for life, just as when you go to school you remain a member of all the classes that you were initiated into even when you cease attending them.'

Gbongbokode and *Tulbare* are both voluntary associations, but few boys wish not to join. Isolation from the group ('sitting alone' or 'sitting with women') is considered to be as bad as being ostracised from the group. Like the *Tatatie* and the *Forubandi binye* groups which perform during initiations, these childhood groups are characterised by a strong play element. They prefigure the adult cult associations whose adepts acquire the knowledge of powerful medicines (*besekoli*) and make contact with powerful extra-social forces. In the play-groups, the boys imitate and anticipate the activities of these associations whose general purpose is the maintenance of social and self control.

Kome

A boy can join this cult association in the year preceding his initiation, that is, when he is still a *bilakore*.[17] The association is widely known throughout the Mande-speaking area (usually as *Komo*). Among the Kuranko, *Kome* is the name of a powerful and dangerous bush spirit. The activities of the cult centre around the use of the powerful *korte* and anti-*korte* medicines.[18] Three kinds of medicines are distinguished. First, *korte* itself—a kind of 'arrow medicine' or 'missile' which can kill a victim within ten minutes. The symptoms of *korte*-poisoning are severe nose-bleeding, trembling and convulsions of the body. Even more potent is *senekorte* (*sene*: 'gold'), but this is rarely made today. The second kind of medicine is called *koli*—it is made up of sharp objects which penetrate the victim's foot when he 'steps' on the place where it has been placed. The symptoms of *koli*-poisoning are comparable to those of septicaemia. The third class of medicines includes *nyenkofuri*; this is a kind of 'itching powder' which is scattered to the wind and so carried to the victim. The symptoms of *nyenkofuri*-poisoning are severe skin-irritation and scabies; it is said to cause death within 12-14 hours. These powerful medicines (*besekoli*) are divided into two categories: those which penetrate the body as missiles, and those which are thrown onto the body as irritants. The antidote for all these medicines is called *yobe* and, after initiation into the *Kome* cult, a man is instructed in its uses. It is considered imperative that a man take precautions against other people using various *besekoli* in indiscriminate or malicious ways. As a dispenser and controller of these medicines and antidotes, the *Kometigi* enjoys considerable prestige in the community. Even chiefs must obtain protective medicines from him. And today, most Kuranko men still 'wash' themselves with *yobe* as a defence against sorcery.

Apart from learning how to use *besekoli*, members of the *Kome* cult make contact with or 'see' *Kome*. Certain magical verses (*haye*) and songs enable the adepts to conjure the bush spirit.[19] It is openly acknowledged that the punishment for divulging any of these cult secrets is death. The protective powers of *Kome* are called upon during initiations when the neophytes are thought to be particularly vulnerable to witchcraft attack. But a man may seek the protection of *Kome* at any time when he feels threatened by enemies, sorcerers or witches.[20]

Saran Salia Sano was the *Kometigi* at Firawa and his house was almost always occupied by several small boys whose parents had sent them to him for protection against witchcraft. Saran Salia had been orphaned when he was still a child. He was sent to Guinea to be apprenticed to a famous medicine-master (*besetigi*). Twenty-two years later he returned to Firawa where he has since built up a considerable reputation as a *besetigi*. His unique knowledge of medicines has also enabled him to rise to the position of *Kometigi*. But, as he once told me, his professional commitments have prevented him from marrying and he has also been obliged to renounce his Muslim heritage. His paternalistic attitude to the boys of Firawa is widely admired. Many of the boys who live with him are parentless; some are apprenticed to him. And whenever an altercation arose among a group of *bilakorenu*, he would always be there to intervene and settle the dispute. It is this protective and paternalistic role which he emphasises. Although he acquired knowledge of harmful medicines during his own apprenticeship, he disdains the use of that knowledge. He regards his primary responsibility to be a curer and preventer of illness (*kiraiye*). Techniques of bone-setting, the use of herbal remedies, and the dispensing of antidotes to sickness caused by sorcery constitute the most important part of his practice.[21]

Among the Bambara and Malinke, the *Komotigi* administers a fund which is made up from seasonal contributions, offerings and fines 'paid in' by members.[22] It is possible for any member to borrow from this fund when in need, although the debt binds the borrower to *Komo* in a rather ominous pact: if the debt is not discharged within a given period, then the defaulter may be poisoned. I found no evidence of this practice among the Kuranko. But cult members can 'beg' (*tarle*) assistance from *Kome*. The petitioner offers a chicken to *Kome* by throwing it onto the ground at *Kome's* feet. If it dies, it signifies that *Kome* agrees to assist the suppliant. If it does not die, then *Kome* has refused the request. Kola could be offered in a similar manner: if the two cotyledons of the kola come up 'even' then *Kome* agrees to the request, if they come up 'odd' then *Kome* refuses. These ways of approaching *Kome* for assistance are, however, used only when a person seeks *Kome's* protection against sorcerers or enemies (*morgofian*, literally 'people black'). It is a common reliance upon the cult medicines for protection (*kandan*) that binds the members of the cult together. All members are said to be 'as one' (*morgo keli*, literally 'person one') in relation to the superior powers of *Kome*. As one man expressed it, '*Kome* is feared above all else; you can never abuse/joke with (*tolon*) *Kome;* the powers of *Kome* are beyond our understanding'.

Complete subordination to *Kome* is required of the cult members. The most unforgiveable kinds of insubordination are betrayal of cult secrets and boasting. Boastfulness (*yunke*) implies that a person has powers and abilities equal to those possessed by *Kome*, that he is either immune to the *Kome* medicines or has medicines which are even more powerful than those of *Kome*. Betrayal of cult secrets is even more reprehensible, for the secrets may be passed on to women or enemies. The exclusiveness of cult membership is stressed by the Kuranko. The *Kome* cult serves to reinforce the principles of social structure in two ways: it maintains a strict separation between male and female domains, and it effects a firm division between superordinate and subordinate roles. In the context of the cult, these category distinctions are cermonialised. The masquerades[23] and ceremonies of the cult enable members to transcend idiosyncratic or personality differences and to define their solidarity in terms that eclipse kinship, affinal and descent-group identifications. Significantly, the cult always meets out of town, in a 'secret' bush house known as the *Komebon*. Mystical association with the bush spirit, *Kome*, indicates still further that it is only by stepping outside the confines of the ordinary social world that the Kuranko can overcome the divisions and influences that tend to contradict the ideal principles of their social order.

Sometimes the *Kome* cult does in fact enter the village and give public performances. The levity and licence which characterise these occasions are in complete contrast with the serious mood of activities in the *Komebon*. It may be that by associating with the village world the cult is dissociated from the source of its power (which lies beyond the village) and thus relinquishes momentarily its authority. Among the Bambara, when *Komo* performs for amusement (publically and within the village), normal codes of conduct are reversed. *Komo* insults the mothers of cult members, remarking their lustful proclivities, criticising them for not being virgins. In turn, the cult members insult the mother of *Komo;* *Komo* then replies that he will disregard the insults on this occasion because it is only in jest.[24] The Kuranko *Kome* cult also performs on certain occasions for amusement only. As *Kome* approaches the village, some of the cult members begin to sing one of the cult songs. *Bilakorenu* who have been recently inducted into the cult respond in chorus to the song, but from the village. Women may hear the songs and commit them to memory. It is said that they sometimes sing *Kome* songs when working on the farm, but never in the presence of men. On these occasions, it is common for members of *Kome* cult associations in other villages to participate in the festivities. Evidently, it is important that the powers of *Kome* be demonstrated periodically in the presence of those who do not belong to the cult. The sanctioning powers of *Kome* seem to require the maintenance of a subtle balance between accessibility and inaccessibility, nearness and distance, exclusiveness and inclusiveness. A glimpse caught, a song overheard . . . these inspire a greater sense of mystery and awe than would be the case if the cult remained utterly inscrutable.

Konke *and* Gbangbe

When the male initiates leave the *fafei* at the conclusion of *biriye* they are entitled to join the *Konke* cult association. The *Konketigi* ('master/owner/bearer of *Konke*') lives with the initiates during their period of seclusion in the *fafei*. His responsibility is to prevent women or witches approaching the site and he also 'steps' and raises the long heavy pole (*lumbon*) that stands at the centre of the *fafei*.

I was told that should any uninitiated boy see *Konke* then he would be seized and forcibly circumcised. Apparently some boys use this as a way of getting circumcised when they have reached adolescence and their fathers have proved reluctant to have them initiated.

Activities associated with the cult are generally concerned with trials of strength such as weightlifting, but the major occupation of the cult is hammock-bridge construction. This requires secret techniques and engineering skills which are considered fit for only men to know about. Kuranko hammock-bridges are built at the beginning of every rainy season to span the large rivers, such as the Bagbe and Seli, which cross Kuranko country. The bridges are impressive structures and their construction involves a large number of men and takes several weeks. It can be difficult and dangerous work, and it is not surprising that it should have become the focus of ceremonial activity, expressive of the superior powers of men and the values of cooperation. Moreover, like most social, economic and recreational activities which are carried out in the bush (*fera*), bush spirits must be appeased or conjured as allies if the activities are to be successful.[25]

Also after initiation, young men are introduced to the first stages of knowledge of the men's witch-finding cult: *Gbangbe* or *Kuruwe*.[26] The *Gbangbe* cult is perhaps the most dramatic expression of those social attitudes which prescribe exclusive domains for men and women. In the *Gbangbe* cult a man acquires anti-witchcraft medicines (*sase*) and is introduced to the secret objects and techniques with which cult leaders can disarm witches and nullify the powers of witchcraft. Witchcraft is always associated with nefarious and uncontrolled female influence, and it is through the periodic purgings of *Gbangbe* that the male social order defends itself against such inimical forces.[27] The master of the cult, the *Gbangbane*, is always a man of extraordinary power, usually accredited with having 'four eyes' (*ya nani*) or 'second sight'. This enables him to 'see' in the dark and to penetrate the walls of houses with his gaze, so locating the hidden armouries of witches. No one knows exactly how he robs witches of their secret powers, but the terror which the cult inspires when it 'comes out' is considerable. The cult is 'called out' when it is suspected that deaths or illnesses in the community have been caused by witchcraft. The approach of *Gbangbe* is signalled by a man who passes around the village, knocking a piece of wood with a small baton. Immediately, women and children retire indoors. Then the cult members circulate among the houses during the night, the *Gbangbane* chanting muffled incantations into a medicine horn.

Due

Kome and *Gbangbe* are the two most important male cult associations. Both cults are regarded with awe and respect, although *Gbangbe* is distinguished from *Kome* in terms of its greater secretiveness and seriousness. While *Kome* sometimes performs publically for entertainment, *Gbangbe* never does. The Kuranko often remark on a man's grave or inscrutable character by using the phrase, '*i tura i yusu ma i ko gbangbane* (or *gbangbe*)' ('you are always deadly serious like *gbangbane*'), implying that the person never jokes or relaxes his guard.

The male cult association—*Due* (or *Doe*)—is, by contrast, a more informal group. In the words of Keti Ferenke Koroma (the leader of the *Due* association at Kondembaia), the *Due* is 'simply an association of clever people'. Although uninitiated men cannot join (they cannot be trusted to keep the *Due* secrets), very old women who are past childbearing age may become members.

The leader of the cult is called the *Dobe* or *Doka' morgo* (literally '*do* teacher'), and the members are known as *Dodannu* ('*Doe* children'). *Dobe* can be roughly translated as *Doe* mother, on an analogy which the Kuranko draw with *Sisibe* ('brooding hen') and *Sisidannu* ('the chickens which are hatched'). A special *do* language is learned and used; it is completely incomprehensible to the uninitiated and it enables members of the cult to communicate in public when they do not want others to know what they are talking about. Code words, special forms of greeting and special handshakes also form part of the cabalistic lore of the cult. Members acquire, moreover, knowledge of various mind-reading techniques and verbal tricks for interrogating strangers; this knowledge permits *Doe* adepts to divine the hidden thoughts of others. I was told that this knowledge was very important during warfare when it was imperative to ascertain whether a stranger was a spy or not.

The exclusiveness of the cult is also strengthened by the members' knowledge of various wire puzzles and riddles. When I first expressed an interest in the cult, Keti Ferenke asked me several riddles. For example, to the question 'How many people are there in the world?' one must give the answer 'Two' and explain that they are 'Man and woman'. To the question 'How many steps does a person take in a single day?' one must reply 'Two', for there are only two steps: one with the right foot and one with the left foot.

Keti Ferenke also elaborated upon the notion of cleverness (*hankili*). He used the analogy of a container full of liquid. An ordinary person's common sense or intelligence 'fills the container to the brim'. A dull-witted person 'fills the container half-way'; he is described as *hankili mama*, as 'empty in the head' (*kun' to kolon*) or as being 'half clever, half stupid' (*hankili mama yua fa na ma*). An exceptionally gifted person 'fills the container to overflowing' (*hankili me*); his 'head is full' (*a kunye faan dun*). Keti Ferenke's extraordinary and renowned talents as a story-teller (*tile sale*, literally 'one who puts down or lays down stories') make him, in the opinion of the community, a very clever person *(hankili me)*. As the 'mother' of the *Doe* cult, he gains even greater prestige. However, the genius or power which the *Kometigi* or *Gbangbane* possesses is of a different kind. The phrase, *'ke ro kolo ma'* ('this person or thing is not empty') implies the possession of potentially dangerous powers such as sorcerers and bush spirits have; alternatively it may imply the power inherent in certain medicines or magical properties.

The problem which cult organisation serves to resolve is one which pervades Kuranko thought: how is it possible to make exceptional and individual powers serve a collective purpose? Phrased another way, how is it possible to systematise and exploit contingent or randomly-distributed powers, talents and capabilities?[28] By assigning exceptional persons an approved social role as leaders of a cult association, it is possible to go some way towards the solution of this problem. The institutionalisation of 'marginal' roles inhibits 'marginal' individuals from threatening the system of values and norms. The cults transform potentially negative and inimical forces (symbolised by the bush spirits) into socially-beneficial powers. Dangerous medicines are hedged around by strict rules prescribing their proper use. The secrecy with which they are guarded and the penalties which exist to deter individuals from using them for private gain or vendetta, reinforce these rules. The cults resolve the conflict between unrestrained personal power and social control by making the former serve the latter. Thus, clandestine affairs are considered to be socially negative.[29] yet the principle of secrecy is transformed into a positive force for social control within the context of cult organisation. Medicines may be acquired that empower a person to kill or injure others for personal reasons (envy, hate, spite, jealousy), but within the cults these medicines are used for collectively-approved purposes only.[30] They serve as potent sanctions for maintaining the category distinctions between male and female, elder and younger, insider and outsider. A common fault of secular authority is the discrepancy between personal weakness and the demands of the role. In the cults, this fault is corrected, for the *principle* of authority is made to transcend the domain of its ordinary practice.

Individual power does not, however, always find its outlet in socially-beneficial forms. In the first case, cult leaders themselves sometimes misuse their powers. The young man who died of a curse *(danka)* in Sukurela (details of the case are given in chapter 6) was in fact the *Kometigi*. Here the interest in this case lies in the fact that the cursed man considered that his powers as *Kometigi* exempted him from certain conventional responsibilities (he ignored a court injunction) and made him invulnerable to mystical attack. To break these powers the man's girl-friend's father-in-law journeyed beyond the chiefdom and sought the aid of one of the most renowned and powerful medicine-owners in the *ferensola*. It is of only marginal significance that the onset of the man's illness (encephalitis) coincided with the curse; it is of more value to note that there is, in the Kuranko view, always a higher authority whose powers are largely inaccessible to man. The Kuranko speak of God *(Ala* or *Altala)* as the ultimate and omnicient authority, although in particular contexts this kind of external constraint may be said to have its immediate source elsewhere: in the ancestors, the bush spirits, the elders or the chief. In the ascending and expanding frame of supernatural reference which the Kuranko employ, authority and power are always relative. The crime of the cursed man in the case which I have alluded to was that he acted as if his authority was absolute. He acted in terms of personal interests rather than in conformity with group necessities and values.

The second category of gifted individuals whose talents are regarded ambivalently includes a number of ritual experts who, unlike the cult leaders, act alone. I have already made a passing reference to the mori-men, and I have published elsewhere details of the Kuranko beliefs concerning persons who can transform themselves into certain wild animals *(yelamafentiginu,* literally 'change-thing masters', i.e. shape-shifters).[31] Other similar experts include the 'rain-catcher' *(bande brale)* and the 'thunder master' *(sangbalmatigi)*. All these persons 'own' certain medicines and incantations and have non-inherited gifts which enable them to harm or protect people. From a mori-man one can purchase medicines, fetishes or *haye* which can be used either for personal protection or for harming others. The 'thunder masters' can use their powers either to command respect or to kill people and livestock. The great Barawa chief, Belikoro, possessed this power and used it to bolster his chiefly position. One man told me that 'In those days, when many powerful Paramount chiefs were in their heyday, meetings would sometimes be called in Kabala. Then the chiefs would demonstrate their powers. Belikoro would use the thunder to great effect and all the other chiefs feared and respected him. As he approached Kabala he would make the thunder crack and the lightning flash[32] and, seeing this, people would say "the Barawa chief has come". Wherever he went, people would bring gifts for him, such as a cow, lest he use the thunder and lightning to kill their cows'. The powers of the *bande brale* are similarly ambivalent. If a farmer wants the rain to stop so that he can burn off or hoe his farm, he may enlist the services of the 'rain catcher' who can 'wash' leaves through the air and so cause the rain clouds to move away from that area. But if a farmer wants to disrupt another man's farmwork, then he could ask the 'rain catcher' to call rain down on that man's farm. In the case of the *yelamafentiginu*, there are some who use their shape-shifting powers to ravage other people's farms or kill domestic livestock; others employ their powers within social structure. Thus, Mara who can transform themselves into their totem, the leopard *(kuli)*, can reinforce the awe and respect which should be shown to them as rulers.

Women's Cult Associations

The most important women's cult association is called *Segere*. The Kuranko sometimes compare it with the men's *Gbangbe* cult because it too has the power to locate and disarm witches. The main function of *Segere* is, however, to support and defend the rights and privileges of women. The women may 'take out' *Segere* on the following occasions: if men invade the privacy of the women's part of the stream, if a man trespasses in the vicinity of a house where a woman is giving birth, if men infringe the women's rights to privacy during *dimusu biriye*. As we noted in chapter 5, these kinds of actions signify a blatant disregard for the boundaries between the male domain *(ke dugu)* and the female domain *(musu dugu)*. Sometimes *Segere* is summoned when the community as a whole is afflicted by misfortune: when stealing is rife, in times of serious epidemics, when witches are active. During the 1971 farm season at Kamadugu Sukurela, continual rain made burning impossible after brushing had been completed. The *bande brale* tried, without success, to stop the rain. The men's cults also failed. Finally, the men asked the women to 'take out' *Segere*. *Segere* managed to bring the rains to an end and burning became possible on the farms.

There are no childhood associations for girls and there is no organisation among the Kuranko comparable to the Malinke *fla-nse*.[33] Several female groups perform during initiations; some, like the *Tatatie*, are always children's groups, others, like *Kamban* and *Sewulan*, are restricted to initiated women. But the purpose of all these various groups, which have both disciplinary and recreational functions, is said to be 'to keep distance and respect between the sexes'. As with the male cults, the female cults 'own' secret objects *(sumafen)* which empower the cult leaders to injure or kill any man or non-initiate who disregards the privileges of women or 'insults womanhood'. Thus, *Segere* is sometimes called out to deal with men who have made obscene remarks about female sexuality in public. Whenever men speak of *Segere* it is with awe and reserve. Any derogatory or abusive reference to a women's cult may be answered by a frightful retribution, usually said to be some disease of the sexual organs which will lead to impotence and death. This belief may be an institutional elaboration of the personal power which women command, namely their ability to withold their sexual favours from men. If a man does not have children, then his lineage will die out *(ban)*. In the Kuranko view, to show disrespect to women is tantamount to inviting one's own destruction. If the boundaries between the sexes are confused or transgressed then this implies an irregularity in reciprocal relationships between men and women. The cults must then re-impose regularity and confirm the pattern of reciprocity and complementary roles by ritually segregating the sexes. This transformation of irregularity into regularity is effected by dramatic demonstrations of secret powers. In this way, the momentary *absence of sharing* serves to discriminate between the sexes they have been corrupted by *indiscriminate sharing*. In Kuranko thought, the worst vices of women (adultery, lust, gossip, witchcraft and treachery) are all united by a common theme, namely sharing indiscriminately or sharing with the wrong category of persons. Against these proclivities, the cults constitute one of the most important agencies for social control in the Kuranko community.

Secrecy, or restricted sharing, not only segregates certain categories of people (male-female, elder-younger), it binds together those who share a secret. Saran Salia Sano told me that the purpose of the secret things *(sumafen)* was 'to train people in the keeping of secrets, for when I share a secret with you, then we are bound together'. This idea of a pact or trust which binds people together at the same time as it separates them from others, is of tremendous importance in Kuranko social life and thought. In the cult associations these social distinctions are expressed terms of certain fundamental oppositions: restricted/elaborated codes, esoteric/common knowledge, sacred/profane objects, bush/village, night/day, restraint/familiarity. These symbolic oppositions make up a system of 'objective correlatives' through which the abstract principles of the Kuranko social order are made to transcend the context of ordinary social existence. It is the very marginality of the cults to ordinary or secular existence which gives them their meaning and force.

The role and mystique of the cults are today, however, diminishing in significance. Many Kuranko contemplate external or supernatural powers, less in terms of the ancestors and the bush spirits than in terms of the European world and the administrative system of the national government. For many Kuranko, schooling (which is often compared with the traditional hierarchical organisation of the cults) has become a kind of symbolic replacement for the cult system and for initiation ritual. Command over knowledge and scarce resources is seen as a function of literacy and the control of money. As the prestige and power of cult offices decline, and with the inevitable migration of young men away from their villages to attend school or earn wages in the diamond districts, the cults and the mystical forces which they embody (as medicines or as bush spirits) disappear.

Notes

1. They are also comparable, in some respects, with the Masonic lodges of the Creoles in Sierra Leone (see Cohen 1971 : 427-48).

2. 'The word *ton* can be used to describe any grouping of people, either permanent or temporary, for the achievement of common goals' (Imperator 1972:5). 'Roughly, a *to* is a group of people from the same village or neighbourhood, selected according to a common characteristic (age, belief, activity), who submit to a certain number of rules and organize themselves hierarchically' (Meillassoux 1968:49-50). These definitions also describe what, in the Kuranko case, I refer to as associations or cult associations.

3. Cf. the Mende *Poro*, 'In terms of their institutional personnel and apparatus of hereditary officials, masked spirits, rituals, etc., the secret societies are an embodiment of and a means of canalizing supernatural power . . . In the old days, it supplied the mystical quality of authority which is apparently lacking in the purely secular figure of the Mende chief . . . It is probable that individual chiefs, like Nyagua of Panguma, who held sway over a local hegemony of chiefdoms, owed most of their success to the use they were able to make of Poro organization. On the other hand, *the Poro could be an equally powerful check on rulers who attempt to usurp their position*' (Little 1961 : 199-200, 204, 205; my italics). Among the Temne, the office of the Paramount chief was also deeply involved in the cult system)Dorjahn 1960). But of the Limba, Ruth Finnegan notes that 'The "secret societies" do not seem to form an important check against the chief (1965 : 40).

4. Membership of some associations (hunters, blacksmiths) and professions (medicine-owners) was acquired through a lengthy apprenticeship; in other cases (e.g. the *gbansogoron*) membership was acquired through the payment of fees. Visions, dreams (sing. *chio*), or the gradual realisation of innate gifts all play their parts in a person's becoming a diviner *(bolomafelne)* or sorcerer *(besetigi* or *besebole)*; there are, however, no formal associations of diviners or sorcerers.

5. Ruel 1969 : 200.

6. Nevertheless, the *boya tolon* (joking relationship among contemporaries, especially those initiated in the same year) has ambivalent connotations. The Kuranko fully recognise the difficulty of keeping secrets, particularly personal secrets. Hence the saying, *bolo kunde mera kure koro nyaonya a si bo* ('however hard you try to keep a secret, one day it will be divulged'); the phrase means literally 'hand short, long clothes under, however, it will come out/appear'.

7. See chapter 5 for a fuller discussion of this attitude.

8. There is no formal age-set system among the Kuranko; nor is there any organisation which corresponds exactly with the Bambara *fla-bolo* (a group comprising all initiates of the same sex who were initiated in the same year).

9. See Gluckman 1970 : chapter 2.

10. See Little 1961 : 204-5.

11. Tauxier 1927 : 280.

12. Ibid. Among the Kuranko, one of the *Kometigi's* main functions is to protect the neophytes from witchcraft attack during *biriye* and to provide entertainment as part of initiation festivities. On these occasions, secular rulers are subject to the authority of the *Kometigi*; officially, the village is temporarily under his command.

13. See Tauxier 1927 : 279.

14. Parents often conjure up fearful images of the *nyenne* in order to curb a child's unruliness. The ancestors are never alluded to in this way. It may be suggested that the *nyenne* are, in such contexts, symbols of the ambivalence associated with parental authority; the cannabalistic attributes of the *tutu* may signify the devouring and coercive parental figure who inhibits the wilful desires of the child. Certainly, it is through making contact with and 'mastering' the *nyenne* that a child passes beyond the constraints of the kinship order and attains an identity independent of that given by the circumstances of his birth.

15. Details of the manner in which children learn and use stereotypes about witches are presented in my paper on Kuranko witchcraft beliefs (Jackson 1975).

16. The price a person may have to pay for allying themselves with a bush spirit is said to be possible insanity (*yuwaye*), barrenness, impotence, or the death of a child. Such alliances, when they occur outside the cult context, are always regarded as dangerous because a person will be subject to the caprice of the bush spirit.

17. Meillassoux translates the Bambara term *bila-koro* as 'wearer of drawers' (*bila*, drawers; *koro*, to wear). Imperator translates the same term as 'old cache sex' (*bila*, the cache sex worn by small boys; *koro*, elder) (Meillassoux 1968 : 50; Imperator 1972 : 4). The latter translation is correct for the Kuranko term *bilakore*, the term referring to boys who have almost attained the age for initiation (they are thus 'senior' than very young boys).

18. *Korte* is always a men's medicine, classified under the general heading of medicines 'which shoot' *(ka bon)*. Poisons *(daberi)* are always associated with nefarious female activity. The curse *(danka)* and the power to curse *(ka gburu)* are not associated with one sex or the other, although the most powerful curses (*gborle fan*, literally 'curse thing') tend to be associated with male sorcerers. It is noteworthy that *korte* is known among the Gonja of Ghana, where it is associated with female witchcraft (Esther Goody 1970 : 237-9); it is also known among the Mende of Sierra Leone where it is called *kuete* (allegedly borrowed from the Kuranko) Harris and Sawyerr 1968 : 82).

19. Members of the hunters' 'society' also use special medicines and *haye* to enlist the support of certain bush spirits, e.g. *Komokunde* ('the short/dwarf *Komo*') who is renowned for his strength, and *Sogorei* or *Kayan* who helps

the hunters sight the game animals. It is said that *Sogorei* can kill a cow by mystically sucking away its blood. If a cow is dying as a result of such an attack, its throat is cut to prevent its death being entirely a consequence of *Sogorei's* influence.

20. Sorcerers *(besetiginu)* are divided into three categories: those concerned with therapeutic and preventative medicine, those concerned with contagious magic and harmful medicines, and those concerned with techniques of cursing. For a more complete account of witchcraft and sorcery among the Kuranko see Jackson 1975.

21. Saran Salia also mentioned that he was able to cure a disease that is contracted when an uninitiated boy or a woman accidentally 'sees' *Konke*. The disease is probably yaws (Framboesia).

22. See Tauxier 1927 : 280-1; Labouret 1934 : 89.

23. Carved masks are unknown among the Kuranko, but the cult masters may use other kinds of ceremonial apparel or disguises.

24. Tauxier 1927 : 286-9.

25. For example, farm sacrifices made to the *nyenne* (Jackson 1977a) and hunters' recruiting various bush spirits (see footnote 19).

26. The cult is comparable to the Limba *Gbangbani* association (see Finnegan 1965 : 77-8); Kuranko informants often claimed that the Limba cult was a borrowing from Kuranko. The term *Gbangbe* or *Gbangbane* is said to be onomatopoeic; it means literally 'jump jump' or 'knock knock' and refers to the way in which a man knocks two pieces of wood together as a signal that the 'devil' is about to come out.

27. For futher details of actual situations when *Gbangbe* was summoned see Jackson 1975.

28. I have discussed this problem elsewhere (Jackson 1977b).

29. Refer chapters 5 and 6.

30. The problem of restricting the illegitimate and private use of harmful medicines is exacerbated by the presence of Muslim medicine-makers in the community. Many of the *alphas* or mori-men act alone. From them a person may purchase medicines which he can use to injure or kill others. Many of the *morenu* are not Kuranko. Marginal to the community in both religious and tribal affiliation, they are often feared and blamed as the indirect agents for much sorcery; the uses and formulae of their medicines are not controlled by any Kuranko social group.

31. Jackson 1975.

32. Lightning is referred to by the phrase *saan a nyi ma sorgola* (literally 'the sky is showing its teeth').

33. Among the Malinke, 'Boys who have undergone circumcision and girls who have been excised during the same year belong to two parallel groups bearing the name, *fla-nse*, which are clubs whose members have a similar relationship as twins, *fula-ni* or *fla-ni*. They are called either by this term or by the phrase *de-nn' oro*: "children same": as proof of their unity and solidarity' (Labouret 1934 : 96).

13. Comparative and Theoretical Aspects

Dunia toge ma dunia; a toge le a dununia (The name of the world is not world; its name is load)
  —Kuranko proverb

The point of view which I have endeavoured to develop in this monograph study of the Kuranko world is epitomised by the Kuranko proverb which prefaces this final chapter. The proverb, like many other Kuranko sayings (*sarenu*), exploits oxymoron and pun; *dunia* ('world') and *dununia* ('load') are near homophones. In translating it my field assistant, Noah Marah, emphasised both its stoical connotations and the fact that the 'world' is largely arbitrary, provisional and problematic. 'The Kuranko think of the world as a load, and everything depends on how you carry it; the world is not what it is, it is what you make of it.'[1]

Throughout this study I have adopted implicitly the theoretical perspective of the sociology of knowledge. Its main tenet is that 'Society is constituted and maintained by acting human beings. It has no being, no reality, apart from this activity.'[2] I regard this point of view as parallel to Sartre's view of the personal life as 'constituting-constituted', as a synthetic unity of what we make out of what we are made.[3] I have worked with the basic assumption that man's 'ontological vocation' (to use a phrase of Paulo Freire's) is to be a Subject who acts upon and transforms his world. This world to which he relates is not a static and closed order, a given reality which man must accept and to which he must adjust; rather, it is a problem to be worked on and solved.[4]

My intention in this study has been to present an account of Kuranko social existence, emphasising both structural-functional problems of social order and control, and the existential problematics of Kuranko being-in-the-world. This project has meant understanding Kuranko social existence dialectically, as a continual and often intentional oscillation between contrasting dimensions of reality, and as an interplay between subjective and objective modalities of experience and knowledge.

Of the anthropological project, Godfrey Lienhardt writes: Eventually, we try to represent their conceptions systematically in the logical constructs we have been brought up to use; and we hope, at the best, thus to reconcile what can be expressed in their languages, with what can be expressed in ours. We mediate between their habits of

237

thought, which we have acquired with them, and those of our own society; in doing so, it is not finally some mysterious 'primitive philosophy' that we are exploring, but the further potentialities of our thought and language.[5]

Clearly, this project involves far more than a sociological re-presentation of what one observes and learns in the field; this avowed goal is often confounded at the outset by the variability of individual perspectives and motivations, by the privileged character of the dialogue between the ethnographer and his informants, and by the provisional and relative status of world-views. One often feels that every movement towards an objective and collectively-valid definition of another culture (or of its symbols) is simultaneously a tendency towards depersonalisation, a move away from the realities of actual experience and interpretation as these are realised in particular social contexts. There is, nonetheless, some consolation in the fact that the arbitrariness of the anthropologist's account shares the same problem of authentication that the people themselves face. Even though the 'social' confronts man as pre-ordained, inert, and externally-factitious, it is in truth always an invention of the human mind. As we discover the unending dialogue between the mind and its productions, between nature and culture, we come to realise the vigour of a consciousness that transcends or opposes the anterior conditions of its existence. Reality is then construed as merely 'one subset of the possible'.[6]

The objectivist form of theoretical knowledge has tended to seek to understand social reality as some 'thing', independent of consciousness, and it has invoked the notion of unconscious structures or contents, or has reduced mind to behaviour in order to do so. Man is presented as a passive receiver of culture, and culture is presented as a common code or even as a common catalogue of answers to recurring problems.[7] 'The viewpoint disguises as given a world which has to be continually interpreted.'[8]

I have tried to show in this book that it would be absurd and futile to analyse Kuranko social activity without reference to the constructions which they themselves put upon that activity. Even if many Kuranko believe that their social order has a transcendent origin, this should not inhibit our awareness that this conviction is not completely valid for describing the meaning of actual social activity. This activity must work to approximate or actualise these beliefs, and it must also work to make good discrepancies within the belief system and resolve contradictions which lie between ideology and actuality.

The Dialectics of Identification

From a comparative point of view, one of the most interesting aspects of Kuranko social organisation is the manner in which 'locality' and 'descent' define groupings or social categories which, at different levels and in different contexts, either complement or displace each other.[9]

Except in the case of farm hamlets (*senbekinu*) or small settlements comprising only single *luiye*, the local community includes many clans, diverse in origins, unrelated by descent, and disproportionate in number. Some clans, particularly those of the ruling estate, are divided into several *kebile*. The heterogeneous composition of each local community and territorial unit undoubtedly reflects the processes of migration, dispersal and warfare which characterise Kuranko history. The absence of corporate unilineal descent groups reflects the abundance of land for farming, the low population density, the absence of hereditable land rights—factors which also enable young men to exercise considerable choice in where they will live and with whom they will live.[10] I have also noted how geographical dispersal of members of a lineage results in a weakening of effective kinship ties and an atrophy of genealogical knowledge. Residential contiguity complements, but also supercedes, genealogical proximity in determining the composition of actual corporate groups. The primary jural and property-owning unit is the household. But even though this unit is ideally based upon close kinship (as is the *luiye*), it tends to incorporate distant kin, affines and strangers. The Kuranko emphasise that amity should exist among people who live together; they recognise that this amity is not invariably correlated with the fact of close kinship. Beyond the level of household organisation political, legal, economic and ritual groupings tend to be based on local and neighbourhood ties. Although the village is a network of ramifying affinal and cognatic relationships, kinship and affinity do not constitute the idiom for all social grouping. Neighbourhood and friendship networks play an important part in the organisation of farming and production. Craft specialisations are only loosely associated with the clan system. Political and legal matters are discussed and settled by the chief acting in concert with a council of elders, made up of representatives from all *kebile* in the community. And various clans in the community are inter-related not by any notion of common descent but in terms of the system of estates.

Descent in Kuranko society implies differentiation and division. I have shown that kinship has a metaphorical importance that goes far beyond the area of its actual operation, but the distinction between idiomatic and operational significance must be made. Even clan totems and inter-clan joking alliances differ from locality to locality, indicating that clan identifications are continually adjusted in order to produce a simulacrum of unity in a single village.[11] Against the tendency towards descent-group separatism and despite the instability of affinal ties, each local community maintains collective alignments which transcend those given by kinship and descent. Cooperative groupings such as the *kere,* which are based on neighbourhood and friendship ties, have their ritual counterparts in the various cult associations of the village. The cult groups, like ritual assemblies for sacrifice, burial and initiation, differentiate people in ways that both transfigure and supercede descent groupings, kinship affiliations and affinal networks. The ritual groups cut across residential and descent-group boundaries; they mitigate the separatist or fissive tendencies of descent and kinship.

Two general principles can be stated at this point. First, actual social groupings beyond (and sometimes at) the domestic level are best described as 'strategic' or 'compromise' groupings; they reflect a high degree of choice in place of residence. The activities of such groupings are carried out both within the jurally-given system of descent and affinity and within the context of local-non-descent relations. Kinship relations at the level of *kebile* and clan tend to be only quasi-operational and thus ambiguous; descent connotes an idiom of thought rather than a system of rules determining patterns of action. Second, cooperative and ritual groupings beyond the domestic level tend to 'play down' descent and kinship affiliations and emphasise values based on local contiguity. Category distinctions such as male-female and elder-younger mediate between the domain of kinship organisation and the domain of community organisation, particularly in ceremonial contexts and in the system of cult associations. These abstract category distinctions (sex and age) enable the Kuranko to eclipse kinship, descent and affinal identifications; in doing so they deflect attention from and momentarily resolve contradictions and tensions in the field of kinship and affinity.

In several West African societies, relations between local groups are usually thought of in terms of relations between lineages; apical ancestors of the lineages provide points of intellectual and ritual focus for members of local groups. This ubiquity of the lineage principle has been noted in such societies as the Tallensi[12] and Konkomba[13] of Ghana. Among the LoDagaaba, Goody has emphasised the manner in which locality-based ties take precedence over descent ties when the territorial unit ceases to be coterminous with a homogeneous descent grouping.[14] This principle is borne out in studies of the Nuer. Although the Nuer, like the Tallensi, have a 'classic' segmentary lineage system, they conceptualise their social universe 'primarily as actual relations between groups of kinsmen within local communities rather than as a tree of descent . . . Nuer think generally in terms of local divisions and of the relations between them'.[15] When we turn our attention to the Mande, Southern Nigerian and Cross River peoples of West Africa, we find that locality far more than lineage is emphasised in tribal conceptualisations of relations between groups.[16] One major difference between these societies and the Voltaic peoples lies in the pattern of settlement. Whereas the Voltaic pattern is a neighbourhood of dispersed family homesteads within a clan or sub-clan territory, the Mande-Southern Nigerian-Cross River pattern is characterised by the presence of compact villages and dispersed hamlets related in terms of politically-discrete, centralised units. The multi-lineal (and often multi-tribal) composition of these units is accompanied by a lack of overall integration in terms of descent. It is characteristic of such societies that lineage fragmentation rather than segmentation has resulted in heterogeneous communities[17]; common territory and local contiguity rather than common descent and kinship figure prominently in the conceptualisation of community values.[18] Age-grades and age-sets, hereditary professional associations, cult groups, political assemblies, credit associations, work groups and title associations often cut across, compromise and transcend descent ties and lineage identifications.

I have endeavoured to elucidate the manner in which Kuranko social life involves a continual interplay or oscillation between these two principles of identification—descent and locality—and further to show how in specific contexts of social and ritual activity these principles are manipulated in order to define the values most appropriate for giving solidarity to the grouping.

Similar transformations have been traced out in my discussion of the interplay between 'biographical' and 'social' time, and in my examination of the interplay between the idiosyncratic and cultural personality. The immediate, sensible, biographical and contingent aspects of human nature are continually transformed in favour of conventional codifications and patterns of systematic attribution. Socialisation is, from this point of view, a process whereby the range of the possible is reduced to the inventory of the given. In Sartre's terms, it is a process by which a person learns to judge that 'the appearance (which he is to others) is the reality and that the reality (which he is to himself) is only appearance'.[19] Nowhere is this transformation so clear as in the context of initiation rituals. The implicit contrast which the Kuranko make between the 'influence' of women and the 'structure' of society (which is associated with male control), also indicates the nature of this problematical interplay between contingency and necessity, between uncontrolled subjectivity and the determinate rules of the social order. These abstract conceptualisations of the relationship between male and female are, as we have seen, related metaphorically to other contrasts such as inner-outer, community-wilderness. I have noted the Kuranko concern for the ritual control of the boundaries between these and other categories or domains. But there is always a tacit acknowledgement that the social order can only maintain its viability by accommodating the very elements and influences which are regarded as marginal to it. The mediatory significance of women within the officially agnatic structure, the male arrogation or imitation of the female child-bearing role during initiation, the ritual exploitation of the powers of bush spirits in the context of cult activity, and the influence of the *jelis* and *finas* exemplify this principle.[20]

One of the fundamental problems of human existence is that 'we can be ourselves only in and through our world and there is a sense in which "our" world will die with us although "the" world will go on without us.'[21] Subjective experience is not necessarily homologous with behaviour; nor are the officially recognised patterns and rules of conduct in a given society necessarily determinant. I have advanced the view that each individual strives to place himself in a particular relation to time, a relation in which he can subjectively experience both personal freedom and active control over events.[22] This freedom may be illusory and the control spurious, but in the words of Dostoyevsky 'the meaning of man's life consists in proving to himself every minute that he's a man and not a piano key.'[23] In my discussion of Kuranko initiation I emphasised this point: that the Kuranko do not so much change physical events such as life and death as change or modify their experience of those events. [24] The dialectical movement towards and away from order, and from one mode of identification to another, which I have described in this book can, in my opinion, be understood in terms of an inner existential imperative. The social 'givens' are manipulated, rules are broken, the inevitable is denied, not because man is inherently anarchistic, but because his own identity in a world of things is defined through *praxis*, through a project in which he comes to makes himself out of the conditions which make him.

Infringements of the law, rebellion and refractoriness, ritual manipulations and inversions of conventional codes—these are not merely aspects of a sociological necessity which demands that ideals be defined periodically in terms of their contradiction. They are perhaps the ways in which man transforms himself from object to subject, from category to categoriser, placing himself in a position of world-producer in a world which simultaneously produces him. It seems to me that only an existential account can enable us to understand the impulse towards *bricolage*, that process in which the given world is shattered only to be reconstituted and shattered again, in which the frozen circumstances are forced to dance by singing to them their own melody.[25]

Notes

1.   Noah Marah 1973 (personal communication). The point of view is reminiscent of Victor Uchendu's summary of the Igbo attitude to the world: 'If you ask the Igbo why he believes that the world should be manipulated he will reply' "The world is a marketplace and it is subject to bargain" ' (Uchendu 1965:15).
2.   Berger 1969:7
3.   Sartre 1963:49
4.   Freire 1972:13
5.   Lienhardt 1963:96-7
6.   Bruner 1961
7.   Bourdieu 1971:192
8.   Esland 1971:75
9.   See Jackson 1977a. On the relation of locality to descent in India, see Dumont 1964:71-6.

10. Cf. Rigby (on the Gogo) 1967:637-58; Meggitt 1965:266
11. Refer Jackson 1974:401
12. Fortes 1969
13. Tait 1970
14. Goody 1967:102
15. Evans-Pritchard 1971:202, 203
16. For examples see Ruel (Banyang) 1969:73; Horton (Kalabari) 1962:197-8; Forde (Yakö) 1950:267-89; Nadel (Nupe) 1942:393; Ottenberg (Afrikpo-Igbo) 1968:142; Smith (Kagoro and Kadara) 1969:162; Bascom (Yoruba) 1944:46; Little (Mende) 1951:111; Hopkins (Mandinka) 1971:103. In certain East African societies there is no lineage system at all: Willis (Fipa) 1972:369; Gulliver (Ndendeuli) 1971.
17. See Balandier on 'mixed villages' among the Fang (1970:138) and Hopkins on the Mandinka (1971:99).
18. Adherence to agnatic organisation of territorial groupings can also be correlated with the degree of pressure on scarce resources, especially land (see Meggitt 1965:266-7).
19. Sartre 1963:35-6
20. As Devereux has noted: 'Each culture contains also the negation of its manifest pattern and nuclear values, through a tacit affirmation of contrary latent patterns and marginal values. *The complete real pattern of a culture is a product of a functional interplay between officially affirmed and officially negated patterns* possessing mass' (1967:212, italics in text).
21. Laing 1966:19
22. Lyman and Scott 1970:192
23. Dostoyevsky, *Notes from the Underground* 1961:115. Cf. 'We are not lumps of clay, and what is important is not what people make of us but what we ourselves make of what they have made us' (Sartre 1963:49) See also Wolf 1964:46-7.
24. Cf. Lienhardt 1970:291
25. Marx, quoted in Fromm 1973:83

APPENDIX A Bridewealth Refunded at Divorce

(Compiled from District Court Records, Sengbe Chiefdom, 1946-59)

1946 (9 cases)
    Highest: Le.34, 1 bull, 1 cow, 1 sheep, 2 goats.
    Lowest: Le.22, 1 bull.
    (Note: Money, domestic animals, country cloth, cooking pots, rice were the main commodities refunded. A cow or bull was valued at Le.12, a pot at Le.2, a bolt of country cloth at Le.3.33.)

1947 (16 cases)
    Highest: Le.22, 5 goats, 1 cow, 1 bull.
    Lowest: Le.21

1948 (12 cases)
    Highest: Le.18, 2 bulls, 2 cows.
    Lowest: Le.15

1949 (8 cases)
    Highest: Le.35, 2 cows, 1 bull, 3 goats.
    Lowest: Le.36

1950 (8 cases)
    Highest: Le. 32, 3 bulls, 3 sheep, 1 goat, 1 pot, 1 bolt of country cloth.
    Lowest: Le.9, 1 bull, 1 sheep.

1951 (12 cases)
    Highest: Le.32, 4 bulls, 2 cows, 3 goats.
    Lowest: Le.5, 3 bulls, 1 sheep.

1957 (8 cases)
    Highest: Le.70, 2 cows, 1 sheep, 1 gown.
    Lowest: Le.15, 4 cows.

1958 (20 cases)
    Highest: Le.92, 3 cows, 2 sheep.
    Lowest: Le.32, 1 cow

1959 (26 cases)
    Highest: Le.82, 2 cows, 2 sheep.
    Lowest: Le.20, 3 cows, 1 sheep

Notes

1. There are no detailed records for the years 1952-6.
2. Records from 1957-8 indicate a much greater amount of money being used in bridewealth transactions. In 1965 the highest refund was Le.109.35 and 4 cows, while the lowest was Le.0.50 and 1 cow. In 1966 (19 cases) the highest refund was Le.196.50 and the lowest Le.12.80 and 3 cows and 1 sheep. However, though the amounts of money involved have risen, the numbers of domestic livestock in marriage transactions have remained constant.
3. Up to 1957-8 the variations in amounts of bridewealth are noticeably small. From this period on there has been a sharp increase in the variations of amounts paid, reflecting the growing inequalities of wealth in Kuranko country as a result of the migration of young men to the diamond districts where they amass wealth for marriage by wage labour.
4. A Ministry of the Interior memorandum (P3/5 of 11 April 1963) directed that in cases of divorce the only legal claim in refund of bridewealth concerned the wealth given on the marriage day together with initiation expenses. All other prestations given before and after the marriage day, including brideservice, had to be reckoned as civil debts and claimed independently.

APPENDIX B

Kinship Terminology

m'bimba	'my grandfather'; 'my ancestor'	FF, MF, FFB, MFB, FMB, MMB, and generally any male of these generations.
m'mama	'my grandmother'; 'my ancestress'	FM, MM, FFS, FMS, MFS, and generally any female of these generations.
m'fa	'my father'	F, FB, FMBs, FFSs, FFBs, FMSs.
n'na	'my mother'	M, MS, MMSd, MFBd, MMBd, MFSd.
m'berin	'my maternal uncle'	MB, MMSs, MFBs, MFSs, MBs (if MB deceased).
n'tene	'my paternal aunt'	FS, FFBd.
n'koroke	'my elder brother'	B, MSs, FBs, MMSds, FSs, MBs (if MB alive), FFBss, MFBds, FMSss, FFSss, MFSds, FMBss, when older than ego.
n'doge or *n'dogone*	'my younger brother'	Same as above, when younger than· ego.
n'koromuse	'my elder sister'	S, MSd, FBd, MMSdd, FSd, MBd, FFBsd, MFBdd, FMSsd, MMBdd, FFSsd, MFSdd, FMBsd, when older than ego.
n'dogemuse	'my younger sister'	Same as above, when younger than ego.
na dan	'my child'	If male: s, Bs, FBss, MSss, FSss, of a man; but: s, Ss, MSds, FBds, of a woman. If female: d, Bd, MSsd, FBsd, FSsd, of a man; but: d, Sd, MSdd, FBdd, of a woman.
m'berinne	'my nephew/niece'	Ss, Sd.
mamane	'grandchild'	Any child of a person whom ego calls *dan*.
tolobire	'great-grandchild'	Any child of a person whom ego calls *mamane*.
kegiye	'great-great-grandchild'	Any child of a person whom ego calls *tolobire*.
kinkinkegiye	'great-great-great-grandchild'	Any child of a person whom ego calls *kegiye*.
fu fa fuye	person of the 6th descending generation	

Terms of Affinity and Other Kinship Nomenclature

n'dinyon	'joking partner'	Woman speaking: older brother's wife, husband's younger sister.
numorgo	'joking partner'	Woman speaking: older sister's husband, husband's younger brother. Man speaking: elder sibling's spouse, wife's younger sister.
m'biranke	'my male in-law'	*Wife's* F, MB, FB, younger sister's husband and brother (when older than ego), daughter's husband.
m'biranmusu	'my female in-law'	*Wife's* M, FS, MS and sister (when older than ego).
n'tersan	any sibling or classificatory sibling of the opposite sex	
n'tenne	'my nephew/niece'	Woman speaking: Bd, Bs.
m'buin *na ke*	'my husband'	
na muse *nanyagane*	'my wife'	
n'sine	'my co-wife'	
n'na kura	'my new mother'	Mother's co-wife.

Notes

1. Abbreviations used: F—father; M—mother; B—brother; S—sister; s—son; d—daughter.

2. In the first ascending generation the age of classificatory fathers and mothers may be denoted by adding *kinema* (older/bigger) or *dogoma* (younger/smaller) to the kinship term, e.g. *fa kinema* (father's older brother), *fa dogoma* (father's younger brother). The status of a brother or sister may be designated by reference to whether or not he or she is initiated; thus: *n'dogo bilakorene* ('my uninitiated younger brother'), *n'dogo kemine* ('my initiated younger brother') etc.

3. Sex is denoted by the suffixes *muse* or *musu* (female) and *ke* (male); thus: *n'koroke* ('my older brother'), *n'koromuse* ('my older sister'), *maman'ke* (grandson), *mamanemuse* (granddaughter), *dimuse* (daughter), *denke* (son).

4. The 'quality' of a relationship may be indicated or signified by the use of a kinship term in conjunction with the personal name, e.g. *m'berin* Tamba ('my maternal uncle Tamba'), *m'fa Sewa* ('my father Sewa'). This usage also enables clear distinctions to be made among various persons who stand in the same relationship to ego.

Bibliography

Works which contain references to the Kuranko

Chevalier, A. 1909. 'La Région des Sources du Niger', *La Géographie*, 14:337-52.

Drummond, D. B. and Kamara, K. 1930. 'Some Kuranko Place Names', *Sierra Leone Studies* (Old Series), 16:27-34.

Kamara, K. and Drummond, D. B. 1930. 'Marriage Customs Amongst the Kurankos', *Sierra Leone Studies* (Old Series), 16:57-66.

Kamara, K. 1932. 'Notes on some Customs of the Kurankos', *Sierra Leone Studies* (Old Series), 17:94-100.

———— 1933. 'Kuranko Funeral Customs', *Sierra Leone Studies* (Old Series), 19:153-7.

Kewule. 1932. Postscript to 'Notes on some Customs of the Kurankos', *Sierra Leone Studies* (Old Series), 17:100-1.

Laing, Major A. G. 1825. *Travels in the Timanee, Kooranko and Soolima Countries*, John Murray, London.

Luke, Dr. J. Fashole. 1939. 'Some Impressions of the Korankos and Their Country', *Sierra Leone Studies* (Old Series), 22:90-4.

Person, Y. 1961. 'Les Kissi et leurs Statuettes de Pierre dans le Cadre de l'Histoire Ouest-Africaine', *Bulletin de l'Institute Français d'Afrique Noire*, Series B, 23(1):1-59.

———— 1962. 'Tradition Orale et Chronologie', *Cahiers d'Etudes Africaines*, 2:462-36.

Sayers, E. F. 1925. 'The Funeral of a Koranko Chief', *Sierra Leone Studies* (Old Series), 7:19-29.

Sayers, E. F. 1927. 'Notes on the Clan or Family Names Common in the Area Inhabited by Temne-Speaking People', *Sierra Leone Studies* (Old Series), 12:14-108.

Thomas, Northcote W. 1916. *Anthropological Report on Sierra Leone, Part I. Law and Customs of the Timne and Other Tribes*, Harrison and Sons, London.

Trotter, Lieut.-Col. J. K. 1898. *The Niger Sources*, Methuen, London.

Other works to which reference is made

Balandier, G. 1966 *Ambiguous Africa* (translated from the French by Helen Weaver), Chatto and Windus, London.

———— 1970. *The Sociology of Black Africa*, André Deutsch, London.

Barnes, J. A. 1962. 'African Models in the New Guinea Highlands', *Man*, 62:5-9.

Bascom, W. R. 1944. 'The Sociological Role of the Yoruba Cult-Groups', *Memoirs of the American Anthropological Association*, no. 63.

Bateson, G. 1958. *Naven*, Stanford University Press, Stanford.

Berger, P. 1963. *Invitation to Sociology*, Penguin Books.

———— 1969. *The Social Reality of Religion*, Faber and Faber, London.

Berger, P. and Luckmann, T. 1971. *The Social Construction of Reality*, Penguin University Books.

Bettelheim, B. 1954. *Symbolic Wounds*, The Free Press, Glencoe, Ill.

Bloch, M. 1971. 'The Moral and Tactical Meaning of Kinship Terms', *Man* 6(1):79-87.

Borges, J. L. 1964. *Other Inquisitions*, Simon and Schuster, New York.

———— 1975. *Fictions*, John Calder, London.

Bourdieu, P. 1971. 'Systems of Education and Systems of Thought', in *Knowledge and Control* (ed. M. F. D. Young), Collier-Macmillan, London.

———— 1972. 'The Three Forms of Theoretical Knowledge', *Social Science Information*, 12(I):53-80.

Bowlby, J. 1971. *Attachment and Loss*, Volume I., Penguin Books.

Brown, P. 1951. 'Patterns of Authority in West Africa', *Africa*, 21(4): 261-78.

Bruner, J. 1961. *The Process of Education*, Harvard University Press, Cambridge, Mass.

Cendrars, B. 1956. *Moravagine*, Grasset, Paris.

Clarke, J. I. (ed.) 1966. *Sierra Leone in Maps*, University of London Press, London.

Cohen, A. 1971. 'The Politics of Ritual Secrecy', *Man*, 6(3):427-48.

Dalby, T. D. P. 1962. 'Language Distribution in Sierra Leone', *Sierra Leone Language Review*, 1:62-67.

Dawson, J. 1964. 'Urbanization and Mental Health in a West African Community', in *Magic, Faith, and Healing* (ed. A. Kiev), The Free Press, Glencoe, Ill.

Devereux, G. 1961. 'Two Types of Modal Personality Models', in *Studying Personality Cross-Culturally* (ed. B. Kaplan), Harper and Row, New York.

———— 1967. *From Anxiety to Method in the Behavioural Sciences*, Mouton, the Hague.

Diamond, S. 1969. 'Plato and the Definition of the Primitive', in *Primitive Views of the World* (ed. S. Diamond), Columbia University Press, New York.

Dieterlen, Germaine. 1957. 'The Mande Creation Myth', *Africa*, 27:124-38.

Dorjahn, V. 1960. 'The Changing Political System of the Temne', *Africa*, 30(2):110-39.

Dostoyevsky, F. 1961. *Notes from the Underground*, Signet, New York.

Douglas, Mary. 1968. 'The Social Control of Cognition: Some Factors in Joke Perception', *Man* 3(3):361-76.

Dumont, L. 1964. 'A Note on locality in Relation to Descent', *Contributions to Indian Sociology*, 7:71-6.

Eliade, M. 1959. *Cosmos and History*, Harper and Row, New York.

Esland, G. M. 1971. 'Teaching and Learning in the Organization of Knowledge', in *Knowledge and Control* (ed. M. F. D. Young), Collier-Macmillan, London.

Evans-Pritchard, E. E. 1969. *Kinship and Marriage Among the Nuer*, Clarendon, Oxford.

———— 1971. *The Nuer*, Clarendon, Oxford.

Finnegan, Ruth. 1965. *Survey of the Limba People of Northern Sierra Leone*, H. M. Stationery Office, London.

———— 1967. *Limba Stories and Storytelling*, Clarendon, Oxford.

Forde, D. 1950. 'Ward Organization Among the Yakö', *Africa*, 20(4):267-89.

Fortes, M. 1959. *Oedipus and Job in West African Religion*, Cambridge University Press, Cambridge.

———— 1962. Introduction to *Developmental Cycle in Domestic Groups* (ed. J. Goody), Cambridge Papers in Social Anthropology, I, Cambridge University Press, Cambridge.

———— 1969. *The Web of Kinship Among the Tallensi*, Oosterhout, N.B., Netherlands and Oxford University Press, London.

Freire, P. 1972. *Pedagogy of the Oppressed*, Herder and Herder, New York.

Fromm, E. 1973. *The Crisis of Psychoanalysis*, Penguin Books.

Gamble, D. P. n.d. *Economic Conditions in Two Mandinka Villages: Kerewan and Keneba*, Report to the Government of the Gambia, Colonial Office, London.

Gellner, E. 1964. *Thought and Change*, Weidenfeld and Nicolson, London.

Gluckman, M. 1954. *Rituals of Rebellion in South-East Africa*, Manchester University Press, Manchester.

———— 1970. *Custom and Conflict in Africa*, Blackwell, Oxford.

Goody, Esther. 1970. 'Legitimate and Illegitimate Aggression in a West African State', in *Witchcraft Confessions and Accusations* (ed. Mary Douglas), A.S.A. Monograph 9, Tavistock, London.

Goody,.J. 1967. *The Social Organisation of the Lo Wiili* (2nd edition), Oxford University Press, London.

———— 1969. *Comparative Studies in Kinship*, Routledge and Kegan Paul, London.

Griaule, M. 1973. 'The Mother's Brother in the Western Sudan', in *French Perspectives in African Studies* (ed. P. Alexandre), Oxford University Press, London.

Griaule, M. and Dieterlen, Germaine. 1970. 'The Dogon of the French Sudan', in *African Worlds* (ed. D. Forde), Oxford University Press, London.

Gulliver, P. H. 1971. *Neighbours and Networks*, University of California Press, Berkeley.

Haas, A. W. 1974. 'Diffusion of Innovations in Sierra Leone, West Africa', cyclostyled report to the Institute of Cultural and Social Studies, Leiden State University, the Netherlands.

Hallpike, C. R. 1972. *The Konso of Ethiopia*, Clarendon, Oxford.

Harris, W. T. and Sawyerr, H. 1968. *The Springs of Mende Belief and Conduct*, Sierra Leone University Press, Freetown.

Heisenberg, W. 1958. *The Physicist's Conception of Nature*, Hutchinson, London.

Hopkins, N. S. 1971. 'Mandinka Social Organization', in *Papers on the Manding* (ed. C. T. Hodge), Indiana University Publications, Bloomington.

Horton, R. 1962. 'The Kalabari World-View: an Outline and Interpretation', *Africa*, 32(3):197-219.

———— 1971. 'African Traditional Thought and Western Science', in *Knowledge and Control* (ed. M. F. D. Young), Collier-Macmillan, London.

Hubert, H. and Mauss, M. 1968. *Sacrifice: its Nature and Function*, Cohen and West, London.

Imperator, P. J. 1972. 'Contemporary Masked Dances and Masquerades of the Bamana Age Sets from the Cercle of Bamako, Mali', unpublished paper presented at the Conference on Manding Studies, London 1972.

International African Institute. 1962. *Practical Orthography of African Languages*, Memo. I, I.A.I., London.

Jackson, M. 1969. 'Literacy, Communications and Social Change: the Maori Case 1830-1870' unpublished M.A. Thesis, University of Auckland, New Zealand.

———— 1974. 'The Structure and Significance of Kuranko Clanship', *Africa*, 44(4):397-415.

———— 1975. 'Knowledge and Event: Witchcraft Confession Among the Kuranko', *Man*, 10:387-403.

———— 1977a. 'Sacrifice and Social Structure Among the Kuranko', *Africa*, 47 (forthcoming).

————1977b. 'Dogmas and Fictions of Birth-Order Position', *Yearbook of Symbolic Anthropology* (forthcoming)

Koch, K-F. 1974. 'Sociogenic and Psychogenic Models in Anthropology: the functions of Jalé Initiation', *Man*, 9(3):397-422.

Koinadugu District Intelligence Diary (1900-25). Original in the Koinadugu District Office, Kabala, Sierra Leone.

Kup, A. P. 1961. *A History of Sierra Leone*, Cambridge University Press, Cambridge.

Kuper, H. 1961. *An African Aristocracy*, Oxford University Press, London.

La Barre, W. 1972. *The Ghost Dance*, Dell, New York.

Labouret, H. 1934. *Les Manding et leur Langue*, Libraire Larose, Paris.

Laing, R. D. 1966. *The Divided Self*, Penguin Books.

Leach, E. R. 1967. 'Magical Hair', in *Myth and Cosmos* (ed. J. Middleton), Natural History Press, New York.

———— 1971. *Rethinking Anthropology*, Athlone Press, London.

Lévi-Strauss, C. 1963. *Structural Anthropology*, Basic Books, New York.

———— 1967. *The Scope of Anthropology*, Cape, London.

———— 1969a. *The Elementary Structures of Kinship*, Eyre and Spottiswoode, London.

———— 1969b. *Totemism*, Penguin Books.

Lienhardt, G. 1963. 'Modes of Thought', in *The Institutions of Primitive Society*, Blackwell, Oxford.

———— 1970. *Divinity and Experience*, Clarendon Press, Oxford.

Little, K. 1951. *The Mende of Sierra Leone*, Routledge and Kegan Paul, London.

———— 1961. 'The Role of the Secret Society in Cultural Specialization', in *Cultures and Societies of Africa* (eds. S. and P. Ottenburg), Random House, New York.

Littlejohn, J. 1960. 'The Temne House', *Sierra Leone Studies* (New Series), 14:63-79.

———— 1963. 'Temne Space', *Anthropological Quarterly*, 36:1-17.

Lyman, S. M. and Scott, M. B. 1970. *A Sociology of the Absurd*, Appleton-Century-Crofts, New York.

Mannheim, K. 1968. *Ideology and Utopia*, Routledge and Kegan Paul, London.

Marah, N. B. 1973. Personal communication.

Mbiti, J. 1969. *African Religions and Philosophy*, Heinemann, London.

Mead, Margaret. 1935. *Sex and Temperament in Three Primitive Societies*, Routledge and Sons, London.

Meggitt, M. J. 1965. *The Lineage System of the Mae-Enga*, Oliver and Boyd, London.

Meillassoux, C. 1968. *Urbanization of an African Community*, University of Washington Press, Seattle.

Merleau-Ponty, M. 1964. *Signs* (translated and with an introduction by R. C. McCleary), Northwestern University Press, Evanston, Ill.

———— 1965. *The Structure of Behaviour* (translated by A. L. Fisher), Methuen, London.

Murdock, G. P. 1959. *Africa, Its Peoples and Their Cultural History*, McGraw-Hill, New York.

Musil, R. 1954. *The Man Without Qualities*, Secker and Warburg, London.

Nadel, S. F. 1942. *A Black Byzantium*, Oxford University Press, London.

———— 1957. *The Theory of Social Structure*, Cohen and West, London.

Niane, D. T. 1965. *Sundiata: an Epic of Old Mali* (translated by G. D. Pickett), Longmans, London.

Ottenberg, S. 1968. *Double Descent in an African Society*, American Ethnographical Society Monograph, no. 47.

Paques, Viviana. 1954. *Les Bambara*, Paris.

Paulme, Denise. 1948. 'The Social Condition of Women in Two West African Societies', *Man*, 48, art. 45, p. 44.

———— 1949. 'Formes de Ressentiment et de Suspicion dans une Société Noire', *Journal de Psychologie*, 4:467-80.

———— 1964. *Les Gens du Riz*, Plon, Paris.

———— 1973. 'Blood Pacts, Age Classes and Castes in Black Africa', in *French Perspectives in African Studies* (ed. P. Alexandre), Oxford University Press, London.

Piaget, J. 1971. *Structuralism* (translated and edited by C. Maschler), Routledge and Kegan Paul, London.

Pocock, D. F. 1967. 'The Anthropology of Time Reckoning', in *Myth and Cosmos* (ed. J. Middleton), Natural History Press, New York.

Pouillon, J. 1971. 'Traditions in French Anthropology', *Social Research*, 38:73-92.

Radcliffe-Brown, A. R. 1952. *Structure and Function in Primitive Society*, Cohen and West, London.

Rigby, P. 1967. 'Time and Structure in Gogo Kinship', *Cahiers d'Etudes Africaines*, 7(28):637-58.

———— 1968. 'Joking Relationships, Kin Categories, and Clanship Among the Gogo', *Africa*, 38(2):133-55.

Rivière, P. G. 1971. 'Marriage: a Reassessment', in *Rethinking Kinship and Marriage* (ed. R. Needham), A. S. A. Monograph II, Tavistock, London.

Róheim, G. 1971. *The Origin and Function of Culture*, Anchor Books, New York.

Ruel, M. 1969. *Leopards and Leaders: Constitutional Politics Among a Cross River People*, Tavistock, London.

Sahlins, M. 1968. 'On the Sociology of Primitive Exchange', in *The Relevance of Models for Social Anthropology* (ed. M. Banton), A. S. A. Monograph I, Tavistock, London.

Sartre, J-P. 1963. *Saint Genet* (translated from the French by B. Frechtman), George Braziller, New York.

———— 1967. *Search for a Method*, Alfred A. Knopf, New York.

Schutz, A. 1962. *Collected Papers*, Volume I, Nijhoff, The Hague.

Sierra Leone Population Census (1963). Central Statistics Office, Freetown.

Simmel, G. 1968. *The Conflict in Modern Culture and Other Essays* (translated and with an introduction by K. P. Etzkorn), Teachers College Press (Columbia University), New York.

Smith, M. G. 1969. 'Differentiation and the Segmentary Principle in Two Societies', in *Man in Africa* (eds. P. Kaberry and M. Douglas), Tavistock, London.

Strathern, Marilyn. 1972. *Women in Between*, Seminar Press, London.

Tait, D. 1970. 'The Territorial Pattern and Lineage System of the Konkomba', in *Tribes Without Rulers* (eds. J. Middleton and D. Tait), Routledge and Kegan Paul, London.

Tauxier, L. 1927. *La Religion Bambara*, Paris.

Thomas, L. V. 1973. 'Le Pluralisme Cohérent de la Notion de Personne en Afrique Noire Traditionnelle', in *La Notion de Personne en Afrique Noire* (ed. Germaine Dieterlen), Editions du Centre National de la Recherche Scientifique, Paris.

Trimingham, J. S. 1962. *A History of Islam in West Africa*, Oxford University Press, London.

Turay, A. K. 1972. Personal communication.

Turner, V. 1970. *The Forest of Symbols*, Cornell University Press, Ithaca.

———— 1972. *Schism and Continuity in an African Society*, Manchester University Press, Manchester.

Uchendu, V. C. 1965. *The Igbo of Southeast Nigeria*, Holt, Rinehart and Winston, New York.

Van Baal, J. 1970. 'The Part of Women in the Marriage Trade: Objects or Behaving as Objects?', *Bijdragen tot de taal-, Land-, en Volkenkunde*, 126:289-308.

Voorhoeve, C. L. 1975. Personal communication.

Wagner, R. 1975. *The Invention of Culture*, Prentice-Hall, New Jersey.

Westermann, D. and Bryan, M.A. 1970. *Handbook of African Languages Part 2: Languages of West Africa*, International African Institute, London.

Whiting, J. W. M. 1961. 'Socialization Process and Personality', in *Psychological Anthropology; Approaches to Culture and Personality* (ed. F. L. K. Hsu), Dorsey, Homewood.

———— 1962. 'Comment' to F. W. Young, *American Journal of Sociology*, 67:391-4.

Willis, R. G. 1972. 'Pollution and Paradigms', *Man*, 7(3):369-78.

Wolf, E. 1964. *Anthropology*, Prentice-Hall, New Jersey.

Young, F. W. 1962.'The Function of Male Initiation Ceremonies: A Cross-Cultural Test of an Alternative Hypothesis', *American Journal of Sociology*, 67(4):379-96.

Index

ADAM AND EVE, in myth, 57, 88-9, 92
Adultery, 62, 79, 98, 101, 116, 121, 123
Affinity (*biranye*), 105-9
Age: in succession and inheritance, 161-3; significance of age differences, 163-4
Age status differentiation: Kuranko theory of, 149-50; and clanship, 151-3; between rulers and *nyemakale* clans, 156-8
Agnatic descent, 67-9, 87, 91
Altala (God), 57, 58, 231
Ancestral spirits, 17, 18, 29, 57, 58, 138
Angels, 33
Avunculate (*see also* Marriage), 114, 132

BALANDIER, G., 14, 243
Bambara, 4, 54, 89, 158, 219, 223, 226, 234
Barnes, J., 24
Bateson, G., 217
Behaviour: ideal, 17-8; kinds of misdemeanour, 60-2
Berger, P., xiv, 242
Betrothal (*see also* Marriage), 95-6, 98
Bettelheim, B., 208, 215, 217
Birth, 38, 67, 82, 139
Birth-order position, 161-80
Bloch, M., 80
Borges, J. L., ix, 214
Bourdieu, P., xiv
Bowlby, J., 214
Brideservice (*see also* Marriage), 95, 118
Bridewealth (*see also* Marriage), 95-6, 126-7, 243-4
Brothers, non-uterine, 142; 144-6
Brother and sister, relationship between, 123, 125-31
Brown, P., 215
Bruner, J., 242

CHIEFTAINCY, 6, 25, 26-7, 36, 60, 221-2
Childhood: stages of, 23; recreational associations in, 223-5
Clan: distribution of clans, 24-5; origins of clans, 3; intermarriage between clans, 26; hierarchical organisation of clans, 151-2; joking partnerships (*sanakuiye tolon*), 25, 34, 153-6; ruling clans, 26, 28; totems, 25-6; endogamy, 26
Clarke, J. I., 29
Cohen, A., 234
Co-wives, relationships between, 141-6, 178
Craft specialisations, 12-13, 86
Cross-cousin marriage (*see also* Marriage), 114-16, 117, 118, 119, 130, 131, 137
Cult associations, 82, 219-36
Curse (*danka*), 57, 85, 126, 135

DALBY, D., 14
Dankawali, village of, x, xv, 58
Dawson, J., 79
Death (*see also* Mortuary rites; Homicide), 57, 62
Debt, 73-77
Dembaiye (family; household), 9, 28-9, 46-8, 51, 106; organisation of, 69-70; patterns of authority in, 65
Descent (*see also* Clan; *Kebile;* Lineage), 24, 65, 239
Devereux, G., xiv, 135, 214, 215, 243
Diamond, S., 215
Dieterlen, G., 30
Disputes, categories of, 28-9, 63-4, 122
Divination, 90
Divorce (*see also* Marriage), 97-105, 116, 121, 122
Dogon, 89, 135
Dorjahn, V., 234
Dostoyevsky, F., 242, 243
Douglas, M., 123
Dreams, 37

253

DATE DUE

HIGHSMITH 45-220